PORTRAITS IN LEADERSHIP

PORTRAITS IN LEADERSHIP
Six Extraordinary University Presidents

Arthur Padilla

AMERICAN COUNCIL ON EDUCATION
PRAEGER
Series on Higher Education

Library of Congress Cataloging-in-Publication Data

Padilla, Arthur.
    Portraits in leadership : six extraordinary university presidents / Arthur Padilla.
        p. cm.—(ACE/Praeger series on higher education)
    Includes bibliographical references and index.
    ISBN 0–275–98490–7 (alk. paper)
    1. Universities and colleges—United States—Presidents—Biography.
  2. Universities and colleges—United States—Administration.   3. Leadership.
  I. Title. II. American Council on Education/Praeger series on higher education.
  LB2341.P315 2005
  378.1'11'092'2—dc22   2004028377

British Library Cataloguing in Publication Data is available.

Library of Congress Catalog Card Number: 2004028377
ISBN: 0–275–98490–7

First published in 2005

Praeger Publishers, 88 Post Road West, Westport, CT 06881
An imprint of Greenwood Publishing Group, Inc.
www.praeger.com

Printed in the United States of America

The paper used in this book complies with the
Permanent Paper Standard issued by the National
Information Standards Organization (Z39.48–1984).

10 9 8 7 6 5 4 3 2 1

For my father

CONTENTS

ACKNOWLEDGMENTS

I t is customary in these pages to thank individuals for their help in projects such as this one, and I am proud to follow this tradition. First I want to thank the students who endured the lectures in my class "Leadership and Management" at North Carolina State. Even though I had considerable experience in the senior administration of a very complex organization, the sixteen-campus University of North Carolina, I could not have written this book ten years ago. The massive scope of what had been written about leadership, along with the complicated nature of the topic, required a significant amount of time to digest and comprehend. My students helped considerably in sharpening my understanding of the literature.

The six presidents included in the case studies set aside major chunks of their time to help with this project and answered every question posed of them without hesitation. They also read drafts of chapters and provided very helpful comments and corrections. I regret very much that Clark Kerr passed away before the project was completed but he had a chance to comment on earlier drafts, as did several of his associates at Berkeley, including Marian Gade, Neil Smelser, and Gene Lee. In addition, I was able to visit several times with close colleagues of each of the individuals highlighted here. These include: Ray Dawson, Felix Joyner, and Molly Broad at UNC; Brit Kirwan, Chuck Sturtz, and William Thomas from Maryland; Father Ned Joyce at Notre Dame; Bill Baumol (Princeton and NYU) and Neil Rudenstine (Princeton and Harvard) at Princeton; and Jonathan Kleinbard (Chicago) and John Hope Franklin

(Chicago and Duke) at Chicago. In addition, Mitch Maidique at Florida International University, Stan Ikenberry of Illinois and ACE, Charlie Reed (California State University system), and Barry Munitz (Getty Trust) in California, were amazingly helpful and generous with their time. Their participation is greatly appreciated.

My good friend Dick Robb has been a terrific encouragement and his concerns for humanity have been a real inspiration to me over the years. I am also grateful for the research advice that my wife Laura Lunsford has given me throughout. As a psychologist and expert on mentoring, Laura alerted me to the latest work on resiliency and mentoring and her insight has been invaluable. Finally, my colleagues at NC State and throughout the country, including Rob Kaiser, Jon Bartley, Beverly Tyler, Lynda Aiman-Smith, Paul Mulvey, Ray Dawson, Jim Leutze, Bart Craig, Jerry McElroy, and Mitzi Montoya-Weiss, read various drafts and provided me with important comments. Rob Kaiser was especially helpful with the chapter on leadership. Former Park Scholars at North Carolina State, Tomás Carbonell, Jenny Chang, Eva Feucht, Danny Malechuk, and Matt King, all provided meticulous research assistance and contributed significantly to the final product. Ed Hoffman has been a splendid editor and advisor from the beginning and his many suggestions improved the final versions of each chapter materially. Myra Strober of Stanford University and the Atlantic Philanthropies was an unexpected source of encouragement and her support is appreciated. Finally, the assistance provided by the Park Foundation and the Atlantic Philanthropies made the research for this project possible and is gratefully acknowledged. Unfortunately, none of these people or organizations can be blamed for any shortcomings in the book.

CHAPTER 1

Introduction

All the politics that are in me I learned in New Jersey.
—Woodrow Wilson

When U.S. President John F. Kennedy quoted the British poet John Masefield (1878–1967) during his commencement speech at American University in June of 1963, noting that there "are few earthly things more beautiful than a university," he was not referring to ivy-covered rock walls or quadrangles or towers. Instead, the former president was alluding to beauty of ideas and of opportunity and personal challenges, a beauty that transcends the visible and the apparent. The university is indeed a vital force for society and its culture and science, one of the few places left on earth where one thinks critically about the world and where young people are prepared to shape its future. At times, its most important obligation to the society that supports it might be to refuse to do what that society wants.

President Kennedy could have added that the university is not only a beautiful place, but also a very complicated one. As such, it offers a particularly useful organizational setting for the study of leadership, precisely because it is so complicated and because there are so many different demands upon, and boundaries on the power of, its leaders. Former Yale University president Bart Giamatti, whose term was not entirely uneventful, likened the university presidency to holding "a mid-nineteenth-century ecclesiastical position on top of a late-twentieth-century corporation."[1] One of Kennedy's predecessors in the White House, Woodrow Wilson, could have verified Giamatti's contention. Wilson, who led the United States through the first World War and who won the Nobel Peace Prize in 1919 for his leadership in shaping the League of Nations, cut his proverbial teeth as president of Princeton University between 1902 and 1910. As university president, Wilson would enact some truly revolutionary educational reforms. But he also confronted a level of opposition and intrigue that later would cause him to remark he had learned nothing new about politics after leaving the university.[2]

Wilson was the son of a Presbyterian minister who did not learn to read until he was nine, probably because of a mild case of dyslexia. But from that point forward Wilson became an outstanding student, and like many sons of Presbyterian clergy, he attended Princeton. He flourished there, participating as one of the leaders of the debating society and as editor of the student newspaper, *The Princetonian*. After graduation in 1879, he went to law school at the University of Virginia and practiced briefly in Atlanta. But the law was not for him and he entered Johns Hopkins University for further studies in history and politics; his doctoral dissertation, entitled *Congressional Government*, brought him acclaim as well as faculty appointments at Bryn Mawr and then at Wesleyan. He was invited to return to his alma mater as a professor in 1890, eleven years after his graduation. He quickly became one of Princeton's most outstanding faculty members and a favorite among students for his superb teaching and for his kindness and generosity of spirit. He continued as a prolific writer of biography and history and lectured routinely at Johns Hopkins and New York University in the law.

In 1902, the Princeton trustees unanimously elected Wilson as Princeton's thirteenth president. Wilson immediately proposed to the trustees several initiatives to transform Princeton into one of the world's great universities, tightening enrollments and creating a formal organization with departments of instruction and deanships, all antecedents to a major curricular reform. Wilson's new academic configuration replaced a random, elective system of courses with a more coherent set of general courses for the first two years of college, followed by concentrated, discipline-based studies during the junior and senior years. He added an honors system for more ambitious and gifted students.

Wilson next turned to the faculty and the teaching. He started the first alumni fund-raising campaign in Princeton's history and used the funds to strengthen the faculty ranks, adding fifty assistant professors called "preceptors," who guided students in small-group discussions and readings. Eventually, he recruited an outstanding group of young scholars who brought great acclaim to the university. Wilson also separated science and religion at the university, putting biblical instruction in the hands of secular scholars and insisting that research in the sciences be based on scientific research and appointed the first Jews and Roman Catholics to the faculty. It was an impressive whirlwind of change and innovation, based on the overarching intention of excellence and distinction. But he was not finished.

Recognizing that some aspects of student social life at Princeton were harmful to the intellectual strength and individual equity of the university, Wilson took on the "eating clubs" on Prospect Avenue. Much of the undergraduate life centered on these clubs, and Wilson considered them sideshows that encouraged exclusivity, elitism, and ostracism. Aware that he would face major opposition, he nonetheless presented a plan to the trustees based on the creation of quadrangles, areas where undergraduates would live, each with its own recreational and dining facilities and faculty preceptors. Membership would be determined randomly and the eating clubs would be eventually eliminated. But while the trustees approved the plan in principle, the alumni in New York and Philadelphia did not. Wilson had gone from preaching to meddling; he was, they said, eliminating a splendid tradition of freedom of social choice. "He's ruining a fine country club," one alumnus reportedly grumbled, and an influential donor, M. Taylor Pyne, threatened to withdraw his support if Wilson persisted. The episode would transform Wilson into a radical social democrat, but by then he was in the middle of another controversy, this time involving the graduate school.

Latin scholar and Princeton dean Andrew F. West established the graduate school at Princeton in 1900, two years before Wilson assumed Princeton's presidency. West, a 1874 Princeton graduate and no doubt a well-connected member of one of the notorious eating clubs, wanted the graduate school to remain secluded from collegiate life (that is, the undergraduate college) and thus preferred a Gothic-style school in Oxbridge fashion, away from the bustle of campus, "above the golf links," as West was wont to say, referring to a place overlooking the Springdale golf course, about a half mile from the main campus. Wilson, who had worked hard to bring outstanding research faculty to Princeton to strengthen the graduate teaching, felt the graduate school should be the driving force of the intellectual life of the university and that the graduate students should interact with the undergrads. The trustees agreed with Wilson and voted for the graduate school to be built on the Prospect grounds, but Dean West continued working in opposition: an ally of West, William Procter, of Cincinnati, Ohio, said he would donate half a million dollars for the graduate school, but only if it were located "above the links." Wilson fought the Procter offer, finally accusing West of having exclusive social ideas; the real source of debate was personal animosity between the two men. The same New York and Philadelphia group of conservative alumni, led by Pyne, once again brought the fight to Wilson. Following months of protracted controversy, Procter withdrew his offer. But then another alumnus, Isaac C. Wyman, of Salem, Massachusetts, died and left his entire estate, considered initially to be worth $3 million (but later discovered to be worth only $794,000) to the graduate school, naming West as one of executors. Wilson gave up: "We've beaten the living," he told his wife, "but we can't fight the dead." He was about to quit ("My inclination is to resign and leave them to their own devices," he wrote) when he was asked by local Democrats to run for the governorship of New Jersey, a challenge Wilson must have accepted with relief. The graduate school headquarters (in its full medieval splendor, complete with gargoyles and spire) remains located above the golf links. Princeton students now know it as "Goon Castle." The removal of the graduate school from the main campus had lasting effects, as Alvin Kernan, a graduate-school dean at Princeton under Bill Bowen during the early 1970s, observed. "The graduate school grew and flourished, but the university remained basically collegiate."[3]

Given such a string of battles, some won and some lost, it is not surprising that the twenty-eighth president of the United States would feel that the university presidency had provided rigorous preparation for the political tribulations of the nation's top job. The unusual number of publics or followers that depend on the university, and upon which the university in turn depends for support and nurturing, along with the unique role of faculty in the governance and operation of the enterprise, all combine to make the university a complex and fascinating organization for study. As Princeton's president, Wilson would learn about the university's multiple challenges firsthand; he would discover the tremendous importance of effective communication across diverse interest groups. As the chief executive of the United States, Wilson would benefit from his experiences at Princeton as he would once again encounter many of the same challenges and obstacles, magnified, of course, by the enormity of running a nation at war. The issues faced by Wilson at Princeton are in many ways similar to the experiences of the university presidents examined in this book: the struggle for change, the resistance by opponents, and the politics of leading such a wide array of publics. But the question of what makes a person capable of leading a university, or a nation, is as important to examine as the details of a presidency. What general organizational lessons might be learned by examining the way the university functions and how its stakeholders behave? Is the ability to lead innate or learned? What traits and experiences do leaders share?

PURPOSE AND METHOD

As the twenty-first century begins, humanity appears confronted by several critical challenges. One is the danger of a nuclear disaster, either intentional or accidental, a menace that ironically the collapse of the former Soviet Union has not alleviated (and perhaps has even aggravated). Another is related to health and environment: an ecological catastrophe or some rampant epidemic or virus resistant to the best vaccines and antidotes. But a third, less-noticed challenge might be more significant than either of the first two: a crisis of leadership. One has only to look at some the world's large corporations or to the heads of states of several nations to recognize the problems. Yet, as discussed in the chapters that follow, our knowledge about leadership and followership remains at relatively embryonic levels.

The idea for this project came when I returned to the classroom after nearly two decades as a university officer. In my late twenties I became a senior administrator for the sixteen-campus University of North Carolina, and instead of teaching and conducting research, I helped manage a very complicated organization, one of the nation's largest and most diverse multi-campus universities. For nearly twenty years I was immersed in the politics, economics, and sociology of universities as a witness to the pressures that bear upon this unique organization. The diversity of the "publics" of the university—students, faculty, alumni, athletic boosters, parents, legislators, businesses, philanthropies—certainly contributes to its complexity. And the presence of academic tenure creates unique employment relationships that make leading these enterprises a true challenge. The distance afforded by teaching and thinking again about leadership and organizational behaviors highlighted the intricacies of the university and the trials that confront its leaders.

This is a book is about the phenomenon of leadership, using a complicated entity, the university, as the organizational lens through which to view and understand it. Leadership principles, patterns, and behaviors are illustrated and examined through detailed case histories of six well-known university leaders of recent times. The interaction between these leaders, their followers, and their organizational situations are at the center of this analysis. Three overlapping circles may be used to describe the basic framework and approach.

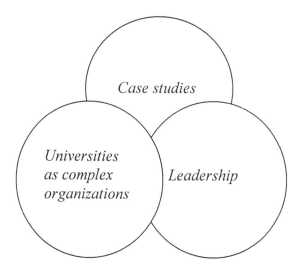

The first circle represents a unique and ancient organization that is singularly difficult to lead—the university. It is, paradoxically, both traditionalist and progressive, a place where research knowledge expands swiftly and where the noise of social argument often reaches deafening, and occasionally silly, levels, all in the midst of tradition and ceremony. The second circle is leadership: its patterns, theories, and commonalities; it includes a synthesis of leadership factors and elements that inform the content and format of the cases. The final circle denotes the case studies of six extraordinary university leaders that highlight their early experiences and important leadership behaviors and actions. The overlap of the circles defines the conclusions and synthesis.

Readers familiar with John Kennedy's *Profiles in Courage* will recognize a certain similarity between the approach used here and the one Kennedy employed in his Pulitzer-prize winning study of members of the U.S. Congress. Kennedy's book apotheosized great Americans in Congress who were courageous precisely because they did not follow their constituents. In essence, Kennedy looked at the phenomenon of political courage within the organizational context of the U.S. Congress. In this book, I begin with an analysis of the university as an organization in Chapter 2, exploring the commonalities between universities and other organizations and examining those characteristics of universities that make them unusual entities; Kennedy did this, of course, for the Congress. It then turns to an analysis of leadership and followership and develops a general framework about leadership applicable to a broader range of organizational contexts and settings (Chapter 3). These two chapters on organizational context and on leadership essentially define the structure of each of the case studies. The book's subsequent chapters and sections are devoted to in-depth case studies of the six university leaders:

- Clark Kerr, the creator of the University of California and controversial leader who was (in Kerr's famous words) "fired with enthusiasm" by Governor Ronald Reagan following the student riots of the 1960s;
- William Friday, who served as president for three decades of arguably the nation's most complex university system, the University of North Carolina, and who headed the American Council on Education and the Association of American Universities;
- Father Theodore Hesburgh of the University of Notre Dame, best-selling author who served on countless presidential commissions, including as chair of the Civil Rights Commission in the 1960s, and whose efforts transformed his institution into a major research university;
- Hanna Gray of the University of Chicago, the second woman president of a major and certainly unique university and the only female chair of the Association of American Universities, the world's most prestigious society of universities;
- John Slaughter, a former head of the National Science Foundation and of the NCAA's Presidents Commission, and only the second African American to lead a major university, where he dealt with racism and an explosive athletic scandal surrounding the death of basketball superstar Len Bias at the University of Maryland;
- William Bowen, leader of Princeton for fifteen years during which time that Ivy League institution was converted into a major force in higher education through controversial decisions about admission of women and minority students and expansion of graduate programs.

The cases present detailed overviews of the areas defined by the discussions about organizations in Chapter 2 and the leadership synthesis developed in Chapter 3 and build upon the findings of these two chapters. They begin with the leader's background and then move to formal education, including a discussion of important mentors and influential adults. In each case, the discussion of the formative period is followed by an analysis of senior leadership roles and major defining events, successes, and failures. Each case includes a section on managerial and leadership styles and contains significant discussions about the organizational environments and situations. While Chapter 4, "Prologue to the Cases," lays out in detail the methods and approaches used in the case studies, as well as the factors involved in the selection of the six university leaders, it is important in this introduction to highlight some of elements examined in each case.

In discussing the young leader, the cases analyze those dimensions of adult leadership and creativity that have their roots in childhood and the patterns of formative experiences. The questions that arise include:

- What were the important family, cultural, and societal factors that these future leaders experienced as children?
- In what ways did these six leaders differ from their peers? Did they possess distinguishing physical features?
- Did they achieve unusually early as compared to their peers?
- A basic level of intelligence is indispensable in leadership positions, but without the ability for expression, it may be overlooked: how well did the young leaders speak and write and did they have special opportunities to perfect these skills?
- Are there early signs of great perseverance in the face of substantial odds or of unusual or otherwise extraordinary behavior at an early age?
- For those leaders who were dealt a "poor hand" as young people, is there evidence of resiliency and of playing the poor hand well?
- Were there early opportunities for travel and patterns of understanding diverse points of view and cultures?
- Was there an early exposure to the top of their organizations, a position from which they could "see" the entire enterprise from above and understand the interrelations of the various pieces?

For the adult leader the cases focus on ways in which leaders reached their positions, how they dealt with the various publics, and how they affected the behavior of others. Within the context of universities, examination of the political pressures facing leaders who work in collegial or collaborative domains is vital. The specific areas of inquiry included:

- The leadership and managerial styles employed in dealing with the wide variety of "publics" or stakeholders. How did they manage communications across the various groups?
- Experiences and circumstances as they rose to the top of their organizations.
- The extent of their prior connection to their organizations.
- Specific behaviors and traits shared by the six leaders in work habits, communication patterns, or interpersonal skills.

- Relationships with key associates and colleagues and delegation of responsibilities.
- Cadence of life.
- Presence or absence of behaviors typically associated with "career derailment."

Chapter 2, "The University as a Complex Organization," analyzes the organizational characteristics of the university, with special attention to its main elements and how they affect and limit its leaders. It could be argued that there is no such thing as "the university," and to some extent the case studies support this notion. The University of Chicago, for example, is quite different from Princeton in its size, scope, and traditions, and those two institutions in turn are very different from the University of Maryland at College Park. But there are also important similarities in leadership traits and behaviors among leaders of different types of institutions and even of a broader set of organizations, characteristics, and traits such as physical and psychological stamina and communication and interpersonal skills. Nonetheless, the importance of "situation" emerges from these cases, as five of these six leaders accumulated specific "human capital" in their particular organizations, learning about organizational cultures and developing affinities and ties to their traditions and organizational idiosyncrasies. In fact, one general finding is the deep connectedness of leaders to their organizations as a predictor of leadership success.

Chapter 3, "Leadership," reviews the major streams of research in the study of leadership over the last century, as well as several of the more comprehensive, broader works on leadership. Based upon a synthesis of these research efforts, the chapter develops a general template for identifying the factors that make leadership and followership possible to provide a framework for viewing the six case studies. A prologue to the cases follows next, a shorter chapter that serves as a guide for the six individual case studies. The last chapter presents a summary and conclusions. Each of the cases has been written in a similar format to enable easier comparisons and contrasts. In the instances of Clark Kerr and William Friday, the cases are slightly longer due in part to the wider availability of biographical materials and the longer lengths of their tenures and because of the wide range of events during their presidencies and scope of their responsibilities.

A final note for readers with limited time or interest is in order. Readers more interested in the particular stories of selected presidents can proceed directly from this introduction to "Prologue to the Cases" (Chapter 4) and then to the particular case studies. Reading Chapter 2 and Chapter 3 will provide a theoretical framework for interpreting the case studies, but each case is written essentially to stand alone. The concluding chapter provides a general summary for the entire book, including the main findings from the case studies.

NOTES

1. A. Bartlett Giamatti, *A Free and Ordered Space* (New York: W. W. Norton, 1988), 17.

2. This passage about Woodrow Wilson at Princeton is based on the following sources: Kendrick A. Clements, *The Presidency of Woodrow Wilson* (Lawrence: University of Kansas Press, 1992); Kendrick A. Clements, *Woodrow Wilson: World Statesman* (Boston: Twayne Publishers, 1987); Alexander Leitch, *A Princeton Companion* (Princeton, NJ: Princeton University Press, 1978); Jon Blackwell, "1913: The President from Princeton," *The Trentonian*, November 1, 1998; and http://www.educatetheusa.com/Wilson28.html.

3. Alvin Kernan, *In Plato's Cave* (New Haven, CT: Yale University Press, 1999), 206.

CHAPTER

The University as a Complex Organization

Being president of a university is no way for an adult to make a living. . . . It is to hold a mid-nineteenth-century ecclesiastical position on top of a late-twentieth-century corporation.
— A. Bartlett Giamatti, former president of Yale

Humans are primarily social creatures. They associate and connect with others within the context of societies, institutions, and traditions that have evolved slowly over decades and even centuries, as in the case of the university. Since the processes of leadership and followership are inextricably tied to the workings of the culture and the institutions within which leaders and followers interact, it is important to examine the nature of the university as an organization before exploring a general framework of leadership to guide and inform the content of the six individual cases of university leaders. In this chapter I treat the "university" in a general fashion, and, in the main, from the perspective of the larger institutions, although I try to distinguish among public and private, large and small, or individual campuses and university systems, where appropriate. This is primarily due to limitations of space: it would take much longer to describe and analyze the various types of institutions in the detail they each deserve. There are other factors involved in focusing on larger entities. The larger universities are among the most complex, most publicized, and most subject to intense social and political pressures; they educate one-fourth of American college students and produce nearly all of the nation's Ph.D.'s; and their presidencies and other high-level posts have been among the most highly sought jobs in any labor market. I also found that the historical records at many of the smaller institutions often were not as complete or readily available as they were at the larger campuses. Thus, expediency and accuracy were important reasons for choosing presidents of the larger universities for the case studies in the chapters that follow. There remain, nonetheless, significant differences in areas like finances, curricula, enrollments, and traditions, between Princeton and Berkeley or between Chicago and Chapel Hill. But it is also true that many of the organizational issues and managerial challenges found in the larger campuses also exist in smaller ones, though perhaps in slightly different forms. Nevertheless, I plead guilty to the charge that in the process I might neglect some of the particular circumstances of the smaller colleges or of those of institutions that focus less on research or on big-time college sports by choosing this approach. In no way is my choice of these six presidents meant to slight many truly outstanding leaders of the smaller institutions.

ANCIENT AND COMPLEX ORGANIZATIONS

It was Heraclitus, the most significant of Greek philosophers until Socrates and Plato, who proposed the idea of a universe in a constant state of change. Nothing endures, he said, but change (or flux, as Heraclitus called it). With all respect due to Heraclitus, however, Clark Kerr points to seventy-five western enterprises and organizations still recognizable today that existed over five hundred years ago; the institutions have changed, certainly, but they retain similar purposes and relatively unbroken histories. The list includes the Parliaments of England, Iceland, and the Isle of Man; the Roman Catholic Church; the Bank of Siena; the governance structures of several Swiss cantons; and sixty-one universities, some of which are nearly one thousand years old. These universities in fact occupy many of the same buildings and conduct similar functions as they did at their founding.[1]

The enduring role of the university over the course of a millennium would seem to challenge Heraclitus' model of an ever-changing universe. Of course, this is not the case, although universities are not typically viewed as agile enterprises that adapt quickly and seamlessly to change. To outside observers, they often appear as lumbering elephants, or even dinosaurs, resistant to change and glacially bureaucratic in movement. Changes to the academic calendar, a system of classes and vacations designed around an agricultural age that is now two centuries old, is often likened to moving a graveyard.

However, the most rapidly evolving aspects of universities—the activities in classrooms and in research laboratories—are also their least visible and understood from the outside. Internally, the pace of the university is at times frenzied, gripped with intellectual debates and with the excitement of discovery. It is a place where the very society that supports it is often bitterly criticized or fundamentally challenged, sometimes to the mortification of its leaders who must defend, for example, the adoption of a controversial book for freshman seminars or a professor's unsympathetic stance toward the state's primary industry. As E. M. Forster once said about Greek poet C. P. Cavafy, it is a place that stands at a slight angle to the universe.[2] Its longevity must therefore involve a largely unseen component: its ability to adapt. Without such internal change and responsiveness in its most basic teaching and scholarly functions, the organization arguably would not have survived all these centuries.

Consider, for example, the changes that have taken place over the last fifteen or twenty years in disciplines like computer science and genetics. A typical undergraduate computer science program at a major American university in the early 1980s would have offered between ten and fifteen courses, including principles of systems programs (like the use of tapes, disks, drums, and other hardware obsolete today), as well as courses on digital signal processing and on digital computers. Today, such departments offer between seventy and ninety courses for undergraduates, including two- and three-dimensional raster graphics, Web page development, and computing in the Java programming language. Similarly, genetics departments (if they are still called that and not bioinformatics or genomics) in the mid-1970s would have had ten to twenty graduate classes, many on crude methods of plant and animal breeding. Now they offer some fifty courses on gene manipulation, recombinant DNA, computational molecular evolution, and genetic mapping. In mathematics, the computer has revolutionized how calculus is taught. In the humanities and social sciences, technology has brought unprecedented analytical power to research and to teaching. Central or inflexible management controls of these rapidly changing activities are as unwise as they are unworkable.

EMBLEMATIC CHARACTERISTICS

These apparently contradictory characteristics—a long history, couched in tradition, combined with the capacity for rapid adaptability—

suggest that the university is indeed a complicated institution; it tests the abilities of leaders as perhaps no other modern organization does due to significant constraints upon, and challenges to, the power and autonomy of university leaders. The challenges facing university leaders stem mainly from two of the emblematic characteristics of these institutions:

- the variety of publics or stakeholders (or followers, in the more usual jargon of leadership) to whom then must respond and with whom they must work
- the unique employment relationships between the organization and its main employees, the faculty

Examples of the influence of stakeholder or follower groups are many: the student protests of the 1960s and 1970s; the effects on the organization of the increased vocationalism of students today; the impact of athletic team "boosters" and alumni; "star" faculty and big-name coaches who outshine college presidents and provosts in influence and popularity; legislators who manipulate decisions and choices. Employment relationships add to the complexity of the institutions. Faculty members are the university's main employees and form the heart of the enterprise; their loyalties go in large part to their disciplines rather than to the organizations that employ them. Tenure systems provide an independence and insulation that make leadership solely by coercion and force virtually impossible. The associations between universities and faculty are more akin to loosely defined contracts than they are to traditional employment relations where a boss can define the job content and its direction: as long as professors achieve acceptable teaching evaluations and occasionally publish in the proper journals, they are essentially free to conduct whatever research and seek whatever funding they wish. The time of faculty is theirs and the notion of requiring specific forms of organizational behavior (such as office time or work in teams to achieve organizational goals) is largely foreign, particularly at the large, research universities.

The employment conditions of faculty result from the emphasis on research and specialization that defines the modern American research university, conditions that have been unquestionably successful, widely envied, and produced an elite cadre of experts in a huge variety of fields and specialties. It is not unusual, for example, to find a Caribbean tourism expert in Indiana or an authority on Middle Eastern culture in California at some university. Whenever there is a catastrophe such as an earthquake or an oil spill or a school shooting, the American public, primarily

through television or other media, turns to a university expert for expla-
nation and analysis and even reassurance. Rosenzweig exaggerates when
he writes that it would be hard to find a chief executive as powerless as
the president of a major university.[3] But it is true corporate CEOs have
much more control over their enterprises and expenses and over how
they spend their time. Decision making is much faster in the corporate
world and, in general, corporate chiefs have many internal groups of support, in contrast to the lonelier work of the university leader. Thus, in
certain important respects, the university leader is more like the head of
a highly creative enterprise such as a "think tank" or a symphony or-
chestra, where the knowledge resides with the researcher or the instru-
ment players and where the senior management constantly walks the line
between control and entrustment of duties and functions. But, more
specifically, what type of an organization is the university? What similarities or differences does it share with other organizations involved in
the creation of knowledge and in the management of creativity? Are they
in fact particularly complex and difficult to lead? And what are the leadership implications of their structures?

I turn next to a brief discussion of organizations generally and then to
a detailed analysis of the university's organization and structure.

ORGANIZATIONS GENERALLY

The study of organizations and their behavior is traveled largely on the
foundations of psychology, business management, sociology, social psychology, political science, anthropology, and economics. The familiar
economic term "division of labor" is a classic departure point toward a
definition, although clearly organizations do much more than simply decide how work is divided. Organizations define and redefine objectives
and goals that participants attempt to reach through their performances.
They induce participants to contribute their services and talents and provide a social structure defining relationships among participants. They
perform coordinating and control functions, allocate resources, and select and train participants. And they often provide important services
and resources to (and sometimes create problems for) the communities
and the physical, cultural, political, and social environments within
which they exist. In fact, the importance of organizations can be missed
if they are viewed exclusively as arrangements influencing the activities
of individuals: they are also independent corporate entities in their own
right that consume energy and resources.

The problems facing organizations arise when different things are being done by two or more persons toward a common goal and in definite cooperation with each other.[4] It is the combination of specific goals and formal job roles or titles that separates organizations from more informal arrangements like flea markets or bazaars, which serve as a common ground for many individual transactions. Certain elements of a university, such as the budget office or the physical plant, fit what may be called a "rational system" perspective of organizations, where there exist formal job roles and where cooperation of participants is conscious and deliberate.[5] The more informal elements like the individual research efforts of faculty fit an "open systems" view of organizations, where loosely interdependent activities link participants with differing interests but with some general concern for the survival of the enterprise.

Complex organizations are thus distinguished by the presence of various formal and informal elements, of the rational or traditional forms of organizations and of the bazaar, with direct implications for how they can be managed and coordinated. Organizations might be further categorized in terms of agreement on goals and on what they mean: goals might be very explicit and easily quantified and understood in one enterprise, and they might be ambiguous, too vague or broad, or not widely shared among members of another organization. Function and job roles might be rigidly prescribed in one organizational setting and loosely defined in another. In the case of a complex enterprise like the university, it is probably most useful to think of an organization consisting of various related elements—its governance structure, internal operations, the academic function—each exhibiting distinctive characteristics and organizational qualities.

UNDERSTANDING ORGANIZATIONAL STRUCTURES

Beyond these general observations about formal and informal elements, however, what is of special interest is how an enterprise is structured, how tasks are divided among workers, and how their efforts are coordinated. Three factors, each one clearly manifested in the case of the university, are particularly relevant in understanding why different structures exist: complexity, unpredictability, and interdependence.

Complexity essentially involves the number of different elements with which an organization must deal and it is one of the defining features of the university or university system. Organizational complexity is typically identified by the following:[6]

- horizontal differentiation of jobs (marketing, finance, public relations, research, and so forth);
- vertical or hierarchical managerial structure (for example, president, vice presidents, assistant vice presidents, deans, directors) and considerable spatial, or geographical, dispersion;
- extent of the competitive situation facing the organization (and competition is of course not limited to for-profit businesses);
- rapidly changing organizational environment due to technological, political, social, or cultural factors; and
- size of the enterprise, which leads to greater differentiation of work, geographical dispersion, and decentralization.[7]

Like other complex entities, universities exhibit both an extensive vertical hierarchy of managers and a significant horizontal differentiation across a range of activities. Some parts are highly formalized, even bureaucratized, while others, like the classroom or research activities, have virtually no form or consistency from department to department. Centralization of function ranges from very high (the hiring of secretaries) to very low (the hiring of professors). Major universities, and especially the public ones, are characterized by having an unusually varied group of "publics" or stakeholders; their actions affect the university and they in turn are affected by it. A variety of "sunshine" and public records laws add to organizational complexity by creating a fishbowl effect for decision-makers where many internal decisions and processes are subjected to considerable external publicity and scrutiny. In universities, formalization of function among departments and functional areas (like research and development, human resources, marketing, IT, and finance) is similar to that found in profit-making organizations. Manufacturing divisions in business firms, with a premium on efficiency and consistent reproducibility, tend to be the most formalized, with well-defined jobs and managerial structures. Fundamental research and development units, with great value placed on inventiveness and creativity, are typically the least formal.[8]

Uncertainty or unpredictability in the environment that organizations face is another relevant factor, where the environment is defined to include all persons and elements that affect the organization and that in turn are affected by it. Examples include rapid technological advances in the business environment, such as advances in the communications industry, or instabilities arising from changes in the industry, such as the transformations in the airline industry. Hugh McColl, longtime CEO of

the Bank of America (formerly NationsBank), once observed that technological change in the banking industry was proceeding so rapidly that
he had to trust more people with different parts of his business and no
longer felt as much in control as he once did when change was less rapid.
Greater complexity and greater instability or change in the business environment thus invariably lead to fewer decisions being made at the top
as senior managers have more distance from, and less knowledge of, the
different parts of the organization. With less complexity or differentiation, or with more stable and less changing environments, knowledge
throughout is not as specialized and top executives can have a good understanding of activities and processes in all of the major divisions. More
uncertainty or unpredictability would be expected if there is significant
heterogeneity in the environmental elements, as in the case of the university.

Intercollegiate athletics at universities with big-time athletic programs
are an important environmental element that adds to unpredictability.
This well-coordinated and orchestrated external entity often carries an
agenda that conflicts with internal goals of the organization. The hiring
or the firing of a football coach typically exposes these competing concerns and goals: some athletic donors might want what is in the best interests of the football program; the faculty, if they even speak about these
matters, might be concerned about academic issues such as graduation
rates and entering SAT scores of the student-athletes; and the president
and the trustees might be worried about institutional control and image.[9]

Finally, interdependence of the various entities of an organization also
determines structure. Some organizational outcomes depend critically on
other parts of the organization and others do not. In universities, the English department depends upon the history department to offer the required history classes necessary for the English majors to graduate on
time. Similarly, the internal functioning of universities—the coordination of residence halls, parking, student registration and records, student
billing, classroom scheduling, and physical plant operations—grows in
interdependency (and in bureaucracy) as the size of the institution increases. On the other hand, interdependence can be very weak in the research function of the institution, particularly so at the major research
institutions where independent faculty initiative working within disciplinary boundaries largely determines what is studied, when it is studied,
and by whom it is studied.

It becomes obvious that to treat universities as single, homogeneous
blobs, either as totally open organizations with very little coordination
among units (as some faculty might wish) or as standard for-profit busi-

nesses (as is occasionally suggested by more than a few trustees) is not very useful in understanding the implications for their management and leadership. This discussion about structure points to a more sophisticated and complicated perspective, one that reflects the organizational complexity of the university.

THE UNIVERSITY'S ORGANIZATION SPECIFICALLY

Universities have developed their structures literally over the centuries as a function of their environments, characteristics, and purposes. Their principal work is teaching and research driven by a faculty guild that autonomously governs the educational processes. The independence of faculty and of academic departments in determining their own rules and practices is sometimes criticized, and just as often misconstrued, but it is uniquely matched to the strengths of the organization and to educational functions that demand flexibility and the management of creativity.

Parts of a university's organization resemble organized anarchies, as Cohen and March have provocatively written.[10] This means in part that organizational goals are unclear or not widely shared; that its "technology," or the processes through which the organization does its work and provides its services or products, are not entirely understood by its members. It also implies that participation in university processes is fluid in the sense that participants vary in the amount of time and effort they devote to different domains from year to year. Parts of the university also resemble more of a market or a bazaar than an organization, as Scott or Knight would define an organization; that is, they lack common and specific goals toward which the organization moves in a coordinated fashion. As Kerr says: "[S]ellers make and sell what they want to make and sell, and buyers buy what they want to buy. Most participants want to preserve the environment, but a few occasionally want to change or destroy it."[11] These more loosely organized divisions would include, in the main, the academic and research enterprises, particularly given the presence of academic tenure. However, the internal operations and the budget and finance functions, along with the external development and fund-raising operations, are clearly formalized and subject to well-understood goals and coordination activities. They exist alongside the bazaar. The university, and particularly the large, public research institutions, can thus be seen as a five-part operation, and a rather complex one at that, each component requiring different managerial skills and leadership behaviors and embodiments:

- governance and senior administration
- external development and entertainment
- internal support operations
- student affairs
- academic enterprise

GOVERNANCE AND SENIOR ADMINISTRATION

Like for-profit organizations, a key part of the governance of a university is in the hands of a board of directors (variously called trustees, visitors, regents, or governors). In theory, the board is responsible for the policy of the organization, rather than for its day-to-day operations, which is the primary responsibility of the institution's administrators or managers. In practice, many boards have been known both for their preaching as well as for their meddling. The lay university board, composed of members whose lives and careers are totally outside the universities they oversee, is uniquely American, but in recent years, boards have become more democratic and are now populated with a variety of ad hoc, voting and non-voting student, faculty, and staff members, diluting some of the value of an exclusively "outsider" or lay board. In sharp contrast to university boards, about one-third of corporate boards in the for-profit sector are typically made up of operating officers such as the president and several of the vice presidents. The chair of corporate boards in normal situations is also the CEO of the company, and the CEO in effect chooses many of the other board members. Thus, the corporate CEO has considerable control over his or her board in most cases.[12]

There are appreciable differences in the way boards are chosen in public and private American universities.[13] In general, boards of private universities are still chosen much as they have always been chosen: from the ranks of alumni and other close supporters through a private vote of members of alumni associations. They also typically serve significantly longer terms than do board members of public universities. Public university board members are chosen in more "public" ways: either by the governor or the legislature or the system-wide governing board or by some combination of these groups. In rare instances, as in Michigan, the voters at large elect board members of public universities. The definite tendency toward shorter terms of office among public board members affects negatively institutional "memory" and familiarity with how the university works and how its internal university processes and financial practices function. Owing perhaps to the manner in which they are selected, public university trustees are less likely to defer to the judgment of their presidents or chancellors and more likely to confront them.[14] In comparison to private university trustees, public trustees exhibit more turnover due to their shorter terms of office, and they may feel a need for more responsiveness or loyalty to those responsible for their election or appointment, causing them to carry their issues and agendas to the board meetings.[15] One consequence, according to William Bowen, is that

> it becomes harder to recruit board members, board leaders, and even presidents who have old-fashioned beliefs in liberal education, old-fashioned beliefs in supporting perhaps unpopular fields, and who want to see the university retain its sense of obligation to a broad social mission. That mission includes opportunity, support of the arts, and doing something to address racial divides, which have little to do with money but which are enormously important in our country.[16]

The senior administrators of the university include the president or chancellor (CEOs), as well as the vice presidents in academics, budget and finance, student affairs, and other areas of greater or lesser importance, depending on the university and the person filling the position. Boards of trustees are usually the closest allies and supporters of university presidents since they have some significant stake in presidential success. Boards hire and fire presidents and they are responsible for evaluating their performance. Kerr and Gade have correctly observed that the care of the president is in the hands of the board: a board cannot perform much better than its president, although it can be a good deal worse. When the trustees evaluate a president they are effectively evaluating themselves and their own performance in selecting, advising, and supporting the president.[17]

Differences between the corporate world and the university are significant in terms of advancement to managerial jobs and also in the constraints and requirements facing leaders. In the university, the academic route is typically the most common way to a college presidency; in industry there are several roads: from marketing, production, finance, and design, for instance. The paradox, however, is that in most cases "the academic route does not train or test the breadth of skills needed to be a president."[18] Internal leadership development also seems much more effective in the corporate sector. Most corporate CEOs (nearly 80 percent) are promoted from within the organizations they lead, but university presidents come largely, and increasingly, from the outside; the succession of leaders in the corporate world is more of a baton-passing than it is a brand new race.[19] Like five of the six case studies highlighted in this study (Kerr,

Friday, Hesburgh, Gray, and Bowen), most corporate leaders have been in the same environment and have important learning opportunities within their organizations (the average CEO has been with the same company for twenty-three years); this is not usually the case with college leaders. The "absence of these chances to observe by the board and to learn by the individual are severe handicaps both to those who make the selections and to those who are selected."[20] The increased use of search firms for university presidential jobs, particularly among the public universities, has been a factor in the trend toward the hiring of more external candidates,[21] although this is not a universal pattern. Promotion from within has been the policy used by the Massachusetts Institute of Technology (MIT) and by many Catholic universities for most of their histories with great success.[22]

The length of service of presidents, or their "survival" in office, is a measure of the mutual satisfaction between presidents and those for whom they work. In recent decades, there has been a marked decline in presidential tenures, especially among presidents of public universities. A study of a population of more than two hundred Research I university presidents (excluding all interim or acting presidents) that defined presidential service as the number of years in office from their start to their retirement or other separation reached the following conclusions:[23]

- Presidential tenure has been declining over the last thirty years in both public and private universities.
- The tenure of public university presidents is significantly lower than that of private university presidents.
- Average total tenures of the recent cohorts of presidents are at historically low levels, in spite of the vigorous economic conditions in the 1990s that would tend to lengthen presidential tenures.
- The use of interim or acting presidents is more prevalent today compared to thirty years ago, particularly among public universities.

What explains these trends? The list of external pressures, described in Kerr and Gade as "more barbed wire around smaller corrals," is long.[24] It includes

- increased government controls and greater involvement by the legal system,
- more influence by students and parents as costs rise,
- more university goals and greater ambiguity in their definition,
- more frequent board involvement in day-to-day operations,

- bureaucratization of staff and greater influence by outside experts, including search firms and consultants,
- commercialization of college athletics, and
- less acceptance of the authority and autonomy of many American institutions, including universities.

Some of these forces have a greater impact on public universities than they do on the private sector. For example, many public university presidents report increased involvement by trustees in the daily operations of their campuses—a tendency increasingly favored by legislative and other external bodies since boards of universities can thus become extensions of legislative influence and control. More frequent turnover of trustees, as noted earlier, can be caused by and lead to greater political influence by the governors and legislators who appoint them. By contrast, the trustee selection process and length of tenure at most major private universities have remained essentially unchanged for decades.

Another factor affecting the tenure of presidents is the dramatic escalation in presidential salaries. In the mid-1980s, the typical president of a doctoral-level university was paid about 70 percent more than the typical full professor. About one-third of that difference reflected the difference between the academic year (nine-month) salary of the professor and the calendar year (twelve-month) pay of the president. However, by 2000, the pay advantage presidents enjoyed over senior faculty had risen to over 200 percent.[25] Exploding presidential wages have been both a response and a contributor to conditions making the presidency more challenging. Economists refer to "compensating wage differentials" paid to workers in hazardous or disagreeable jobs. The higher pay of presidents might be an acknowledgment that the jobs have become more difficult, but at the same time the higher salaries have added to the difficulty of the jobs by creating even higher expectations. Consistent with research on executive pay in the private sector, higher compensation often generates increasing impatience on the part of constituents, whose expectations for presidential performance rise in tandem with salary levels. There are also differences in average tenures or lengths of service between internal and external presidents. Individuals promoted to the presidency from within the institution tend to have longer tenures than do those who are hired externally. Public universities have recently been more likely to hire persons whose immediate previous employment was at other institutions and this has contributed to the decline in presidential tenures at the public institutions.

Effective presidencies would seem to need more than five years to man-ifest themselves, yet 5.2 years is the current estimate of presidential tenure among the public research universities.[26] Moreover, around each side of a presidential transition, both at the start and at the ending, there is a period of several months—or even a year or two—during which the de-parting president is, in effect, a lame duck and the institution is running on automatic controls. After a new president arrives, there is a period during which the institution and its various publics become acquainted with the new leader, and the new leader with them. In this environment, an absence of short-term continuity and focused direction can transform such complex projects as capital campaigns into formidable undertakings. With more frequent turnover, periods of discontinuity tend to multiply, which weakens leadership on campus and relocates vital decisions and initiatives off campus, to external boards or legislatures.

Furthermore, the turnover among other administrators whenever pres-idents depart can contribute to organizational distraction. The experi-ence of the two public research universities in North Carolina (UNC at Chapel Hill and NC State University) is illustrative, and perhaps repre-sentative, of many public universities. Between 1989 and 1999, these two institutions had seven different chancellors (three acting, one of whom became permanent), fifteen different provosts (interim and permanent), and countless deans and department heads. Leadership changes often bring dramatic shifts in styles and strategies, taxing the adaptability of faculty and administrators. One former dean put it: "You get used to one style and then another one comes in. After a while, you just wait 'em out because you know there's no continuity at the top, no institutional mem-ory. It makes my job harder because I really can't do it independently of the university." Ironically, increased turnover at the top ultimately results in slower change and less responsiveness throughout the organization.

There is surprisingly little information on what happens to university presidents after they leave. Yet, for those who enter the job at age fifty or below, it is statistically clear that they probably will not complete their careers as presidents at that institution. One study indicates that about 15 percent of "immediately previous" presidents at the research univer-sities were retired and that slightly more than that proportion (19 per-cent) left for other presidencies.[27] The remaining former presidents had either returned to the faculty or were consultants, employed in some other capacity elsewhere, or deceased. An earlier report estimated simi-lar proportions: 25 percent in retirement or semi-retirement; 15 percent who went on to another presidency; 20 percent who returned to the fac-ulty; and the remainder going to another administrative post or to a job outside the academy.[28] Thus, for many university presidents, the presidency is a sort of dead-end job: they are not likely to find another one with the same level of prestige and responsibility unless they shift to another similar position.

THE EXTERNAL AND ENTERTAINMENT FUNCTION

The most visible and publicized sector of the organization, by far, is the external and entertainment function. Included in this sector are fund-raising, public relations, alumni events, concerts, plays, art exhibitions, and big-time sports, a term that applies to some seventy-five of the largest American universities that choose to compete in the sports of football and men's basketball at the highest collegiate levels.[29] Large universities will entertain hundreds of thousands of sports fans and concert-goers each year. Given the influence of television in modern society, it is not unusual for some coaches, athletic directors, or even star student-athletes to command far more attention and publicity than the head of the institution.

To be sure, many members of the university community have ambivalent feelings toward these activities. Nevertheless, the external and entertainment functions are increasingly significant and they are also taking larger chunks of presidential time. In the arena of fund-raising, the aphorism by Penn State football coach Joe Paterno summarizes the ambivalence cleverly: "We want your money, but not your two-cents' worth." Some faculty, though certainly not all, historically have had low regard for this increasingly prevalent money-raising function, although they are usually willing to spend the funds. Big-time athletics also evoke mixed feelings. Many faculty are either indifferent or cynical about big-time sports and their increasing commercialization, and unlike other university staff members, many professors actually hold sports allegiances to the teams of their own undergraduate institutions. Alumni are generally supportive, especially during the relatively infrequent periods of extraordinary athletic success or national championships, but many will also decry quietly the inevitable scandal or NCAA probation, or the compromises made in admission of academically unprepared star athletes. Many boosters, sometimes not graduates of the institutions whose teams they support, will demand success. For university presidents with typical career profiles, the management of intercollegiate sports can be, to mix metaphors, a steep learning curve with a slippery slope. The president delegates much of the work of the enterprise to the coaches and the athletic director, but when problems arise, as they invariably tend to do, the president is inevitably the responsible individual at the center of media frenzy. Moreover, the rampant commercialization of this function, and the fact that the athletic director typically reports directly to the president of the institution, ensures that an increasingly disproportionate amount of the organization's time relative to the main academic purpose of the university will be devoted to its management and control. Indeed, during times of major crisis, the time involvement by top management becomes all-consuming and has, on repeated occasions, led to the firing or forced resignation of a president. One of the more recent and troubling developments in this area, the increased influence of the major athletic conferences in the conduct of intercollegiate athletics, remains largely unexamined.[30] Declining presidential terms of service make it more difficult for presidents to provide continuity and meaningful oversight to this highly visible "entertainment" element of the university.

Fund-raising or university development has similarly taken on more importance on university campuses, especially among the public universities. Capital campaigns to raise billions of dollars over a relatively short period of time are now common among the largest public and private universities. The management of fund-raising divisions has become much more professionalized, like that of athletic departments, and is increasingly supervised by nomadic administrators. Successful fund-raisers are highly mobile from institutional campaign to campaign and their loyalties gravitate more to their professions than to the institutions currently employing them; some university fund-raisers do not even have offices on campus and may actually reside in other states. Several factors have contributed to the rise in prominence of the external activities of universities: the commercialization of college sports; the central role major universities now play in providing community entertainment in various areas; limits on the amount of tuition that institutions are prepared to charge; and the declining support from government and state legislatures in the face of enrollment and cost pressures.

These changes hold implications both for the leadership of the university and for its traditions and independence. The role of presidents, with some rare exceptions, has become preponderantly an external one.[31] While this fact is not meant to downplay the potential internal importance of university presidents, it has transferred power over academic and student matters elsewhere on the campus as the president's involvement has become more intermittent and less consequential to internal processes. Additionally, the nature of the work of the university, and particularly its academic work, has become more dependent on external, often industry, sources of support.

THE INTERNAL SUPPORT OPERATIONS

Usually the largest piece in terms of employees, the university's internal support bureaucracy—its budget and finance divisions, its physical plant operations, the police force, and the human resources department—is the part that most closely resembles a for-profit business. The structure of many of its divisions is similar to those of comparably sized for-profit firms, but typically they are not as efficient as their private counterparts due to the absence of a profit motive. The head of operations is usually a chief finance officer with an advanced business degree who directly or indirectly oversees literally hundreds of employees, and even more than that if the university includes a medical complex. More traditional leadership styles and organizational relationships prevail here: size, centralization, and span of control present serious coordination and control challenges to managers. Chief finance officers have power bases within and outside the organization, derived from their knowledge of budget processes, their responsibility for procurement of supplies and equipment and construction of facilities, and their relationships with legislators (particularly among the larger, public universities) or donors who provide funding for the organization.

As happens in many types of enterprises, the budget drives, or attempts to drive, the strategic and long-term decisions across the breadth of the organization. This of course might create serious interdivisional conflicts, pitting the bottom-line orientation of budget managers versus the longer-term perspective of other parts of the organization that a president or CEO must mediate and resolve. A skillful leadership style is required if the conflict involves the central strategic direction of the organization, and hiring the right people for the right jobs can be of critical importance, as is a deep understanding of both fiscal realities and strategic demands. A common leadership challenge for a university president is the efficacy of the teamwork between the chief budget officer and the chief academic officer.

STUDENT AFFAIRS

The fourth organizational element, student affairs, is part development of young people; part police, health, and safety; and part litigation and law. With broad responsibilities for student life, health, and conduct, it is a city within a city, a self-supporting hierarchical bureaucracy. Like the athletics, fund-raising, and internal operations divisions, the student affairs division typically reports directly to the president. At a large university, this division will employ hundreds of people in areas like student housing, health services, counseling and guidance, food services, admissions, registration, and financial aid. Its budget can represent 20 percent of the total, much of it coming from student "user" fees, which gives it a fiscal independence of important dimensions.

Because students are adults, but also because they are not quite adults, organizational responsibilities in student affairs are especially complex. When a major student problem emerges—a tragic fire in a fraternity, a drug-selling incident, or a sexual assault on campus—the leadership of the organization writ large is in for a difficult and very public period of scrutiny and introspection. They might also increasingly expect some form of litigation over such incidents. Finally, duplication of services and competition with other public or private entities in areas like student housing, book and supply sales, health care, student safety, and food create special managerial challenges that do not typically confront any other kind of organization.

THE ACADEMIC FUNCTION

The final organizational element of the university—the faculty and its teaching and research functions—is the university's least visible and understood from the outside, but it is also its most important component, the reason for the university's existence in the first place. Financially speaking, it is the most significant area of expense because of its inherent labor-intensiveness. And it is here where real differences from the traditional business model exist. The academic COOs—the provosts or the vice presidents for academic affairs—are loosely responsible for several "strategic business units" (the various colleges and professional schools), each with its own relatively independent leadership. Central management does not control the intellectual direction, or even the leadership, of the business units. It is probably not even managed locally, where most "first-line managers"—the department heads in English, chemistry, mathematics, and so on—show no propensity to manage at all. The equivalent of what would be called product and line services in a for-profit business—the teaching and research missions of the university—depend entirely on local entities within which there is little or no management culture of the traditional corporate kind.

The principal employees, the faculty, are what Peter Drucker calls "knowledge workers," whose allegiances are closer to their professions than to the goals and purposes of the organization that employs them.[32] Clark Kerr refers to the faculty as a guild and to the senior faculty as an oligarchy (or rule by the few).[33] Their research effort, sometimes criticized by outside observers for its narrowness and even its irrelevance, nonetheless attracts hundreds of millions of dollars to each of the nation's major universities yearly for the conduct of basic studies and provides an immense source of unquestioned expertise for the nation and even the world. Many of the world's scientific and technological discoveries and developments of the twentieth century, including the Internet, penicillin, carbon-14 dating, laser eye surgery, motion pictures, and the wine industry of California are the direct result of these university efforts.

The literature on the management of creative talent or knowledge workers speaks to the motivational requirements of these individuals and how they differ from other persons in organizations. Some of this work is therefore useful in understanding the culture of this segment of the university and how it might be managed and led. Research shows that scientists and other highly educated professionals within organizations tend to work within the realm of ideas, engaged in a creative or innovative process that is difficult to define, measure, evaluate, or control.[34] Highly educated scientists and engineers also appear to have a "cosmopolitan" orientation, with greater allegiance to their profession and to their professional peers than to their employing organization.[35] A study of high-tech professionals at a large electronics corporation confirms these patterns of behavior: technical professionals are "more likely to take pride in the quality of the technology" than are their management counterparts, who focused on the health of the business and corporate loyalty.[36] More generally, while managerial work involves predictability and control, creative or innovative activities are irregular and largely uncontrollable. Application of time pressures to innovative processes might even be unproductive. Hence, fundamental conflicts between commitment to professional standards and autonomy on the one hand, and managerial controls that emphasize organizational loyalty and short-term profitability on the other, are often inevitable in the management of knowledge workers.

The new organization implied by these patterns, with the greater prevalence of knowledge workers that futurists predict for the economy, might well come to resemble the structures found in hospitals, symphony orchestras, and in the teaching and research areas of universities. They will be composed "largely of specialists who direct the discipline of their own performance" and populated by autonomy-seeking, highly skilled persons, where the energy for the work and for the creative innovations will come from the "bottom" of the structure.[37] In hospitals and symphonies, the basic functions of caring for and curing patients and for playing the music are entirely within the abilities and discretion of the professional health workers and the musicians, respectively, just as in universities the energy for the direction of the teaching and research thrusts comes entirely from the faculty. This scenario suggests that in these sorts of entities there will be little or no hierarchical control over what work is performed or how it is conducted, either in the hospital, the symphony, or the university.

Universities additionally have the singularity of academic tenure, a system of employment where professionals are closely evaluated during an initial period of employment (typically six or seven years) and then are either awarded permanent tenure or terminated in employment. Except for extreme circumstances involving financial exigency or serious personal or professional misconduct or nonperformance, tenured faculty have life-long employment contracts with their university. At most major universities, the proportion of full-time faculty that is tenured is fairly high, ranging from 60 to 80 percent. To varying extents, universities also employ part-time or temporary instructors who are not eligible for tenure (not on the "tenure track") and this practice gives some additional control over their teaching budgets. However, the use of nontenure track faculty is often subject to significant criticism from quite diverse quarters such as the legislatures, who hear complaints from parents about their children not being taught by "regular" faculty, as well as from teaching unions who worry about the status of employees. In general, tenure is less prevalent and the use of temporary teachers more likely at the smaller, less well-endowed or -supported institutions.

Originally tenure had little to do with performance and much to do with political independence and academic freedom. It is not a particularly old tradition in universities—it began at the University of Wisconsin in 1894—but it does make the relationship between the organization and its most skilled workers administratively more challenging, or at least more interesting. It provides greater independence and autonomy to an already independent and autonomous group of professional men and women. In fact, Kerr argues that faculty power in universities has increased dramatically over the last fifty years, and this is particularly true for the most senior faculty.[38]

So when Father Hesburgh of Notre Dame asserts that the university at its heart is a work of devotion, a charitable act, he is correct. This "heart" beats around the nurturing and development of human potential and the discovery of new ways of understanding the world and its environment and its inhabitants. In turn, this involves important elements of creativity, uncompromising independence, as well as kindness and empathy.[39] And when regents or trustees wonder why the university is not run more like a business, they too are asking a pertinent question. Many of the university's functions—its physical plant operations, its sports entertainment programs, its concerts and symposia, its police force, its health services—are largely self-supporting and while they do not always make a profit, they are expected to break even and provide effective and efficient services.

THE MULTICAMPUS UNIVERSITY

William Friday and Clark Kerr both were presidents of families of universities tied together by a common administrative structure. These multicampus systems, which are typically publicly controlled organizations, are types of "holding companies," headed by an individual who oversees multiple "companies" with either similar missions or with substantial differences in their purposes and functions. From organizational and leadership perspectives, multicampus systems can present different challenges and problems than those facing single universities not part of a larger system, both for the head of the system and for the presidents and chancellors of the individual campuses within the system. The fact is that the stand-alone public university, with its own board of trustees and president making final decisions, although typical in America shortly after World War II, is an exception today. These systems of universities, of course, vary in levels of control and centralization: some have governing boards with extensive central authority over individual campuses while others have more limited coordinating (rather than governing) functions. In all such systems, however, the collective voices of the state legislators and governors are clearly heard, either directly or indirectly, through their boards of trustees or regents.

There are about 120 public systems covering some one thousand campuses. Nearly 80 percent of American college students are enrolled in colleges or universities that are part of a multicampus system, with over three million enrolled in the fifteen largest systems alone. Many public flagships within these systems, such as the more prestigious, older research universities like Michigan, UC-Berkeley, or UNC–Chapel Hill, often have more in common in research collaborations, faculty recruitment, or doctoral education with a university twenty-five hundred miles away than they do with an institution twenty-five minutes away. Three decades ago, when Gene Lee and Frank Bowen conducted their seminal work on multicampus universities,[40] the public flagships within each state held clear advantages in the area of resources, size, and political influence. And all of these flagships are still formidable national treasures, but many of the other institutions have developed significant advantages in recent years. Consider the following changes:

- Six of the nine University of California campuses (excluding the new UC-Merced, which is scheduled to open in 2005), for example, have enrollments now in excess of 18,000 students, and ten of the twenty-two California State colleges exceed that number. Size often tends to translate into votes and alumni and important regional support.
- In the last few years, North Carolina has doubled—from three to six—the number of public institutions that award the Ph.D. in its very heterogeneous system.
- Florida's legislature has recently authorized the establishment of two new law schools, in Miami and Orlando, after disbanding the statewide governing system.
- Campuses in thriving cities, like Charlotte, Miami, and Birmingham, now command considerable political influence and public resources.

These changes indicate that the size dominance and political influence of a system's flagships have been diminished by the growing clout of other campuses within their systems, which in turn has created strains within those organizations. Events and conditions leading to stronger regional institutions probably would have occurred in any case over the last three decades, with or without any governing systems or central boards. For example, it would be politically difficult for any group to oppose improvements to public campuses in a growing, vibrant city like Charlotte, which has become the second-largest banking center in the nation, behind only New York City. Contrariwise, in the case of Florida, it is not obvious that the disbanding of the public higher educational system has been beneficial for the two public flagships because significant state resources for the two new law schools, which the Florida system opposed, are now being allocated elsewhere.

The organizational distance between the heads of university systems and the faculties, students, athletic boosters, and some of the other stakeholders is greater than for the president of a single university. Put slightly differently, the University of California system in Oakland doesn't have a basketball team or an alumni association. On the other hand, system heads are usually much closer to the political scene—the governor, the legislatures, and key legislators and congressional members—than are the individual campus presidents. But system heads, principally those responsible for *governing* systems (rather than *coordinating* systems), are still accountable for the entire enterprise, particularly when things do not go well on a particular campus, as happened in the University of California during the student protests of the 1960s, or when there is a major problem such as an athletic scandal, as in the tragic case of basketball star Lenny Bias at Maryland or the more recent football recruiting scandals at the University of Colorado. The dynamics between the system headquarters and the campus chiefs—whether responsibilities are delegated to the campus, or whether the system head and the campus officers work well together, for example—can materially affect outcomes in such situations.

There can also be some interesting dynamics and "turf" rivalries among system heads and campus leaders. System administrators often find themselves in the simultaneous and ambivalent roles of campus advocates and campus critics. To external audiences like regents and legislators, they appear as advocates of the universities on whose behalf they ask for resources. But they can seem like critics—loving or otherwise—to individual campus heads and alumni who might perceive the systems as obstacles to the aspirations of their individual institutions. While there are some analogies and similarities between corporate holding companies and university systems, it is clear that universities bring additional levels of complexity and unpredictability to leadership compared to the private or for-profit sector. When Ed Woolard was CEO of Dupont, the organization was composed of some twenty-two SBUs, or strategic business units: Conoco Oil, Nylon, Lycra, and so forth. Each of these SBUs was a huge business in its own right, with annual revenues between $3 billion and $7 billion in the mid-1990s. But Woolard, as chairman of the board and CEO, was clearly and directly in control of each of the businesses, with full authority to fire and hire executives and employees in each Dupont division and with the responsibility to set detailed annual financial goals and targets for each of them. University system heads, in contrast, have to contend not only with a variety of public officials and legislators, but also with powerful supporters and alumni of each of the individual institutions, who may or may not agree with the overall goals and directives of the central system.

IMPLICATIONS FOR LEADERSHIP

Bringing to these pages the ideas of students of organizations establishes a useful foundation from which to describe the university in its full complexity. In combination with the chapter on leadership that follows, this section presents a general framework of environment and context within which to examine the six case studies that follow. Like all successful social enterprises, universities have developed systems of management and governance suited to their strengths and peculiarities. The dominant characteristic of the modern university is the exceptional degree of autonomy of individual faculty members and the strengths of the academic disciplines and departments and colleges within which they are organized. Energy for innovation and for the vitality of the educational effort comes principally out of the departments and its faculties, from the bottom up. There is little central ability or inclination to relate the work of the English department with that of genomics or materials science departments, except in very broad institutional ways.

The structure of the university has evolved to contain the five main parts discussed earlier—governance and senior administration, internal support operations, external development, student affairs, and the academic functions of teaching and research. This particular organizational structure has been determined and standardized over the decades, in part as a response to growth and increasing size, but also as a result of social and political trends, as well as by the attention that university leaders devote to each of the parts. The nature of the work within the university also has determined how the various groups of organizational employees can best be managed. The external parts—the big-time sports programs, the fund-raising offices, and the community or political public relations activities—call for a very public persona with above average oratory and written skills and with an instinctive, sensing personality capable of detecting shifts in organizational climate and ambience. Franz Humer, the CEO of the Fortune 100 pharmaceutical Roche, is famously skillful at reading subtle cues that elude less perceptive individuals, a skill he developed as a tour guide when he was young. "Eventually," Humer recalled, "I could predict within ten percent how much I could earn (in tips) from a particular group of tourists" by observing their behavior and sensing some of their cues.[41]

The startling diversity of stakeholder groups is thus a feature universities share with just a few other highly complex entities. Its presence highlights the need to understand the various components intimately and for its leaders to bring a global style to the management of the organization, comprehending its culture as well as the places where interests and demands intersect. Highly effective communication styles across the various publics, including the skill of listening, also become paramount, particularly in defining and presenting a widely accepted mission and purpose for the organization. The innocent-sounding goal of outstanding teaching, for example, might bring forth a heated argument, for example, about the canon of a discipline and about what should be taught and in what order. Similarly, a mission statement containing a reference to an institution's "historical strengths" might trigger debates about the strengths that are left off or about being preoccupied with the past and not sufficiently focused on the future. Whereas a for-profit business might have a clear set of financial goals (such as a 20 percent return on equity or a 30 percent market share in a particular product line), a more complex organization will have more ambiguous goals that are either poorly understood, vaguely defined, or not widely shared across the organization. Greater emphasis on fund-raising, on entertainment (with the attendant problems of the occasional recruiting scandal or other community challenges), on being the engine for regional and national economic growth and global competitiveness, and on external partnerships of various sorts by universities, mostly leading to the continued "privatization" of something that has long been held to be a public good, also adds significantly to organizational complexity and to greater challenges for its leaders. Clearly, highly effective communication skills across a wide diversity of audiences and functions, along with strong interpersonal orientation and a deep understanding of the university and its environments, are important features.

NOTES

1. Clark Kerr, with Marian L. Gade and Maureen Kawaoka, *Higher Education Cannot Escape History: Issues for the Twenty-First Century* (Albany: State University of New York Press, 1994), 45–46.

2. As quoted by William Bowen in "At a Slight Angle to the Universe: The University in a Digitized, Commercialized Age," the Romanes Lecture for 2000, Oxford University, October 17, 2000 (Princeton: Princeton University Press, 2001).

3. Robert Rosenzweig, *The Political University* (Baltimore: Johns Hopkins University Press, 1998).

4. Frank Knight, *The Economic Organization* (New York: Augustus M. Kelley, 1967).

5. W. Richard Scott, *Organizations: Rational, Natural, and Open Systems*, 3rd ed. (Englewood Cliffs, NJ: Prentice Hall, 1992).

6. Ibid., 226.

7. James L. Bowditch and Anthony Buono, *A Primer on Organizational Behavior*, 4th ed. (New York: John Wiley, 1997).

8. Richard H. Hall, *Organizations: Structures, Processes, and Outcomes*, 5th ed. (Englewood Cliffs, NJ: Prentice Hall, 1991), 58.

9. John Weistart, "College Sports Reform: Where Are the Faculty?" *Academe*, July–August 1987, 12ff.

10. Michael D. Cohen and James G. March, *Leadership and Ambiguity: The American College President* (New York: McGraw-Hill, 1974).

11. Clark Kerr and Marian L. Gade, *The Many Lives of Academic Presidents: Time, Place and Character* (Washington, DC: Association of Governing Boards of Universities and Colleges, 1986), 154.

12. There are certainly exceptions in the corporate world: Carly Fiorina, the CEO of Hewlett-Packard, has had a rocky relationship with her board, and others, such as Steven Jobs of Apple, have actually been fired by their own boards.

13. See Arthur Padilla, "Passing the Baton: Leadership Transitions and the Tenure of University Presidents," in *Presidential Transition in Higher Education: Managing Leadership Change*, edited by James Martin and James E. Samels (Baltimore: Johns Hopkins University Press, 2004), for a description of recent trends in university board membership and presidential turnover.

14. Perhaps the private university boards are also likely to confront their presidents, but their meetings are quite private and their deliberations and debates are not usually reported in the media.

15. Rosenzweig, *Political University*.

16. William G. Bowen, "Remarks," AAU Centennial Meeting, Symposium on the Future of Research Universities, Washington, DC, April 17, 2000.

17. Kerr and Gade, *Many Lives*.

18. Ibid., 40.

19. Ibid.

20. Ibid.

21. See Arthur Padilla and S. Ghosh, "Turnover at the Top: The Revolving Door of the Academic Presidency," *The Presidency*, Winter 2000, 30–37.

22. James Killian, Jr., *The Education of a College President: A Memoir* (Cambridge, MA: MIT Press, 1985), for a description of the MIT system.

23. Padilla and Ghosh, "Turnover at the Top."

24. Kerr and Gade, *Many Lives*.

25. Padilla and Ghosh, "Turnover at the Top."

26. Padilla, "Passing the Baton."

27. Padilla and Ghosh, "Turnover at the Top."

28. Robert F. Carbone, *Presidential Passages* (Washington, DC: American Council on Education, 1981).

29. As used here, the term "big-time sports" refers to some seventy-five or so American universities that choose to compete in Division I of the National Collegiate Athletic Association (NCAA). This implies huge investments in the sports of football, men's basketball, and occasionally in some of the women's sports and other so-called minor sports, as well as involvement in television deals and postseason competitions such as bowl games in football and "March Madness" in men's basketball. The typical athletic department budget for the operation of such programs is in the range of $20 million to $40 million per year, making it one of the largest financial operations of a university.

30. The Atlantic Coast Conference initiated a highly controversial and pro-

tracted expansion of membership during 2002 and 2003 that led to a raiding of the Big East Conference and several of its more successful teams, all in an effort to increase marketing attractiveness for television purposes in several large markets like Miami and Boston.

31. Clark Kerr, with Marian L. Gade and Maureen Kawaoka, *Troubled Times for American Higher Education: The 1990s and Beyond* (Albany: State University of New York Press, 1994), 33–47.

32. Peter F. Drucker, "The Coming of the New Organization," *Harvard Business Review*, January–February 1988, 45–53.

33. Clark Kerr, *The Great Transformation in Higher Education, 1960–1980* (Albany: State University of New York Press, 1991).

34. Mary Ann Y. Van Glinow, *The New Professionals: Managing Today's High-Tech Employees* (Cambridge, MA: Ballinger, 1988).

35. T. J. Gerpott, M. Domsch, and R. T. Keller, "Career Orientations in Different Countries and Companies: An Empirical Investigation of West German, British and US Industrial R&D Professionals," *Journal of Management Studies* 25, no. 5 (1988): 439–462.

36. Susan M. Resnick-West and Mary Ann Y. Von Glinow, "Beyond the Clash: Managing High Tech Professionals," in *Managing Complexity in High Technology Organizations*, edited by M. A. Van Glinow and S. A. Moorman (New York: Oxford University Press, 1990), 237–254.

37. Drucker, "Coming of the New Organization," 45.

38. Kerr, *Troubled Times*, 39.

39. The issues posed by what Donald Kennedy (1994) calls "the affluent professor" are increasingly relevant to the perception of the university and its image. They are also relevant to the growing disparities in pay and teaching assignments among the disciplines within the same institutions.

40. Eugene Lee and Frank Bowen, *The Multicampus University: A Study of Academic Governance* (New York: McGraw-Hill, 1971).

41. Robert Goffee and Gareth Jones, "Why Should Anyone Be Led by You?" *Harvard Business Review* 78, no. 5 (September–October 2000): 62ff.

CHAPTER

Leadership

As we survey the path leadership theory has taken, we spot the wreckage of "trait theory," the "great man" theory, and the "situationist" critique, leadership styles, functional leadership, and, finally, leaderless leadership, to say nothing of bureaucratic leadership, charismatic leadership, group-centered leadership, reality-centered leadership, leadership by objective, and so on. The dialectic and reversals of emphases in this area very nearly rival the tortuous twists and turns of child-rearing practices, and one can paraphrase Gertrude Stein by saying, "a leader is a follower is a leader."

—*Administrative Science Quarterly*
(quoted in Bennis, *On Becoming a Leader*, p. 39)

A GENERAL INTRODUCTION

The study of leadership is both an art and a science, a trip involving multiple disciplines and a range of qualitative and quantitative approaches. Its disciplinary roots stem from social psychology, sociology, psychology (behaviorist, cognitive, and psychoanalytical), organizational behavior, business management, literature, anthropology, and other fields. It is an expanding field of study that defies arbitrary disciplinary boundaries and restrictions that may one day, as James Mac-Gregor Burns notes, "join the traditional disciplines" in scholarly recognition.[1] But it is also one with a considerable lack of consensus about

the major questions, where the term "leadership" itself remains controversial. It is used neutrally, for example, to analyze the qualities of a Hitler
and a Mother Teresa, and also with passion, implying a moral dimension,
as in the case of "good" and "bad" leadership. However, lack of agreement
and an absence of a comprehensive and grand theory do not necessarily
invalidate the study of leadership as a serious scholarly topic. After all,
the more "mature" discipline of physics is also without a general theory.[2]

It is undeniable that much of the interest in, or possibly the obsession with, leadership has to do with its outcomes, and particularly its
negative ones.[3] Events of the last and current centuries confirm it: the
world has witnessed the direct and indirect impact on millions of an Idi
Amin or a Stalin or a Hitler or a Castro. And although leadership is a
form of power, it is clearly more than just power. Seeing power simply
as leadership obscures the greater imperative of power in leadership and
conceals the essential relationships between leaders and followers.
Shakespeare illustrates these notions in *Henry V*, as Henry has to resort
to bribery, promises, inspiration, and rewards to get his men to fight and
his cousin Katherine Valois to marry him. Newton's Third Law of Motion indicates that for every action there is an equal and opposite reaction, and for every power move there is a corresponding reaction that
offsets, limits, or modifies that power. Parents of teenagers know about
the limits of power, as do baseball pitchers who have tried to overpower
home run hitters with their fastballs. Limits to power therefore suggest
that leadership is about persuasion and not about domination. Unlike
sheer power or domination, leadership is inseparable from the goals and
the needs of followers. Leadership and followership may thus be regarded as circular or reciprocal relationships involving persuasion and
occurring within specific organizational situations. The relationships between these three elements—the leader, the followers, and the situational and organizational contexts within which interactions between
leaders and followers occur—are therefore inextricably linked in defining the leadership process.

The scope of what has been written about leadership presents a challenge of distillation and synthesis if one is to avoid a representation that
is too simplistic, too trivial, or too much of a condensation.[4] An amazingly diverse array of books and articles has been written about the topic
of leadership—over 8,000 by 1990, according to the most recent edition
of a reference book by Bass and Stogdill.[5] In addition, there are significant differences in what the various disciplines study. Social and organizational psychology, for example, concentrate on leaders in small groups
and complex organizations, while political scientists and psycho-

historians focus fairly exclusively on world and national political leaders. Thus, to discuss leadership systematically and comprehensively takes some courage, particularly because theories purporting to be general are vulnerable to a critical mugging and leave theorists notoriously exposed to the probing of experimental researchers. Given these general concerns, where should an analysis of leadership begin? And for the purposes of this study, how can a conceptual synthesis be developed to frame a fruitful examination of the six cases presented here?

PRINCIPAL APPROACHES TO
THE STUDY OF LEADERSHIP

Four principal scholarly approaches have evolved over the years in the study of leadership: the trait approach (including the "neo-trait" approach, a revival of the "traits matter" school led by scholars such as Timothy Judge), the situational approach, the functional or behaviorist approach, and the transformational approach.[6] Each of these approaches has an impact on this study, but overarching these research streams is also a tension about the use of quantitative (or experimental) versus qualitative approaches that remains unresolved.[7] Sometimes in scholarly work the lives or broad leadership experiences of certain men and women are examined qualitatively in hopes of finding commonalities, some average tendencies, so that appropriate generalizations can be made and a better understanding of the entire process can be achieved. Quantitative approaches, on the other hand, which have dominated the journal literature in recent years, essentially tackle the leadership puzzle by inductively fitting together parts of a picture whose overall composition is presumably known. Qualitative studies, more comprehensive and holistic in their approach, focus instead on creating the picture or composition as new parts of the puzzle are collected and analyzed.

From the days of Aristotle and Homer, through Machiavelli and Shakespeare, writers have explored the phenomenon of leadership and followership. During the early part of the twentieth-century writers tended to focus on traits, rather than on behaviors or on particular situations that made one or another type of trait more successful. The classic quote is from Thomas Carlyle, who wrote that "the history of the world was the biography of great men."[8] These studies examined individuals who had achieved a certain level of authority or responsibility in an effort to identify any unique qualities that leaders might possess. Fundamental to the approach was the notion that some people are innately endowed with characteristics that make them natural leaders: leaders were born, not made. Examples from the classics abound. In his *Nicomachean Ethics*, Aristotle discusses a version of emotional intelligence, popularly known today as "EQ," referring to it as a virtue or intelligence of temperance, the ability to know when and how emotion should be displayed. Sophocles' play, *Antigone*, examines the psychology of leadership and female leadership in particular. Homer's *Iliad* and *Odyssey* contain detailed biographies of leaders, while Shakespeare's *Othello* explores the role of intuition in leadership and his *Henry V* offers original insights on power and leadership styles (many of which have been echoed in contemporary films like *Braveheart* and *The Patriot*). And Machiavelli's *The Prince*, one of the gems from the Renaissance, reminds leaders that "nothing is more difficult . . . more perilous . . . or more uncertain in its success, than to take the lead in the introduction of a new order of things." These classics, along with the other more recent efforts generally categorized under the "Great Man" designation (so named presumably because these writers could find no great women), employed qualitative methods. They focused on the detailed circumstances of selected individuals, on the personal traits and characteristics of individuals identified as leaders, such as intelligence, values, self-confidence, strategic abilities, physical presence, and appearance. In fact, these works revealed some important linkages between personal traits and success as a leader: intelligence, for example, is certainly associated with leadership success.[9] But the diversity of traits found among many effective leaders also suggested that leadership ability and success are not entirely related to personal traits or genetics but also to the situation, to leader behaviors (rather than traits or personality), and even to luck.[10]

By the late 1940s and 1950s, with scholarly advances in psychology and social psychology, research inquiries into the traits of leaders had become more quantitative and survey-based in nature. Researchers sought answers among a broader set of individuals in positions of influence rather than from a smaller number whose lives and styles were examined in greater detail. Innovations in computing technologies and significant progress in the discipline of statistics also assisted scholars in using tests and measures of aptitude to examine broad ranges of attributes among large numbers of situations and people. Intricate quantitative studies and model-building experiments were conducted to test (necessarily narrow) concepts of leadership behaviors by examining data of limited usefulness to the broader issues being studied. The focus, however, remained on leader traits as researchers endeavored to develop a list of leadership attributes.[11] Among the traits examined were extroversion, masculinity, integrity, creativity, self-confidence, age, energy level, fluency of speech, popularity and sociability, persistence against obstacles, and desire to excel. This so-called trait approach pointed to broader characteristics thought to be associated with effective leadership, such as the willingness to be in a position of control and dominance over others and being attuned to the needs of others.[12]

As such traits were increasingly found to be important only under particular situations, trait theory evolved into a second, also largely quantitative approach called situational leadership. Possession of a particular trait was no guarantee for success: its importance was situational, or dependent on the situation. For instance, the trait of creativity, consistent with effective leadership in general, was predictably found to be more important in entrepreneurial situations and in developing new businesses than it was in highly bureaucratic settings: the findings from the trait research led to the trait-situational variant that studied traits in the context of particular conditions.

While traits and situational studies emphasized the individual characteristics of leaders (and occasionally, of followers), the functional or behavioral research stream that followed emphasized the behaviors of leaders; it examined actions and communication patterns that leaders employ, rather than the traits they possess. Since many behaviors can be taught and learned somewhat more readily than traits, the notion that leaders were born began to lose ground among scholars.[13] Leadership, or at least certain aspects of valuable leadership skills, such as communication or time management, could be taught. Early behavioral studies in fact served as the precursors to many of the "empowerment" theories so popular today, which emphasize the empowerment of workers, or the delegation of significant responsibilities to, and the sharing of authority within, "teams" in the management of organizations.[14] Behaviorist research also concentrated on another leadership dichotomy: people-orientation and task-orientation.[15] A resultant implication was that behaviors that might be effective in one situation might not be so successful in others; behavior effectiveness is contingent upon organizational situations.[16] Other, more recent work (like dyadic theory or its modern successor, leader-member exchange) emphasizes the relationship between a leader and a follower and argues that trait and behavior theories oversimplify the relationship between leaders and followers. In particular, dyadic proponents argue that leaders do not uniformly broadcast a trait such as self-confidence or a behavior such as people-orientation that is received equally by each subordinate.[17]

Still, in many quantitative models, principal attention is often given to the statistical reliability of measures and to the relationships among variables, with little or no attention shown toward the overall logical adequacy of the underlying model. Leadership studies may be attempted inductively or deductively, and, indeed, at an early stage of development, inductive and deductive approaches might not be distinguishable from one another. Inductive approaches, as Melcher notes, tend not to focus on the underpinning theoretical frameworks but rather on empirical measures through the application of some statistical technique-like factor or discriminant analysis to determine which measures cluster together. An emphasis on inductive approaches has tended to limit theoretical contributions to what is known about leadership. The practical import of these considerations, of data mining and of letting the data tell the story, is that the allure of a quantitative study with statistical rigor has often precluded approaches favoring a broader theory with testable hypotheses flowing from it.[18]

MORE GLOBAL APPROACHES

Among recent works that take a more comprehensive and dynamic (or intertemporal) view of leadership and followership are James MacGregor Burns' *Leadership* (1978), Ronald Heifetz's *Leadership Without Easy Answers* (1994), and Howard Gardner's *Leading Minds* (1995). In his book, Burns proposed his well-known typology of "transformational" and "transactional" leadership, although Machiavelli, with his discussions about the "lion" and "fox" qualities of leaders in *The Prince*, arguably developed a similar leadership nomenclature 500 years earlier. Leadership, Burns argued, was not simply effective or transactional; there were moral dimensions to it as well. In describing the evolution of the governing and leadership styles of Franklin Delano Roosevelt, Burns notes that FDR's governing strategy during the war was quite different from that of the prewar years, as the war effort was changing the nation. FDR, in Burns' words, had become a transforming leader, just as Abraham Lincoln had done during the Civil War. Roosevelt had been "both a lion and a fox" before the war, but after that Sunday in December of 1941, the lion prevailed.[19] Effective leaders transacted with their followers based on rewards and incentives, but they also transformed them at times. He thus made a distinction between two different but compatible leadership behaviors—transformational and transactional—and many scholars would subsequently use Burns' terminology when describing leadership (transformational) and managing (transactional).[20] For example, Bennis and Nanus distinguished between leadership and management this way:

> Management typically consists of a set of contractual exchanges, "you do this job for that reward . . ." What gets exchanged is not trivial; jobs, security, money. The result, at best, is compliance; at worst, you get a spiteful obedience. The end result of the leadership we have advanced is completely different: it is empowerment. Not just higher profits and wages . . . but an organizational culture that helps employees generate a sense of meaning in their work and a desire to challenge themselves to experience success.[21]

Burns' transformational leadership has been the basis for considerable quantitative research in recent years: nearly six hundred Ph.D. dissertations in various disciplines have "transformational leadership" in the title.[22] Burns recognized explicitly that the focus of research should be on leadership, rather than on leaders, and that the hierarchies of motivations of both leaders and followers are the determinants shaping this reciprocal relationship called leadership. In other words, leadership was a process, not a person, a "rich and pulsating" activity held together by the glue of the motivations of followers and leaders. It was both a qualitative and a multidisciplinary response affirming not only the primacy of political science, Burns' own discipline, but also that of psychology and other fields in the study of leadership. Burns' holistic approach stood in sharp contrast to the quantitative (and generally not cumulative) model building that dominated leadership research for much of the twentieth century. It was a return to the more comprehensive qualitative method that prevailed at the beginning of the 1900s in an attempt to arrive at a more universal picture of leadership. It also tended to avoid the false dichotomies in leadership studies: are leaders born or made? Are they people-oriented or task-oriented?

Burns' multidisciplinary approach also emphasizes the importance of the leaders' early lives and of the vast array of stimuli and influences to which they are exposed and by which they are surrounded, an aspect taken largely from psychology and psycho-history that has not received the attention it deserves among quantitative research efforts. Several other writers who have pondered the determinants of extraordinariness or genius, such as Mihaly Csikszentmihalyi, have emphasized the importance of early childhood: where do leaders find the inner confidence and strength to deal with a high level of uniqueness or otherness in comparison to other people?

Gardner, with his central notion of the leader's "story," brings a cognitive perspective to his framework or anatomy of leadership and further deconstructs leadership within the context of the leader-follower dynamic. His "anatomy" asserts that leaders achieve their effectiveness through the stories that they relate. He explicitly uses "relate" instead of "tell" because "relate" implies a much broader connotation; words are only one way to communicate. Thus, the embodiment of traits, or perhaps the embodiment of codifying symbols, such as Churchill's cigar and the confident "V" sign, or the use of other symbols, become part of a leader's story. Gardner emphasizes the struggle that takes place in the minds of followers as they evaluate both the stories of leaders as well as the counterstories of opposing perspectives as the circular or back-and-forth process of leadership and followership evolves. Gardner's approach is also heavy with the influences of childhood on the eventual leader, including the early socialization of the child, drawing significantly from Erikson, Freud, and Piaget, particularly in the area of the personality of the young child.[23]

Heifetz combines elements present in both Burns and Gardner while emphasizing the process of change or adaptation—the new strategies, the clarification of values, the new ways of operating—that leaders must effect in mobilizing people to do adaptive work and fix their own problems. Gardner's notion of a leader's "story" is consistent with the adaptive processes inherent in Heifetz's concept of the leadership and followership process, if there are, as surely there must be, iterative or dynamic versions to leaders' stories and if the group uses the stories to facilitate adaptive work. Heifetz's approach effectively blends Gardner's "story" or vision idea with the notion of power and persuasion from Burns to arrive at a useful framework through which to define the process.[24]

Leadership has no easy answers, according to Heifetz, because leaders are always a part, but only a part, of the answer. This is what makes his notion of adaptive work crucial to an understanding of leadership. People too often look to leaders for the answers to their problems, when in fact the people themselves are the only ones capable of solving them. History indicates that leaders are commonly placed on pedestals beset with unrealistic expectations about the abilities of leaders to achieve results single-handedly and to solve the problems for their groups. And when the problems persist and the leader has failed to resolve them, then leaders are typically attacked, dismissed, or even killed because they come to represent disillusionment of one sort or another to members of a group or community. Scapegoating authority figures is as unfair as it is prevalent: leaders are given authority to provide direction or to maintain order, but they are resented if or when they try to place the adaptive work back on the people themselves.

Adaptive work is the learning process that addresses conflicts in the values that people hold, or at least it is the process that illuminates the gap within the group between expectations and hopes and the realities it faces. It is a fundamentally important responsibility of leadership and implies a change in values, beliefs, and even behavior. Adaptive work, according to Heifetz and to Burns, is thus the exposure and evaluation of conflict and contradictions within groups to mobilize people to learn in new ways. The clarification of what matters most becomes the heart of the leadership function. And the inclusion of competing values within a group might be indispensable to adaptive success: the international business that ignores the widespread concerns about globalism might not be very successful in the long run. Leadership styles, communication skills, knowledge about the organizational culture and about the external environment facing the organization, among other things, are intimately related to effective adaptive work.

Another implication of leadership and followership concerns the temporary nature of these processes. Part of the temporariness comes from biological imperatives—human beings, of course, have limited life and work spans—but it more often originates in the self-interests of people. Self-interest frequently overcomes the interests of a group or of a leader as individuals return to their personal concerns and put aside group priorities. Put somewhat differently, how often can or should the coach ask the players to win one for the Gipper? Several writers have asserted that evolutionary history tends to make people selfish but also capable of cooperation with others for the welfare of a social unit. Indeed, individual survival sometimes depends crucially on group survival.[25] Here there are implications for short-term and long-term self-interests: actions promoting the group might also serve a person's long-term welfare, but perhaps without external threats people will largely pursue their short-term goals.[26] Under these conditions, the leadership process can in part be viewed as an act of persuasion of limited duration while a common goal is pursued and while personal or short-term goals are temporarily set aside for the good of the group. This perspective is useful as one ponders the success and failures of leaders in a variety of settings with the passage of time. Among the interesting questions are: What personal behaviors determine the longevity of leadership? What explains why some leadership is more lasting than others? Are there specific organizational situations that explain longevity of leadership? How difficult is transformational leadership when transactional exchanges—rewards, punishments, and the like—are limited due to the nature of the situation or the organization?

TOWARD A SYNTHESIS: WHAT IS LEADERSHIP?

The distinctive, or even disjointed, nature of the various pieces of leadership research makes it difficult to summarize comprehensively what has been posited over the past century. Inductive studies have illuminated isolated leadership behaviors and patterns, but as a group they do not provide much of a global picture of the larger, and inherently more interesting, problem of the structure of the leadership and followership processes. In spite of literally thousands of studies, broad qualitative and comprehensive approaches to the study of leadership such as Burns' *Leadership*, Gardner's *Leading Minds*, or Heifetz's *Leadership Without Easy Answers* remain rare, even though these are the sorts of inquiries that would bring overarching insights to a topic where there is still a significant lack of consensus about the major questions. In spite of the problems of summarization, it is useful to attempt to lay out what is known about leadership and followership and in the process to develop a framework to inform the analysis of the six cases that follow.

First, the research increasingly concludes that leadership is *persuasion* and not domination or power.[27] This conclusion would seem relevant in any setting, from the military to the for-profit sector and beyond. The element of persuasion in leadership is particularly compelling in an organizational setting such as the university, where stakeholders are so varied and where so many of them, including the faculty, have great independence of action and intermittent involvement with the organization itself. Compounding the difficulty leaders of such organizations face is the common belief that university presidents are much more powerful than they actually are.[28] In fact, much of a president's time is taken up with "royal" activities: receiving visitors or petitions, giving formal approvals, and appearing at meetings and functions of various sorts. Most of these activities are reactive. So persuasion is even more important in these types of organizations than in others where leaders are more powerful and in actual control of processes.

Furthermore, the prototypical American worker until very recently has been a white, Anglo male with a high school diploma and a job in manufacturing. But recent years have witnessed an amazing change in the American worker: most of the new labor market entrants are now not white males but rather women and minorities such as Hispanics. Educational levels are increasing and the management of a vastly diverse pool of skilled workers will be a new demand on leadership, one that will require more comfort and facility with less familiar forms of behavior and communication.[29]

Leadership is fundamentally a *temporary activity*, even aside from obvious biological limits on life. History suggests that without some external stimuli or threat to a group, people within the group will tend to pursue their own interests over the longer run.[30] This was never more poignantly demonstrated than in the case of Winston Churchill, an amazingly effective war leader, when he was voted out of office as prime minister shortly after the conclusion of World War II. Leadership thus entails persuading, not coercing, other people to set aside for some time their individual needs and pursue some collective or group goal or goals.

But *what goals* and, perhaps more importantly, *whose goals*, should be pursued? For both Burns and Heifetz, leadership involves a reciprocal effort between leaders and followers to mobilize resources and do something that is *socially useful*. In the case of Burns, socially useful goals are those that elevate followers to a higher moral level, such as Kennedy's call to help one's country or Gandhi's appeal for peaceful resistance to an unjust social and legal system. The central responsibility of leadership in Heifetz's view is to carry out the adaptive work that highlights what matters most to the group and that begins to reconcile and eliminate differences and obstacles within the group. What about, more specifically, leadership in an organization like the modern university, with its diversity of stakeholders and with quasi–free agents as the primary employees? According to Cohen and March, because of the nature of the university, almost any educated person could deliver a talk on the goals of the university and nearly no one in the university would want to hear it.[31] They view the university as an "organized anarchy," where goals are neither clear nor widely accepted or agreed upon, where the technology (how things are done) is familiar but unclear, and where there is inadequate knowledge about who is attending to what and where major participants wander in and out. While there is a certain allure to this cleverly provocative description of the university as an organization, it nonetheless seems more of a caricature than a realistic description. Many goals are clear, well understood, and widely accepted, at least internally within the university. Budgetary goals, for example, fit this category, (especially when they concern higher salaries), as do goals about building construction and about the strengthening of the teaching or research functions. Still, the university often makes choices without the benefit of consistent or shared goals. Increased turnover at the top of an organization, as has been occurring during the last decade in the major public universities, tends to compound these challenges: middle managers (deans and department heads) often will delay actions in response to managerial uncertainty in higher levels of the organization.[32] These factors do not make

the university a disorganized or a bad place, but they do make it difficult
to describe and, more importantly, to lead.

INGREDIENTS OF LEADERSHIP

While much of the quantitative research is not cumulative in the sense
of a corpus of advancing knowledge that builds upon and learns from itself, there are some important areas of agreement about the process of
leadership. These general spheres of concurrence are easier to identify, or
are more evident, in qualitative works, such as the studies by Burns and
Heifetz, since one of the fundamental missions of qualitative work is to
create a holistic picture of leadership from the various pieces of the puzzle
rather than, in the case of quantitative approaches, taking small pieces
and analyzing those. There are, in fact, four elements common to the
analyses of Burns, Heifetz, and Gardner that define the broad contours
of leadership and followership processes:

1. the evolutionary roots of authority in humans
2. early childhood experiences of future leaders, including the relatively
   new topic of resiliency
3. formal education in domains and the impact of mentors
4. adult characteristics of leaders, including gifts in the realms of communication and interpersonal understanding

1. Evolutionary Roots

One of the most important criticisms of Frederick Taylor's theory of
management was that it ignored human nature. Today, any modern theory of organizational behavior (and leadership) implicitly or explicitly
depends on certain assumptions about the nature of humans.[33] Freud believed that to understand human behavior one had to understand the
evolutionary origins of humans at the genetic level. Some human tendencies, according to Freud, are unconscious and beyond our ken without the help of a therapist, so that humans often will not know why they
do what they do. Darwin probably influenced Freud, at least in some respects: Freud credited Darwin for his decision to enter medical school
and his theory of psychosexual developments had clear biological and
Darwinian influences.[34] Freud was wrong in implying that at the root of
all human motivation were two basic instincts: eros, (including sex, self-
preservation, love) and the destructive instinct (aggression, the death instinct, hate).[35] Robert Wright, whose work on modern evolutionary
theory amends and extends psychoanalysis, argues forcefully that most

humans are motivated by a wide range of unconscious biological impulses, including Freud's eros and the destructive instinct, but also by a drive for status and a deep concern for how one is perceived by others.[36] In addition, humans tend to be both deeply selfish as well as very altruistic (for example, in their willingness to make sacrifices for family, relatives, and friends). Freudian and evolutionary theories agree on the frequency of self-deception by humans but disagree about the purposes it serves. According to Wright, Freudian theory says humans lie to avoid punishment by the superego, because, in other words, they agree with society that such impulses are wrong; evolutionary theory says people lie to themselves because they want status and acceptance or to get ahead and also get along. Modern Darwinians are certainly more cynical, but they might make more sense in some instances.[37]

The proclivity of humans to imitate and to follow is also well established in anthropologic and biological research.[38] Tracing human behavior to these disciplines does not suggest, of course, that people are monkeys or that their biological origins imply a masculine model of leadership. Research with primates indicates the existence of clear positions of dominance and the group's preference for hierarchical leadership positions for the overall benefit of the group in terms of food and safety: when fighting exists among dominant primates for control of a group, the overall welfare of the group declines and suffers.[39] The dominance hierarchy promotes stability and peace within the group and the community looks to the leader for direction, protection, and for control of conflict. Higher status primates also have higher levels of serotonin in their blood; lower status primates within the group show higher stress and are more likely to bare their teeth in a show of fear and submission when confronted by the dominant group members.

Biological roots of authority have contemporary resonance in a variety of settings. Howard Dean's screams and Michael Dukakis' ill-fitting tank helmet (making him look like Snoopy) during their political campaigns were emblematic of their respective downfalls as U.S. presidential aspirants. Students of body language repeatedly cite imitation that flows from higher status individuals to lower status ones. Examples include imitation in fashion, in speech patterns and slang, and in physical looks. Imitation is not all bad, nor is it limited to teenagers or movie star fans: official "dress codes" of Apple Computer—or lack thereof—in the early days of Steven Jobs were a sign of rebelliousness and solidarity with and acceptance of the dot-com garage culture.

The patterns that emerge in small settings involving adult groups are also instructive. Take, for instance, the classic movie *Twelve Angry Men*, starring Henry Fonda as the jurist who single-handedly took on the jury's chairman and eventually led his eleven peers to reconsider their hasty decision to convict a young boy charged with murdering his father. A group with members who do not know each other will quickly establish a hierarchy when undertaking a task. They will select a "chair" for the group and that leader or chair is expected to perform a role of coordination and direction. During a problem or crisis needing intervention or mediation, the group will look to its leader and expect resolution. If resolution is not forthcoming, the leader will lose status and even the dominant role.[40] Thus, studies of small adult groups suggest a psychological dynamic to authority: when uncertainty and stress arise within a group, the group members will look to a leader for coordination and problem solving. Leaderless situations are possible—hippie communes have often functioned without leaders—but they have been a clear exception in history.

2. Family and Early Childhood

In 1802, Wordsworth suggested a simple answer to the impact of childhood on a person's development: "The child is father of the man."[41] Milton narrowed it to five words: "The childhood shows the man."[42] And while the "entire man" might not be seen in the "cradle of the child," as de Tocqueville wrote, a leader's family background and early life have deservedly received intense attention in leadership literature, particularly from the discipline of psychology with the work of Freud, Piaget, and Erikson.[43] The flow of images, symbols, trends, stereotypes, and experiences around a child in the home is a powerful influence on the adult leader, and the early socialization of children provides powerful clues about future behaviors.

Research highlights the importance of the establishment in early life of a strong and secure bond of attachment between infant and caretaker: a developing sense of trust between child and caretaker, or its absence, colors the way individuals react to authority later in life. Another feature is the gradual emergence in the young child of a sense of self. Children as young as eighteen months are aware they exist as separate beings; they know names, faces, and how they are similar to certain other individuals. Scholars study this process, known as "identification," where children begin to identify with certain people within their immediate circle just as they also begin to develop a sense of self as a distinct person. An intriguing indicator of future leaders exists when a youngster exhibits a capacity at an early age to identify with a more distant authority figure, with someone not in his or her immediate circle, an identification that "manifests itself both in efforts to emulate the leader and in a willingness to challenge that leader under certain circumstances."[44]

Gardner's discussion of what he calls the "five-year-old mind" derives from the work on young children of Freud and Piaget and has important implications for how leaders communicate and how their messages are heard and interpreted, even for leaders of organizations (like universities) with more educated and sophisticated members.[45] Both Freud and Piaget believe that children pass through various stages in their development; Freud believes these emotional stages are cumulative while Piaget believes they are not, that once children achieve a more advanced stage, they no longer retain or relive their earlier stages. By five years of age, even without formal instruction, children already have cemented notions about how their world works—heavy objects fall faster than do lighter ones, things that move are alive and those that don't are not—and they have detailed scripts and stereotypes about their surroundings. Piaget of course highlighted these tendencies of young children, but he was perhaps wrong in assuming these simplistic and unsophisticated preconceptions or misconceptions of the child would necessarily dissolve or disappear by adulthood.[46] Children in fact have a remarkably large number of pre-conceptions: their minds are surprisingly "made up" in a large number of instances.[47] These basic or "unschooled" theories and scripts about the world are well consolidated and in the absence of compelling and disconfirming events that are frequently re-enforced to dislodge prevailing beliefs, there is remarkable persistence over one's life in this phenomenon and "the growing individual shows little inclination to change."[48]

Although Ernest Hemingway probably never heard of the relatively new field of resiliency research, in A Farewell to Arms he did refer to it when he wrote that "the world breaks everyone and afterward many are strong at the broken places." In fact, resiliency, the ability of some children to play a poor hand well, is of special interest under the discussion of childhood influences on future leadership behaviors. There is an apparent correlation between a troubled childhood or an absent father or mother and unusual achievement in later life, and thus the notion of resiliency can provide insights to the ways individuals rebound from difficult and even tragic circumstances during childhood.[49] Researchers studying the lives of successful adults who overcame adversity have cited instances in which children used successes in one area of life to neutralize enduring pain in another.[50] For example, many children growing up in violent situations who were skilled academically or athletically and socially engaging were able to use their school experiences to neutralize some of the turmoil experienced at home. From the first day of school, many of these children felt successful and accepted. They were buffered and shielded by teachers, supported by friends and classmates, and welcomed by their friends' families. They developed a sense of mastery by virtue of their school experiences. One of the leaders interviewed during the conduct of this study (not one of the six cases presented in later chapters) put it this way:

> My father left when I was seven years old and returned three years later with another family. My parents divorced, leaving me at home with a younger sister and my mother, who took on all the familial responsibilities by herself. From the very beginning, reading was a way to escape a very dysfunctional family situation. It was a way to live other lives. It was the emotional "place" where I hid and where I first began how to understand other people and how to interpret their feelings and emotions.

Ironically, society might sometimes gain from individual childhood loss and tragedy. A set of conditions that creates chronic unhappiness might establish a driving interest in a particular goal and the motivation to reach it. As Subotnik et al., ask: "What more could individuals accomplish if they had a 'psychological worm' eating inside them, such as low self-concept or need to prove something to someone or to the world, toward the development of a specific talent?"[51] Barbara Kerr, in her *Smart Girls: A New Psychology of Girls, Women, and Giftedness*, echoes many of these themes between difficult childhoods of girls and later extraordinariness.[52] An awkward adolescence compounded by difficult childhood experiences emphasized a sense of separateness from other people, a consciousness often rooted in a lonely or troubled childhood. These girls understood the advantages, as well as the heartaches and loneliness, of nonconformity. It increased their time alone, which allowed them to focus inwardly on their dreams and intellectual achievements and encouraged compassion for and identification with the suffering of disadvantaged or unaccepted people.

The young people who develop the mental muscle required to overcome childhood adversities and who do well as adults tend to rely on protective influences in their earlier years. These protective shields enable them eventually to deal with the pain they endure and to recognize the special talents they possess.[53] Refuge comes from three primary sources: (1) from within the children themselves, as evidenced by personal qualities or attributes such as unusual athletic ability or looks or intelligence (Katz calls such children "sparkly," possessing qualities that draw others toward them in times of need);[54] (2) from the family, such as a parent or grandparent or sibling who buffered and nurtured a child; and (3) from the community or schools or youth and religious groups, through an external support system that allows meaningful and valued relationships to form and flourish and allows a child to express talents or interests.[55]

What differentiates the children who cope and later succeed from those who do not? The literature lists several factors:[56]

1. **Possession of attributes that produce positive responses from other people.** Such children had an active and social temperament, a "hardy" personality that seemed to draw people to their lives. They gain a sense of pride from their achievements, hobbies, and talents and exhibit a sense of internal control: "I can influence what happens to me." (Management scholars call this attitude toward change an "internal locus of control.") Teachers ranked them as excellent problem solvers and as proactive rather than reactive or passive when solving problems, taking charge of situation as opposed to waiting for others to do things for them or reacting negatively to situations they cannot control. This proactivity requires self-reliance and independence but also social adeptness in order to obtain help from adults and peers.

2. **A close bond with at least one primary caregiver during infancy and early childhood.** This caregiver is not always the parent: it might be a coach or a teacher or another relative. Such children enjoy affectionate ties with grandparents and older brothers or sisters, who served as buffers or as parent substitutes and who shield them from some of the stresses surrounding them and encourage trust and initiative within the children.

3. **An external support system that recognizes and rewards talents and abilities and provides the children with a sense of coherence.** The added support was gained in many different ways, such as through school experiences, involvement in youth groups, or in religious activities.

4. **Ability to interpret their experiences in positive and constructive ways, even for those experiences that are painful or negative.** Resilient children tend to be good-natured and easy to deal with and as a result, they gain other people's positive attention.

5. **A sense of challenge and commitment and a consistent ability to find meaning in what they are doing, another aspect of "hardy" personalities.** These children see the positive aspects of change and are able to get beyond the negative or "scary" aspects of threatening situations. The ability to see meaning behind suffering and hardship is an important quality in resilient, hardy children, often assuming the role of caregiver or peacemaker to others in their negative situation.

A cautionary note is important, as Norman Garmezy warns, when discussing the concepts of adversity or risk on the one hand and resilience on the other. Too much adversity is difficult to overcome no matter how resilient or "sparkly" the child. Research shows that exposure to several sources of stress (such as severe marital discord, low socioeconomic status, overcrowding or large family size, paternal criminality, maternal psychiatric disorder, and foster placement) significantly increases a child's chances of developing serious problems. The trivialization of the concept could lead to a Horatio Alger mythology or to an "American Dream" notion of success: anyone can succeed if they work hard and have the right set of traits and attitudes. Another danger would be the mistaken belief that adversity in early life is a necessary or a sufficient condition for future success or leadership. The keys to understanding lie both within the individual and in the situational context.[57]

3. Formal Education and Mentors

Formal education has come to occupy a central place among western nations, indispensable for professional and political advancement. Chief executives of major corporations normally possess not only a bachelor's degree, but increasingly will have a master's degree in business management, a law degree, or both. Similarly, legislators and other politicians often have a university education and many are trained lawyers. It would be similarly difficult to find a president at a major American university without an advanced degree like a Ph.D. or a first professional (terminal) degree like law or medicine. While this situation varies from nation to nation, the norm is toward higher levels of literacy and formal education in a domain as a necessary condition for holding a position of authority and responsibility. In the United States and other western nations, there are age minima for school attendance and students must stay in school until they reach their early to mid-teens as recognition, at least in part, of the notion that a well-educated citizenry is necessary for the proper functioning of democracy and civic government.

For economic and social reasons, formal schooling is concentrated in students' earlier, rather than later, years. During their formative periods, children, teenagers, and young adults learn from masters in various disciplines and are exposed to increasingly sophisticated notions about people and science, and more generally, about the world and its functioning. Travel and exposure to different cultures and the corresponding need for translation, literally and figuratively, is also associated with future extraordinariness and leadership.[58]

Important relationships are also developed during this time of intense learning and exploration with teachers, professors, and others, or as Erikson says, with "leader figures outside of the family."[59] These "leader figures" can be exceptionally important to a young person's future as they can provide models of behavior and action and, more importantly, can open the doors to the guilds. The process of mentoring is in fact not well understood and only beginning to be studied and examined. It is clearly a reciprocal process between mentor and student, one that requires approval and consent from both parties. The mentor has to be attracted by the student and the student must be coachable in the eyes of the mentor. Some mentors, because of their reputations as great teachers or coaches, are actively sought out by potential pupils, and in certain cases are paid well for their services. Examples of "professional mentors" in sports are Nick Bollettieri, a tennis coach with a reputation for training stars such as Andre Agassi and Anna Kournikova, and Bela Karolyi, the Romanian emigrant who coached Nadia Comaneci and several other Olympic gold medalists in gymnastics.

But pay is not limited to famous sports mentors: successful researchers at prestigious university labs and centers are able to take their pick from among dozens of Ph.D. students and post-doctoral students who willingly "pay" them by conducting valuable research for minimal or even no pay in order to obtain a good job after completing the "training" under the distinguished professor. Clearly, to be accepted by the great mentors, whether in a sports camp or at a great university laboratory, pupils must exhibit great talent and attitude, even if they are paying or providing valuable services for the mentoring.

In less extreme mentoring situations, where mentoring is less formal and more voluntary in nature, many of the same elements have to be present. The mentor has to want to mentor the pupil and the pupil must seek out and accept the mentor. The mentor has to bring certain characteristics to the relationship, either career contacts, professional reputation, or expertise in some area, and the mentee has to be easy to work with, with an appropriate personality, and must possess the appropriate skills or intelligence level.

Bill Smithburg, CEO of Quaker Oats during their highly successful run in the 1980s and 1990s, was himself mentored by the previous company CEO as a young man. He describes the importance of mentoring this way:

> Not everyone has a mentor, but this is usually crucial in getting an opportunity and in recognizing it. You first have to be "mentorable,"

which means you have to have talent and skill and the right attitude. You also have to be in the right place at the right time. Every
young person gets an opportunity, a shot, some time early in their
career; some get more than one. The successful people recognize
their shot, their opportunity, once they see it and they have the talent—and perhaps the luck—to do something with it.

Specifically applicable to the case of extraordinary women—and related to the issue of their separateness or nonconformity when growing
up—is the phenomenon of confluence. A term from psychotherapy, confluence refers to a blending or a flowing with other people, to the point
of losing one's identity. Barbara Kerr highlights the importance of mentors as young women are making their bids to enter and succeed in male-
dominated fields.[60] Due to the relative absence of female role models,
mentors might be especially important to women in opening the doors
to the professions and to the business world. Eminent women seem capable of connecting in mentoring relationships without giving up their
own identities and personal goals. Georgia O'Keeffe was furious when she
was once called the "greatest woman artist" because she felt her gender
should not qualify her status in the world of art.[61] Successful women resolved the problem of confluence by the time they started their life's
work. While there is not much research on the topic, the importance of
mentors to other minorities might be of equal prominence, and in the
absence of such mentors, families might take on greater significance. Put
somewhat differently, talented non-minorities might be able, for example, to weather a troubled family situation more easily than could minorities or women because they might have access to a greater variety
and number of potential mentors.

4. Adult Characteristics of Leaders: Communication and Interpersonal Skills

The entire assemblage of traits and behaviors that constitute the adult
leader, including interpersonal understanding and an unusual facility in
the sphere of communication, including listening, comprises the final ingredients in the factors that make leadership and followership feasible.
Persons who reach levels of significant authority and responsibility typically will have above average intelligence but many also have an extraordinary ability to communicate orally and in writing and a keen

understanding of human behavior. The importance of communication, including listening, cannot be overstated for leaders for these skills emerge as one of the top qualities of effective leaders.[62]

As illustrated in the cases that follow, leaders are eloquent in speech and in other forms of communication as well, whether in the instance of Father Hesburgh articulating the case of a Catholic university that also wants to achieve excellence academically, or Bill Friday receiving an un-heard of standing round of applause from a North Carolina legislative committee on appropriations or Hanna Gray leading creative efforts to rejuvenate an ageing faculty at the University of Chicago. In these con-texts, the linkages between leaders and their communities or organiza-tions are also of vital importance. Their credibility and successes hinge on the strength of their ties to their organizations and on their knowl-edge of the audiences and cultures of the groups, as well as on their level of "technical" knowledge appropriate to their industry or sector.

As Robert Caro has shown in his remarkable books about U.S. Presi-dent Lyndon Johnson, many leaders have great intelligence in the realm of human understanding. Johnson was not a reader of books; he was in-stead "a great reader of men. He had a genius for studying a man and learning his strengths and weaknesses and hopes and fears, his deepest strengths and weaknesses: what it was that the man wanted—not what he said he wanted but what he *really* wanted—and what it was that the man feared, *really* feared." Johnson in fact would instruct his younger as-sistants in reading men: "Watch their hands, watch their eyes," he would say. "Read eyes. No matter what a man is saying to you, it's not as im-portant as what you can read in his eyes." And he urged them to focus on a person's weaknesses because weaknesses could be exploited and to read between the lines: "The most important thing a man has to tell you is what he's not telling you. The most important thing he has to say is what he's trying not to say." Lyndon Johnson himself could "read" with an unerring genius that would be difficult to teach. According to Bobby Baker, one of Johnson's closest aides: "He seemed to *sense* each man's in-dividual price and the commodity he preferred as coin."[63]

More recently, the notion of emotional (or personal) intelligence, ex-hibited at the highest levels by individuals who are exquisitely attuned to the needs, interests, and fears of others, has been of interest.[64] While some of this characteristic might be genetically derived, it certainly is also a learned trait that can be perfected into one's late teens. The CEO of Roche Pharmaceuticals, Franz Humer, is famous for his ability to "read" audiences and groups. He traced his legendary skill back to his youth when he was a tour guide and learned from the reactions and comments of the various groups to predict how much of a tip he would get.[65]

A cadence of life is another important element of mature leaders and in their ability to take time to reflect on fundamentally important issues. Established leaders take the time, whether through spiritual retreats as in the case of Gandhi, or through the lengthy walks of French president Charles de Gaulle, or prayer, or some daily exercise routine, to withdraw and reflect and be by themselves. Reflective time alone is associated with the development of self-awareness, an important marker in many leaders. It helps them to ponder what is truly important to them. Clark Kerr once remarked that he always set aside Sundays for gardening and for his family: "The big weeds were the board of regents and the small weeds were the faculty." Bill Friday still often recalls the advice of one of his former associates, Claude Teague:

> Most of the problems, over 90 percent, you see on a daily basis are slightly different versions of problems you have seen before. These are generally easy to resolve. But the other 10 percent are the ones you have not seen before and the ones you didn't anticipate. It is for these challenges, like the time the FBI agent walked in my office to tell me about point shaving in our basketball games, that you need all of your mental strength and your clear thinking. You need to be ready for those.

Routine withdrawals from the often-intense demands of the office recharge leaders and contribute to their overall balance and to their physical and psychological stamina.

A RECAPITULATION

Before moving to the presentation of the six cases that follow, it is useful to summarize briefly the import of the conceptual framework laid out in the previous pages as a guide to the understanding of the cases. Leadership is a fundamental element of the human condition. It is universal to the extent that society is universal and it is linked to whatever it means to be human: to want, to need, to love, to feel, to control, to belong. It is largely symbolic, which in turn underscores the overarching relevance of communication within and across a society. Leadership is a reciprocal, two-way conversation between leaders and followers that takes place in and around institutions and social systems that have existed for decades and even centuries.

There is power in leadership. More importantly, however, there is persuasion and the process of adaptation. Leaders must learn to face difficult issues and reconcile differences among factions of their followers. The inevitably temporary nature of leadership is also a crucial factor, with leaders seeking to stay the course and grappling with the self-interests of followers as they together attempt to achieve a common group goal. The nature of the university as a complex organization, where goals might not be widely shared and where there is a wide range of stakeholders with different concerns and with intermittent participation in organizational goals, makes these institutions especially difficult to govern and lead.

Discussions about biology might seem peculiar within the context of leadership in complex organizations but such reflections are fundamental to an appreciation of leadership. While humans are not monkeys or lions, the dominance relationships observed among some animal species are also present among pre-schoolers. Dominant youngsters are followed and imitated and they control toys and initiate games. Physical size, intelligence, attractiveness, and personality all contribute to placement in human social hierarchies. Biology offers important lessons in the struggle for dominance and for leadership.[66]

From the early lives of children one sees the seeds of many of the characteristics that later define adult behaviors, particularly the importance of the historical contexts and early environmental influences. The generation of William Friday, Ted Hesburgh, and Clark Kerr witnessed the problems attending the Great Depression, with its deep conflicts and tragic human suffering and with one-third of the labor force either out of work or seriously underemployed. Many in that generation faced significant adversity as children and adolescents at home, and they developed or exhibited patterns of response that research on resiliency is uncovering. Travel and exposure to vastly different cultures is also an early component in the development of an ability to translate and to understand or empathize with people and events that were different from those of their own prior experiences. Exposure to "foreign" cultures, whether through travel abroad or even through extensive travel within an enormously diverse country such as the United States, exposes future leaders to a variety of ways of thinking and behaving at critical stages of development. Thus, these notions inform the content of the cases and provide a useful framework within which to understand the relationships between the leaders, followers and their organizational situations.

NOTES

1. James MacGregor Burns, *Transforming Leadership* (New York: Atlantic Monthly Press, 2003).

2. In *The Elegant Universe*, Brian Greene describes the century-old argument among physicists around the currently irreconcilable differences between the laws of the large, general relativity, and the laws of the small, quantum mechanics. The search for this unified field theory in physics is what consumed Einstein's quixotic efforts during the last thirty years of his life, all in an effort to show that these distinct forces were part of an overarching whole. Einstein was, as Greene points out, ahead of his time once more, and physicists are now focusing on "superstring" theory (strings are microscopically tiny loops of energy that lie deep within all matter) as the framework that could tie modern physics together. See Brian Greene, *The Elegant Universe* (New York: W. W. Norton, 1999).

3. For an excellent discussion of power and leadership, see James MacGregor Burns, *Leadership* (New York: Harper and Row, 1978), especially Chapter 1.

4. I focus here on academic publications. There is also a vast collection of popular books and articles that Hogan and Kaiser have dubbed "The Troubadour Tradition," entertaining but considerably less reliable. See Robert Hogan and Robert Kaiser, "What We Know About Leadership," forthcoming in the *Review of General Psychology*.

5. Bernard Bass and R. M. Stogdill, *Bass and Stogdill's Handbook of Leadership*, 3rd ed. (New York: The Free Press, 1990).

6. For what I call the "neo-trait" approach, see, for example, Timothy A. Judge, J. E. Bono, R. Ilies, and M. Gerhardt, "Personality and Leadership: A Qualitative and Quantitative Review," *Journal of Applied Psychology* 87 (2002): 765–780.

7. Jay A. Conger, "Qualitative Research as the Cornerstone Methodology for Understanding Leadership," *Leadership Quarterly* 9, no. 1, (1998): 107–121. The topic of qualitative research is further discussed in the Prologue to the case studies.

8. Thomas Carlyle, *On Heroes, Hero-Worship, and the Heroic in History* (Boston: Houghton Mifflin, 1907), 18.

9. R. D. Mann's (1959) review is often cited as evidence that personality does not matter, for example. And Mann's interpretation of his results—at least what he chose to emphasize—is indeed negative in this regard. But Mann actually reports consistent trait-leadership relationships, and, more importantly, a recent re-analysis (R. G. Lord, C. L. DeVader, and G. Alliger, "A Meta-analysis of the Relation Between Personality Traits and Leader Perceptions," *Journal of Applied Psychology* 71 [1986]: 402–410) of his data casts some doubt on the credibility of his results. See also Timothy A. Judge, R. Ilies, and A. E. Colbert,

"Intelligence and Leadership: A Quantitative Review and Test of Theoretical Propositions," *Journal of Applied Psychology* 89 (2004): 542–552.

10. R. M. Stogdill, "Personal Factors Associated with Leadership: A Survey of the Literature," *Journal of Psychology* 25 (1948): 35–71.

11. Gary A. Yukl, *Leadership in Organizations*, 2nd ed. (Englewood Cliffs, NJ: Prentice Hall, 1989).

12. Bass and Stogdill, *Handbook of Leadership*.

13. Many personal traits, especially physical ones such as eye color or height, of course, cannot be taught or influenced at all. Others, like sociability or even intelligence, have significant components not related to genetics and thus can be affected by environment.

14. Kurt Lewin, "Field Theory and Experiment in Social Psychology: Concepts and Methods," *American Journal of Sociology* 44 (1939): 868–896.

15. See R. F. Bales, *Interaction Process Analysis* (Reading, MA: Addison-Wesley, 1950), and R. R. Blake and J. S. Mouton, *The Managerial Grid* (San Francisco: Gulf, 1964).

16. F. E. Fiedler, *A Theory of Leadership Effectiveness* (New York: McGraw-Hill, 1967).

17. F. Dansereau, Jr., G. Graen, and W. J. Haga, "A Vertical Dyad Linkage Approach to Leadership Within Formal Organizations: A Longitudinal Investigation of the Role Making Process," *Organizational Behavior and Human Performance* 13 (1975): 46–78.

18. Arlun Melcher, "Leadership: A Functional Analysis," in *Leadership: The Cutting Edge*, edited by James Hunt and Lars L. Larson (Carbondale: Southern Illinois University Press, 1977), 94–108.

19. Burns, *Transforming Leadership*, 23. See also Bernard Bass, "A Seminal Shift: The Impact of James Burns' Leadership," *Leadership Quarterly* 4 (1993): 375–377.

20. A. Zaleznik and M. Kets de Vries, *Power and the Corporate Mind* (Boston: Houghton Mifflin, 1975). Zaleznik and Kets de Vries first distinguished between managing and leading, a distinction that would generate a great deal of interest in the literature.

21. As quoted by Jay A. Conger, "Charismatic and Transformational Leadership in Organizations: An Insider's Perspective on These Developing Streams of Research," *Leadership Quarterly* 10, no. 2 (1999): 150. Conger also quotes Warren Bennis and Burt Nanus, *Leaders: Strategies for Taking Charge* (New York: Harper and Row, 1985), 218.

22. Georgia Sorenson, "An Intellectual History of Leadership Studies: The Role of James MacGregor Burns," paper presented at the 2000 annual meeting of the American Political Science Association, Washington, DC, September 2000.

23. Howard Gardner (*Leading Minds*) acknowledges Erik Erikson as a mentor who inspired his work on leadership and draws from Freud and Piaget in articulating his views of the personality of the young child. Both Freud and Piaget

agreed that children pass through "stages" in early childhood, but disagreed on the nature of those stages.

24. The primary contribution of House's path-goal theory involves the leadership process that aligns the self-interest of followers with the needs of the organization. See R. J. House, "A Path-Goal Theory of Leader Effectiveness," *Administrative Science Quarterly* 16 (1971): 321–339.

25. R. Dawkins, *The Selfish Gene* (New York: Oxford University Press, 1976).

26. I. Eibl-Eibesfeld, *Human Ethnology* (Chicago: Aldine, 1989); Joyce Hogan, "Personological Dynamics of Leadership," *Journal of Research in Personality* 12 (1978): 390–395.

27. Robert Hogan, G. Curphy, and J. Hogan, "What We Know About Leadership, Effectiveness, and Personality," *American Psychologist* 49, no. 6 (1994): 493–504.

28. Michael D. Cohen and James G. March, *Leadership and Ambiguity: The American College President* (New York: McGraw-Hill, 1974).

29. L. R. Offerman and M. K. Gowing, "Organizations of the Future," *American Psychologist* 45 (1990): 95–108.

30. Hogan, Curphy, and Hogan, "What We Know About Leadership."

31. Cohen and March, *Leadership and Ambiguity*, 195–196.

32. Arthur Padilla and S. Ghosh, "Turnover at the Top: The Revolving Door of the Academic Presidency," *The Presidency*, Winter 2000, 30–37.

33. Robert Wright, *The Moral Animal: Why We Are the Way We Are. The New Science of Evolutionary Psychology* (New York: Pantheon, 1994).

34. M. Schur, *Freud: Living and Dying* (New York: International Universities Press, 1972).

35. Patricia Miller, *Theories of Developmental Psychology*, 2nd ed. (New York: W. H. Freeman, 1989).

36. Wright, *Moral Animal*.

37. See also the review by Robert Hogan of Wright's *The Moral Animal* in *Personnel Psychology* 49, no. 2 (1996).

38. See, for example, R. Sapolsky and R. Jay, "Styles of Dominance and Their Physiological Correlates Among Wild Baboons," *American Journal of Primatology* 18 (1989): 1–13, and M. Donald, *The Origins of the Modern Mind* (Cambridge, MA: Harvard University Press, 1991).

39. Edward O. Wilson, *Sociobiology* (Cambridge, MA: Harvard University Press, 1980); George B. Schaller, *The Mountain Gorilla: Ecology and Behavior* (Chicago: University of Chicago Press, 1963); Jane Goodall, *The Chimpanzees of Gombe: Patterns of Behavior* (Cambridge, MA: Belknap/Harvard University Press, 1986).

40. Ronald Heifetz, *Leadership Without Easy Answers* (Cambridge, MA: Harvard University Press, 1994), 56.

41. William Wordsworth, "My Heart Leaps Up When I Behold." The quote has also been associated with aging parents and the passage from childhood to adulthood and to parental care.

42. John Milton, *Paradise Regained*, Book iv, line 220.

43. Alexis De Tocqueville, *Democracy in America*, vol. 1 (New York: Vintage Books, 1945), 28; Jean Piaget, *The Origins of Intelligence in Children* (New York: International Universities Press, 1952); Erik H. Erikson, *Identity: Youth, and Crisis* (New York: W. W. Norton, 1968).

44. Howard Gardner, *Leading Minds: An Anatomy of Leadership* (New York: Basic Books, 1995), 25.

45. S. Freud, *A General Introduction to Psychoanalysis* (New York: Washington Square Press, 1952); Jean Piaget, "Piaget's Theory," in *Handbook of Child Psychology*, vol. 1, edited by P. Mussen (New York: Wiley, 1983).

46. Gardner, *Leading Minds*, 27.

47. Ibid., 28–29.

48. Ibid., 28.

49. Gardner, *Leading Minds*; Mihaly Csikszentmihalyi, *Creativity: Flow and the Psychology of Discovery and Invention* (New York: HarperCollins, 1996); Barbara A. Kerr, *Smart Girls: A New Psychology of Girls, Women, and Giftedness*, 2nd ed. (Scottsdale, AZ: Gifted Psychology Press, 1995); Robert S. Albert, "Family Positions and the Attainment of Eminence": A Study of Special Family Positions and Special Family Experiences," *Gifted Child Quarterly* 24 (1980): 87–95; and John Viney, *Drive: Leadership in Business and Beyond* (New York: Bloomsbury Publishing, 1999), for example, highlight the pattern of missing fathers or of turmoil during childhood or adolescence among many future leaders and creative individuals. Albert refers to a "wobble" effect, where having emotionally distant or absent parents as a result of death or divorce appears to catalyze some talented individuals to develop their capacities to very high levels.

50. M. Rutter, L. H. Taylor, and E. Taylor, eds., *Child and Adolescent Psychiatry*, 3rd ed. (Oxford: Blackwell Scientific Publications, 1994); E. Werner and R. Smith, *Overcoming the Odds: High Risk Children from Birth to Adulthood* (Ithaca, NY: Cornell University Press, 1992); H. Zimrin, "A Profile of Survival," *Child Abuse and Neglect* 10, no. 3 (1986): 339–349.

51. R. Subotnik, L. Kassan, E. Summers, and A. Wasser, *Genius Revisited: High IQ Children Grown Up* (Norwood, NJ: Ablex Publishing Corp., 1993).

52. Kerr, *Smart Girls*.

53. Werner and Smith, 1992; M. Rutter, "Commentary: Some Focus and Process Considerations Regarding Effects of Parental Depression on Children," *Journal of Developmental Psychology* 26 (1990): 60–67.

54. Mark Katz, *On Playing a Poor Hand Well: Insights from the Lives of Those Who Have Overcome Childhood Risks and Adversities* (New York: W. W. Norton, 1997), 26.

55. Werner and Smith, 1992.

56. This list of factors is based on Joanne Joseph, *The Resilient Child: Preparing Today's Youth for Tomorrow's World* (New York: Plenum Press, 1994), and on references cited therein, as well as on Diane L. Coutu, "How Resilience Works," *Harvard Business Review*, May 2002, 46–55.

57. N. Garmezy and A. Masten, "Chronic Adversities," in *Child and Adolescent Psychiatry*, 3rd ed., edited by M. Rutter, L. H. Taylor, and E. Taylor (Oxford: Blackwell Scientific Publications, 1994), 191–208.

58. Gardner, *Leading Minds*.

59. Erikson, *Identity: Youth, and Crisis*, 87.

60. Kerr, *Smart Girls*.

61. Ibid.

62. Whetten and Cameron summarize the findings from a large number of studies where the most important skills of leaders are highlighted. See David A. Whetten and Kim S. Cameron, *Developing Management Skills* (New York: Prentice Hall, 2002), 8.

63. Robert A. Caro, *The Years of Lyndon Johnson: Master of the Senate* (New York: Alfred A. Knopf, 2002), 136.

64. For the original discussions about emotional intelligence, see J. David Mayer and Peter Salovey, "The Intelligence of Emotional Intelligence," *Intelligence* 17 (1993): 433–442; and J. D. Mayer, P. Salovey, and D. R. Caruso, "Models of Emotional Intelligence," in *The Handbook of Intelligence* edited by R. J. Sternberg (New York: Cambridge University Press, 2000), 396–420.

65. Robert Tannenbaum and Warren H. Schmidt, "How to Choose a Leadership Pattern," *Harvard Business Review*, May–June 1973, 162–175.

66. See also C. John Anderson, D. Keltner, and A. M. Kring, "Who Attains Social Status? Effects of Personality and Physical Attractiveness in Social Groups," *Journal of Personality and Social Psychology* 81 (2001): 116–132.

CHAPTER

Prologue to the Cases

I keep six honest serving men
(They taught me all I knew):
Their names are What and Why and When;
And How and Where and Who.
—Rudyard Kipling

Before presenting the six case studies it will be useful to provide an overview of the structure of the cases in this book and what they are meant to illuminate. In doing so, I hope to explain the approach used to understanding the process of leadership in complex enterprises, as well as to recapitulate key points from the earlier discussions. The first two chapters on the organizational characteristics of the university and on leadership serve as the general framework through which to view each of the cases; the cases thus represent the intersection of the first two chapters with the phenomena of leadership and followership. Their content, partly historical and biographical and partly analytical, is designed to illuminate the commonalities and singularities in leadership in order to understand how the individual traits and behaviors of leaders relate to their environments and institutional contexts. Each case begins with an examination of the leader's background and early childhood experiences, within the environmental, historical, and familial crucibles where their personality patterns were shaped; it progresses through their education in domains, including discussion of important mentors and their influence.

Their movement through early careers and subsequent pivotal leadership events follows this. By choosing the university as the organizational vehicle through which to examine the various configurations of leadership, a sort of standardization regarding the environment is made possible, allowing for more detailed examinations of how leader backgrounds and characteristics relate to particular organizational situations. Nonetheless, the notion of a single university or, by extension, of some homogeneous organization or situation across which unambiguous comparisons might be possible seems totally inappropriate. While the choice of six very different individuals within a context of similar organizational challenges and structures provides a rich setting for analysis, the organizational setting and contexts for Hanna Gray were nonetheless quite different from those for Clark Kerr.

THE APPROACH: QUALITATIVE AND QUANTITATIVE

The study of leadership cannot help but involve multiple disciplines and a wide range of approaches and methods, defying academic boundaries and arbitrary restrictions. Often in scholarly work the lives of "great" men and women are examined in the hopes of finding shared tendencies, so that appropriate generalizations may be stated. Other times intricate experiments are conducted that test necessarily restricted models of leadership behaviors by examining data of partial utility to the issue being studied. The present effort tries to be neither exclusively deductive nor inductive and it incorporates findings and successes from both theoretical and experimental approaches and from quantitative and qualitative streams of research. The basic assumption is that idiographic or qualitative approaches that study selected individuals in detail can make valid and significant contributions to the basic foundations of leadership, those general tendencies and principles that help explain a range of phenomena. The analysis of a relatively large number of detailed cases enables certain generalizations and inferences that otherwise might not be possible.

Qualitative approaches to the study of leadership remain fairly rare, but these types of studies are often responsible for radical shifts in the ways scholars think about problems, and they offer longitudinal perspectives that other approaches routinely miss.[1] Disciplines such as anthropology widely use ethnographic methods, a form of research that focuses on close observation of particular phenomena; scholars in business, psychology, social work, and history widely use the case method as a basic scientific investigatory tool for decades. The usefulness of the case approach hinges around its practicality: theories alone cannot provide the confrontation with real world experiences needed to understand a wide array of situations and circumstances. Business cases of course provide detailed information about a particular manager or about conditions and problems in different industries and companies, with each case requiring its own diagnosis and solution. Other cases, such as the famous idiographic study by Gruber in his analysis of Charles Darwin, take an account of a person or group of persons in a situation.[2] Thus, in these situations, there is usually something interesting about the person, the situation, or their interaction. The cases are usually self-contained, relatively short episodes or segments of a person's life, mini-biographies of sorts.

The essential feature of these cases is that they are naturally occurring events in the real world: a business fails; a university president grapples with a huge variety of stakeholders during a crisis; an organization is not adapting rapidly enough to changes in the market; a corporation is involved in financial corruption. They are not experimentally contrived events or simulations. Given enough cases or situations, investigators will classify and generalize and begin to identify certain kinds of patterns, being especially careful not to generalize too readily. From such classifications emerge concepts and testable propositions that may be used in experimental settings. It is important to realize that even individual experiments, simulations, and surveys are themselves "cases," provided they are studied as real world events in their wider context.[3] The merit of the case study method lies in its ability to consider a large number of factors together and in their relationships.

Why not use another technique, such as multivariate analysis? First, because the present concern is with process rather than with specific traits; multivariate techniques, with their reliance on measurement, imply that it is appropriate or even possible to measure most relevant traits or that their interaction is somehow separable. This separation seems implausible in the very complex and complicated processes of leadership and followership. The need is to understand leaders in their setting and situation, but an emphasis on measurement tends to de-emphasize the context of what is being studied. And the numerical need for large numbers of subjects for statistical validity raises the question of the appropriate control group for exceptional leaders, who by definition constitute a small group. What would be, for instance, the control group for Abraham Lincoln and Mohandas Gandhi?

It is sometimes assumed that qualitative work is an antecedent to or a first draft of quantitative research of more authority. Perhaps little is known about the subject, so the purpose is to generate multiple hypotheses that can later become better defined and to which quantitative methods may be later applied, thereby validating the hypotheses with empirical rigor. The notion that qualitative work is better suited for the early stages of research has dominated the thinking in leadership work, although in areas like decision sciences and strategic change, the dominance of quantitative methods has been successfully challenged, even in the more advanced stages of research. Qualitative methods clearly provide major contributions to advances in what is known about leadership and followership, particularly considering that after thousands of studies the field has yet to develop an acceptable general theory that "explains all aspects of the process adequately."[4]

The complexity of leadership, and the corollary need for qualitative approaches, arises because leadership involves multiple levels of relationships: the intrapsychic (the leader), interpersonal (the interaction among leaders and followers), organizational (the specific organization and its culture and characteristics), and environmental (the external forces or trends that affect the process of leadership across all organizations and leaders).[5] One shortcoming of the quantitative approaches is the inability to reach across these multiple levels; the narrowness of focus tends to reinforce the idea that leadership is reducible to a single individual or relationship with followers. Descriptors used in survey-based quantitative work contribute additional problems of interpretation. As Conger notes, a typical descriptor like "actively sets goals for the group" reveals little about the process used to set goals or how one knows whether the selected goals will in fact be effective.[6] Many of the survey-generated leadership descriptors do not reach the deeper structures of leadership phenomena.

In addition, the dynamic nature of leadership creates challenges for quantitative approaches. Relationships between leaders and followers and leaders and their organizations and environments change over time. A leader during the first year of tenure is typically very different from the same leader after five years in office; the static nature of quantitative approaches misses these distinctions. The symbolic and subjective aspects of leadership also have important implications for research approaches. Quantitative methods capture concrete and supposedly objective structures, but there is an ever-shifting reality to leadership where human beings actually shape its creation. Impression management or "spin" control influence follower perceptions, and a qualitative method is more likely to pick up the outcomes as researchers move from external observation to a more internal place from which to view leadership.[7]

But no single measurement approach is perfect and qualitative work would be deficient if it depended on a singular solution. An overreliance on interviews can be an important shortcoming to qualitative work. Method triangulation, through observation and document analysis and discussion with followers and others, is a necessary adjunct to leader interviews. In each of the six cases that follow, such triangulation was carried out; several close associates and contemporaries were interviewed for each of the case subjects, and documents were reviewed and analyzed extensively as a supplement to the leader interviews. There is the related challenge of discerning between operational and presentational data. Operational data is defined as being more "genuine," because it is obtained from candid interviews and activities engaged in and observed by the researcher,[8] while presentational data is more contrived and designed to maintain a certain public image. The study of leadership is particularly prone to the use of presentational data. But whether the approach is qualitative or quantitative, there exists the same dilemma of people answering questionnaires or presenting information as they think they should.

ON THE CHOICE OF THE SIX PRESIDENTS

It is useful to discuss why the particular individuals in this study were chosen: why these six and not another six or even why just six and not thirty? There were, in fact, many excellent choices from many institutions, and there is an element of arbitrariness that cannot be avoided in choosing some and not choosing others. But detailed case studies, which are essentially mini-biographies tied analytically to the formulations and syntheses from Chapters 2 and 3, can only be done for a finite and relatively small number of individuals. Having said this, there were also indispensable categories of experiences, challenges, and situations that I viewed as necessary for the completeness of the analysis.

First, there had to be an assortment of public and private universities due to their significant differences in terms of control, financing, and oversight and having this diversity in the sample of leaders provides for more useful comparisons and contrasts. The challenges that Father Hesburgh faced at Notre Dame in building that small, Catholic institution into a major research campus were quite different from those that Clark Kerr faced when he became the first chancellor of UC-Berkeley, although they required many similar leadership skills. There had to be a significant mixture of issues faced, ranging from challenges involving students, such as the ones faced by Bill Friday, Ted Hesburgh, and Clark Kerr, or intercollegiate athletics scandals such as those of Friday and John Slaughter, or restructuring of systems and graduate and undergraduate educational issues as were faced by virtually all six leaders. It was important that a variety of institutions be represented: four-year, major research, and systems of universities containing a wide range of campuses.

Three of the presidents eventually selected, Kerr, Friday, and Hesburgh, were repeatedly mentioned in preliminary discussions with experts from the higher-education community as this study was being formulated. Thus, half of the individuals ultimately selected were fairly obvious choices who provided as close as one can get to a controlled experiment using case-study analysis. Kerr, Friday, and Hesburgh were close contemporaries who were involved centrally in the student protests during the 1960s at their own institutions, albeit under different conditions and environments. There is considerable evidence that the Berkeley student protests of the early 1960s were relatively isolated events, although it is possible that Friday and Hesburgh might have benefited somewhat from the earlier experiences of Kerr. Regardless, all three essentially dealt with similar problems during the same time period, and this is particularly true for Kerr and Friday. Being at a comparatively small Catholic university, Hesburgh did not have a governor and other government officials to deal with, though he faced most of the other issues Kerr and Friday did.

Another important consideration was availability of persons to interview and materials to read and study. All six of the individuals had either retired or were close to doing so, but all were still professionally active and available for personal interviews, as were several of their closest associates during their periods of leadership. (Clark Kerr passed away in late 2003 but was interviewed three times and had an opportunity to remark on earlier drafts of this book.) Thus, these presidents had all served in relatively recent times, but their presidential careers were largely or entirely behind them so their entire contributions and challenges could be examined and evaluated. Much has been written about each of the presidents selected, and most of them had themselves written a variety of books and articles and given speeches and testimony that could be analyzed. Kerr was in the process of writing his two-volume memoirs during the interviews for this book and so had fresh on his mind, events and situations that otherwise he might not have remembered as easily (In fact, he provided me with various drafts of his memoirs as he was writing them). Friday and Hesburgh had splendidly detailed biographies published about them that made this study much easier than otherwise would have been the case. In addition, the entire Lenny Bias episode was recorded in C. Fraser Smith's *Lenny, Lefty, and the Chancel-*

lor, and this provided an important and detailed record of that tragic incident and of John Slaughter's role in the process. Bill Bowen and Hanna Gray both had written extensively and had been interviewed by a variety of magazines and journals, providing a rich context for studying their presidencies as well. These considerations made the writing of the case studies easier and the conclusions perhaps more accurate.

All six had made significant contributions both to their institutions and to the larger community beyond their institutions, and they had faced relatively difficult and complex situations that were well known nationally and even internationally. They all led complicated enterprises at crucial times and faced major problems and challenges, many of which received national and international attention. All had important challenges of communication with external and internal audiences that involved fundamental changes and adaptations in their organizations. For example, Kerr dealt with the California Master Plan orchestration and decentralization of the university system and the student protests of the 1960s; Friday faced athletics scandals, student protests, the reorganization of higher education in North Carolina, and the controversy with the U.S. Department of Health, Education and Welfare over "desegregation"; Hesburgh addressed the major challenges of institutional upgrading and enhancement and the student protests; Bowen dealt with serious challenges in the areas of cost controls, budgeting discipline, diversity, and graduate program development; Slaughter, in addition to the challenges of being an African American president at a major university, faced issues of campus diversity and a major athletics scandal; and Gray, as the first woman president of the distinguished but uniquely different University of Chicago, tackled fund-raising organizational challenges, major problems with graduate education, the modernization of facilities and accounting procedures, and the establishment of extracurricular opportunities for undergraduate students to offset enrollment declines. And they served for a variety of terms, ranging from seven years to more than thirty years.

But it is as important to state why they were *not* selected. They were not selected because they fit one or another category or because they exhibited some behavioral or personality pattern that fit earlier research findings. Nor were they selected because they fell into some demographic group or geographical region. Finally, while I generally adhere to the belief that one learns more from successful behaviors and models, it is indisputable that there are important lessons in failure, particularly in learning about factors commonly associated with career derailments. The six individuals chosen for this study were unquestionably successful as a group and individually but they were not universally successful across all areas. One was fired by a governor and one resigned to take another presidency at a smaller institution following a long period of turmoil; several ended their tenures under increasing controversy.

The latter issue about controversy and turmoil suggests a question about whether these university leaders could adequately represent presidents who serve today. Some observers might conclude that being president today is more difficult, more perilous, and less attractive than it was twenty or thirty years ago. However, it would be difficult to conceive of a more stressful or trying leadership moment than when the district attorney walked in Bill Friday's office to tell him about a point-shaving scandal, or when Clark Kerr had to address the six thousand people at Berkeley's Greek Theatre at the height of the student protests, or when John Slaughter had to face the press after Lenny Bias' tragic cocaine overdose. Additionally, the major changes that Princeton made in graduate research and in the atmosphere of the university during Bill Bowen's tenure, and the shifts in undergraduate culture, Ph.D. education, and financial procedures that Hanna Gray engineered at Chicago, were fundamentally perilous from a leadership perspective. The issues have changed and their contexts are different, but it seems improbable that today's leadership challenges are inherently more difficult or dangerous to navigate than those involving point-shaving and cocaine overdose athletic scandals or student riots and Vietnam war protests or financial problems associated with the "stagflation" of the 1980s.

STRUCTURE AND CONTENT OF THE CASE STUDIES

Reading biographical materials about recognized individuals involves a bit of voyeurism. Many people are naturally curious about the personal and professional pilgrimages of leaders, particularly if they are familiar with the individuals highlighted or the organizations they represented. But there are other reasons to study exceptionality in all of its human expressions. The voyages of extraordinary people might suggest the way to a better life for others and their patterns of behavior might point to common elements that could be useful in the development of a broader range of people. Of course, elements of luck and of situation are always important ingredients in the recipe for achievement: the luck of unusual gifts such as those of soccer star Mia Hamm or writer Gabriel Garcia Marquez; the fortune of growing up in a wealthy family like U.S. president George W. Bush; the serendipity of being in the right place at the right time like British prime minister Winston Churchill in 1939. But as Csikszentmihalyi observes in the context of creativity, others with similar luck are not as successful or creative.[9] Indeed, the distinctiveness of the lives of extraordinary persons underscores the obvious fact that they were able to follow a less-crowded path, and it is worthwhile and useful to see how and maybe even why they did it.

ORGANIZATIONAL SITUATIONS

It is useful to remark on the importance of the organizational situation and environment prior to an examination of the cases. While there are many similarities between universities and corporations, there are two factors that define the university as an organization: the number and variety of stakeholders and the employment relationships between the university and the faculty. These two factors complicate managerial tasks for university leaders and limit what they can do and when they can do it. The organizational complexity of universities leads to more complicated structures, and more complicated structures are more difficult to manage. The greater the number and the variety of organizational publics or stakeholders, a pivotal feature of the large research universities, the greater the need to design the organization in ways that address and communicate across each of those publics. In addition, the unique fishbowl environment in which many universities must live creates serious challenges for leaders. This is particularly the case among public universities where laws and statutes define the meetings and activities that must be part of the public record and available for inspection by news media and by the public at large. The political influences are clearly evident in the cases of Clark Kerr, Bill Friday, and John Slaughter. At the same time, university leaders may enjoy more institutional loyalty than do corporate CEOs and there are often fewer adjustments to be made in response to competitor challenges and to technological change.

More uncertainty and unpredictability, as a result of greater heterogeneity in the environment, greater orchestration by external actors, or faster change, require more flexibility and greater information by leaders. This in turn implies less centralization of management and, more importantly, even greater expertise and effectiveness in the management of the subdivisions or departments. Universities in general require greater structural complexity to deal with the number and variety of their publics. And a major constraint on leader power and control, as compared to that of a CEO of a for-profit corporation, arises from the unique employment relationships universities have with their main employees—the tenured faculty. This unpredictability, coupled with significant independence in the research activities of faculty, point toward less formalization and less centralization in a vital area of university operations. At the same time, however, other major parts of the university are highly formalized and hierarchically centralized, requiring very different managerial styles.

LEADERSHIP IMPLICATIONS

Building upon the synthesis developed in Chapter 3, the compelling importance of childhood, the impact of families and their backgrounds on the early lives of extraordinary individuals, is a beginning point of inquiry for the cases. There are important dimensions of adult leadership and creativity that have their roots in the patterns of the childhood experiences that shaped them; each case thus begins with the family and early childhood experiences of the leader. What are some of the key early experiences and family patterns? How do these young leaders differ from their peers? Are there early signs of unusual gifts or talents, or distinguishing physical features? Did they do some things unusually early as compared to their peers? Intelligence without the ability to express it is often overlooked, and so it is important to understand how well the young leaders spoke and wrote and whether there was unusual family attention paid to these skills. Are there signs of great perseverance in the face of substantial odds or of unusual or otherwise extraordinary behavior at an early age, as might be suggested by insights from the resiliency theories discussed earlier? Were there significant mentors or important teachers in their lives, and how did they contribute to the development of the future leader?

For the adult leader, interest focuses on ways in which leaders progressed through their careers and how they affected the behavior of others. Their professional mentors and their connections to the organizations they served are carefully examined, as are any opportunities for early exposure to the top of their organizations. Their communication styles and interpersonal skills receive particular attention, given the diversity of stakeholders with which they had to contend. More specifically, what managerial styles were used in dealing with the wide variety of stakeholders one encounters at the university, such as faculty, alumni, trustees, legislators, and athletic boosters? University presidents come from a variety of professional backgrounds, although most travel a traditional academic road: faculty experience in certain disciplines, movement through the administrative ranks, and then the presidency. Others are less orthodox. How do these differing paths affect the leadership styles and how do they intersect with the organizational characteristics and cultures they faced? What values do they tend to bring to the job—do they exhibit charismatic styles or visionary academic leadership, or are they externally-focused on growth and fund-raising—and are there notable or distinctive patterns that depend on their backgrounds and early careers? What pivotal events occurred during their presidencies and how did each president handle them? Finally, what sorts of leadership and managerial styles did they tend to exhibit and what was the cadence of their lives?

NOTES

1. See, for instance, L. Isabella, "Evolving Interpretations as a Change Unfolds: How Managers Construe Key Organizational Events," *Academy of Management Journal* 33, no. 1 (1990): 7–41; N. C. Roberts and R. T. Bradley, "Limits of Charisma," in *Charismatic Leadership: The Elusive Factor in Organizational Effectiveness*, edited by J. A. Conger and R. N. Kanungo (San Francisco: Jossey-Bass, 1998), 253–275. This section also benefited from Conger's fine essay on qualitative research, "Qualitative Research as the Cornerstone Methodology for Understanding Leadership," *Leadership Quarterly* 9, no. 1 (1998): 107–121.

2. Howard E. Gruber, *Darwin on Man: A Psychological Study of Scientific Creativity*, 2nd ed. (Chicago: University of Chicago Press, 1981).

3. See, for example, D. B. Bromley, *The Case-Study Method in Psychology and Related Disciplines* (Chichester, UK: John Wiley and Sons, 1986), and R. G. Miller, Jr., B. Brown, and L. E. Moses, eds., *Biostatistics Casebook* (New York: John Wiley and Sons, 1980).

4. Gary A. Yukl, *Leadership in Organizations*, 2nd ed. (Englewood Cliffs, NJ: Prentice Hall, 1989), 19.

5. B. J. Avolio and B. Bass, "Individual Consideration Viewed at Multiple Levels of Analysis: A Multi-level Framework for Examining the Diffusion of Transformational Leadership," *Leadership Quarterly* 6, no. 2 (1995): 199–218.

6. Jay A. Conger, "Charismatic and Transformational Leadership in Organizations: An Insider's Perspective on These Developing Streams of Research," *Leadership Quarterly* 10, no. 2 (1999): 145–169.

7. G. Morgan and L. Smircich, "The Case for Qualitative Research," *Academy of Management Review* 5, no. 4 (1980): 491–500.

8. J. Van Maanen, "The Fact of Fiction in Organizational Ethnography," *Administrative Science Quarterly* 24, no. 4 (1979): 539–550.

9. Mihaly Csikszentmihalyi, *Creativity: Flow and the Psychology of Discovery and Invention* (New York: HarperCollins, 1996).

Clark Kerr. *Photo by Fred Mertz, Mill Valley, California.*

CHAPTER 5

The Berkeley Quaker

The employers will love this generation (of students). . . . They are
going to be easy to handle. There aren't going to be any riots.
—Clark Kerr, *New York Times*, December 19, 1958

To walk about the campus of the University of California at San
Diego (UCSD), among its eucalyptus groves and buildings overlooking the Pacific Ocean on the bluffs of La Jolla, is to begin to
appreciate the impact of leadership. It is only one of four American
universities to take its place as a leading institution soon after being established (the other three are Johns Hopkins in the 1870s, and Chicago and Stanford in the 1890s, all private and all recipients of great
private fortunes). The campus is tucked away from its crowded neighbors in twelve hundred acres of wooded mesa, and much of its recreational and social life centers on the nearby waterfront, where whales,
dolphins, and sea lions are frequently seen from shore. The university's
art and architecture are as impressive as its physical beauty. Its highlights include the pyramidal Geisel Library, perhaps the most striking
building on any university campus, and Alexis Smith's monumental
"snake" mosaic path that winds 560 feet down its hillside to the Thur-
good Marshall College. The library is named in honor of Theodor Seuss
Geisel, known by children everywhere as Dr. Seuss; many of the author's original drawings and notes are permanently displayed in the
lobby. The building has been used as the backdrop for episodes of *Star*

Trek and *Mission Impossible* and for the cult film *Attack of the Killer Tomatoes.*

The San Diego campus has clearly benefited from the fabulous wealth of the state of California. But it has also benefited from the sweeping vision of the research university provided by Clark Kerr and his associates. The Scripps Institution of Oceanography, a marine research station that has been part of the University of California since 1912, flourished under the charismatic leadership of Roger Revelle during the 1950s and formed the nucleus of exceptional scientific talent around which UCSD grew. The faculty counts among its members six Nobel Laureates, a Fields Medalist, three recipients of the National Medal of Science, Pulitzer Prize winners, and numerous Fulbright, MacArthur, and Guggenheim Fellows. It is routinely ranked among the top universities in America. Yet, despite the achievements associated with the university throughout California, the person most closely associated with this institution and with the other eight campuses of the University of California ended his presidential tenure fired by an ambitious governor and rebuffed by a significant number of the faculty at the system's most prestigious institution at Berkeley.

EARLY LIFE

Clark Kerr, the first chancellor of the University of California at Berkeley in 1952 and six years later the president of the multicampus University of California system, was born on May 17, 1911, at the hillside farm of his parents in the village of Stony Creek, near Reading, Pennsylvania. The only son among four children of Caroline Clark and Samuel William Kerr, his early rural background is not particularly suggestive of a prominent future role in the leadership of American higher education. Kerr's mother, Caroline Clark (to whom Clark owes his first name), was not a highly educated woman, but she nonetheless taught Clark and his three sisters to read and write before they entered school. She vowed not to wed until she had saved enough money to pay for the college education of her children; all four of her children would eventually receive a college degree, but she would not live long enough to see it.

Samuel Kerr, Clark's father, was a well-educated and traveled man. Of Scottish descent, he attended Franklin and Marshall College in Lancaster, Pennsylvania, and after travel in Europe, he returned to Stony Creek to farm and to teach. He spoke Latin, Greek, German, and French, and he earned a master's degree from the University of Berlin. He was an independent thinker and he had a strong influence on young Clark. An avowed Wilsonian pacifist throughout World War I, Samuel Kerr remained so even after President Wilson had changed his pacifist position. This view of American foreign policy was not popular, and Clark Kerr recalled vividly many years later that the family once found their farmhouse splashed with yellow paint.

Religion also influenced Kerr's developing set of values and practical work habits. He was raised in a community where a Quaker meeting was held close to the farm where he lived. But there were also Moravians, Lutherans, and Reformists, and the conflict that arises when different ideologies mix also figured in Kerr's development. Young Kerr grew up thinking of conflict as a natural state of society, as the natural course of life, and the conflict extended to his family life as well. "When I was young, I actually had a mediating role between my parents. They never divorced but they also didn't get along very well." No stranger to conflict as he grew up, Kerr was also no stranger to work. Even as a child, Kerr's work ethic was a strong one.

> I have always worked hard because, even though we always were well-cared for, I grew up on a subsistence farm in Pennsylvania where work was life. We had no alternative: my father was a combination of a schoolteacher and a farmer. We raised vegetables and all kinds of fruit, chickens, and so forth. Some of this work wasn't much of a life, especially when as an eight-year-old I had to go out in the cold and clean chicken eggs. My earliest memories were about cleaning those eggs to take to market. We cleaned them with wet rags and toilet paper, very disagreeable work.

During high school Kerr had afternoon and evening chores at the farm, and this left little time for extracurricular activities at Reading High School. So from the time he remembers anything, he worked and worked hard. "I rather disdain people who seem to think the best thing in life is playing bridge or gossiping with people. I came away from this period of my life believing that the best and proper use of life is work. I also came away with the idea that conflict was a natural part of life. These two things stayed with me throughout my entire life: hard work and trying to work out reasonable solutions in conflict situations."

His father sold the first farm at Stony Creek when Kerr was about ten years old and the family moved to a bigger hillside farm of about 140 acres a little further out of town. Shortly after moving to the new farm, when Kerr was twelve years old, his mother died of cancer. As Kerr's biographer Mary Clark Stuart has noted, Caroline provided for her son's education and also showed him the merits of independence, self-sufficiency, industry, and learning.[1] The loss of his mother marked the end of a happy period in Clark's life.[2] Two years later, in 1925, his father married Margaret Haldeman, the daughter of a wealthy farmer who became part of the local aristocracy after coal was discovered on his land. Just as his new stepmother Margaret was moving in, Clark's two older sisters, Charlotte and Margaret, were leaving for Oberlin College. Clark and Frances, his younger sister by fifteen months, remained at home. By the time his stepmother and his father had their only child, Clark's half-brother, tension and animosity had divided the family. Kerr recalled that at meals Margaret and his half-brother sat at one end of the table while Clark and Frances sat at the other.[3]

Three other people were "very influential" to young Kerr, primarily in broadening his vision of the world and revealing to a rural boy from central Pennsylvania the larger possibilities in travel and work. Granville Clark, his uncle and Caroline Clark Kerr's brother, was a successful attorney and Mina Kerr, an aunt and Samuel's youngest sister, was a professional woman with a Ph.D. from the University of Pennsylvania and also served as executive secretary of the American Association of University Women in Washington, D.C. Kerr saw in their examples the benefits of broad travel, of leaving home to pursue successful and interesting careers, and the advantages of other choices and alternatives.

SWARTHMORE COLLEGE AND THE QUAKERS

Kerr chose Swarthmore in the fall of 1928, one of the options suggested by his father (the other three were Oberlin, where his three sisters had attended, Antioch, and Rollins). The seventeen-year-old was ready to leave home and also for the challenge of a new place; it was at Swarthmore that Clark gravitated to the Quakers. The families of Abraham Lincoln and Daniel Boone, who came from the same area in Pennsylvania as Kerr, also belonged to this Swarthmore chapter (or meeting), which was quite liberal (or "Hicksite," in the terminology of Quakers). Many of Kerr's college friends belonged to this meeting, and he found Quaker teachings and beliefs consistent with his. Kerr's conversion to Quakerism was not so much a crystallizing religious moment in his life as it was an appreciation that he held similar beliefs and principles to those of the chapter members.

As a young boy Clark had shown unusual single-mindedness and determination. Perhaps the Quaker belief that "you do not bend the knee or tip the hat to power" appealed to young Kerr and to his independent and uncompromising vein.[4] At age fifteen, a gritty and determined Clark Kerr tamed a wild and dangerous horse that had killed a man.[5] Quakers also tend to make sense of the world through methodical and practical activity. Benjamin Franklin exemplified this view: his famous "a penny saved is a penny earned" praises frugality and industry and condemns idleness. Education and applied science in support of practical problems were given preference to more abstract concepts.[6] But more important for Kerr's development as a future leader were the opportunities he found through his association with the Quakers to hone his oratory and reasoning skills, to explore ways in which serious conflicts could be resolved, and to travel widely during early adulthood.

He spent three summers during college working as a "Peace Caravaner," one in New England, a second one in Virginia and North Carolina, and the third in California. "We made speeches at Kiwanis or Rotary clubs, before twenty or thirty people, and also at churches, arranging our own presentations on world peace." During his junior year in 1931, in the middle of the Great Depression, he helped to prepare and serve breakfasts to famished children in the poor, black neighborhoods of north Philadelphia, at the Martha Washington School for Colored Children. He accompanied "Ruff" Herndon, a lay preacher and black trainer of the Swarthmore athletic teams, to black churches in the Philadelphia area. "I still remember standing in the center of large and very expressive church crowds, with as many people behind you in the choir as in front of you in the seats." This volunteer work gave young Kerr his first introduction to the hardships of being a non-Anglo in America. "These were desperate conditions, with some really hungry children in these schools, and the experience left an impression that I carried my entire life. Seventy years later, I can still see those young faces." Kerr's experiences with the Quakers, and those with his own family situation, enabled him to view conflict and it resolution in different and perhaps more intellectual ways. The close relationship between the religious beliefs of Quakers and the way they conducted their lives appealed to Clark. His activities enabled him to put into practice his developing views of social needs and concerns, although his attraction with the Hicksite Swarthmore Friends was less theological than it was practical.

"The Quakers really didn't require you to believe in very much. Essentially, instead of believing that there is 'that of God' in every person, we believed there's 'that of good' in every person, and one had the duty to draw that 'good' out of them." With typical Clark Kerr humor, he added:

> I guess I still believe that but I have added a second part: "but it takes me longer to find it in some people than it does in others." I

guess I am still looking for it in some people. At Berkeley some otherwise very intelligent people went crazy when they hit against conflict; they would lose their tempers and would think it was the end
of the world. Most of the issues we would advocate through the
Quakers, when we carried the message of international peace, and
the messages at the black churches about the famished kids, were
controversial. So I came to believe in conflict as a natural thing in
life. It just didn't upset me as much because I could always deal with
it intellectually and not personally.

This ability to remove himself from events and situations even as they
are actually happening, a characteristic trait that Smelser has termed "objectification," was an important element in how Kerr learned to interpret
and understand the world.[7]

Young Kerr was deeply impressed by the educational approach advocated by Swarthmore President Frank Aydelotte. A former Rhodes
Scholar, Aydelotte transformed the culture at Swarthmore into one of
high academic achievement, service, leadership, and, consistent with
Mr. Rhodes' wishes, "physical vigor."[8] Kerr was not initially a great college student, but by his senior year in 1932, the twenty-year-old Kerr
had received High Honors in Social Sciences, a letter in soccer, and, in
recognition of his love for debate, the moniker of "the man with the sil-
ver tongue" from *The Halcyon*, the Swarthmore yearbook. He was also
president of the men's student government and captain of the debate
team. Consistent with the wishes of his mother Caroline, and in admiration of his uncle Granville Clark, the successful attorney, Kerr applied
to Columbia Law School and was admitted for the fall of 1932. But
Swarthmore had expanded his views about careers, and the brilliant
Clair Wilcox, his major professor and mentor at Swarthmore, had
sparked Kerr's interests in economics and in the topical issues of unemployment and labor dispute.

CALIFORNIA DURING THE GREAT DEPRESSION

When Kerr set out in the summer of 1932 for California to see the
Olympics and to work for the American Friends Society Committee,
there were already doubts in his mind about law school.

> I was ready to travel, to see a new world and to explore new things
> and cultures. My popularity wasn't hurt by the fact that I was the
> only one with a car, a 1928 Model A convertible coupe. . . . I prob-
> ably had already decided not to attend Columbia. I had never been

to New York City, but I knew immediately that I liked California a
hell of a lot better. And because of Clair Wilcox, I had already decided that I would study economics and not law.

After the Olympics, he spent his third and last summer as a Peace Caravaner, mostly in southern California. Los Angeles in 1932, without the
traffic and the smog, was a sight for Kerr. At the end of the summer, before heading back east to Columbia, Kerr decided one day in August to
go north and see San Francisco and the Bay area. He wanted to see Stanford and, by chance, it was registration day.

> I was referred to the Stanford registrar, who was sitting just a few
> feet away under a live oak tree. After a quick review of my Swarth-
> more transcript, which by total coincidence had just been mailed to
> me, he accepted me on the spot into the master's program in eco-
> nomics. He just looked over the transcript and announced: "You're
> admitted."

At this same registration line, Kerr met Dean E. McHenry, who had
been student body president at UCLA, and the two former student body
presidents would commence a sixty-six-year-long friendship, beginning
as roommates at Stanford in the fall of 1932. He stayed the year at Stanford, obtaining a master's degree with a thesis on the cooperative barter
movement of the unemployed in California. But the following fall (1933)
he moved to Berkeley and began his Ph.D. in economics under Paul Taylor, a labor economist who had studied at Wisconsin and who was to have
a significant impact on the course of Kerr's studies and professional life.
His professor from Swarthmore, Clair Wilcox, had thought California
was a mistake in the first place, but so long as he was there, he felt Kerr
should transfer to Berkeley, which he thought was the better school and
"more grounded in the real world." Supported by a research assistantship
of $400 per year, Kerr headed across the San Francisco Bay to study eco-
nomics and labor relations.

The town of Berkeley, California, lies just east of the San Francisco
Bay. From its hills the bay is easily observed, and on clear days, one can
see the melon-colored Golden Gate Bridge directly to the west and the
city of San Francisco just to the southwest. Kerr recollected that his first
visual contact with Berkeley was the sight of the Campanile looming up
at the end of Telegraph Avenue. The Campanile remained his favorite
view of the campus, and many years later Kerr would look straight at it
from his window in the President's office in University Hall. "I discovered that Berkeley was much more a part of the real world than was Stan-

ford, and Paul Taylor, my principal professor at Berkeley, was a great expert on farm labor, a practical area that had great appeal to me."

Shortly after his arrival at Berkeley, a cotton-pickers' strike, one of the bloodiest rural strikes in American history, broke out in the San Joaquin Valley. There were massacres in Pixley and Arvin at the southern edges of America's most fertile and productive valley; strikers were living outdoors in disgustingly unhygienic conditions. There was hunger and fighting and there was also pure hatred between the "Okies" and "Arkies" who had gone west during the Dust Bowl and Mexicans who competed for the same farm jobs and who were being led by communists. The unrest, along with other similar events across America, would lead to landmark legislation like the National Labor Relations Act (Wagner Act) of 1935, giving workers the right to form labor unions and forcing employers to bargain, and the Fair Labor Standards Act of 1938, which addressed minimum wages and maximum work hours. The violence and suffering were not lost on Kerr: it was not only a long way from the peaceful Oley Valley in Pennsylvania, but also from the Quakers at Swarthmore and even the relative isolation of the nearby Stanford campus. It was a large measure of rural life in the United States during the Depression.

Under the mentorship of Professor Taylor, Kerr found these events worthy of study because they involved conflict and the resolution of conflict with reasonable solutions. Kerr's master's thesis at Stanford and his Ph.D. dissertation at Berkeley were on self-help cooperatives, enterprises begun by unemployed people that involved bartering, making clothes for one another, sharing food, and other cooperative arrangements. The cooperatives contributed to people's spirits and their sense of independence, things that were in real shortage among Americans during the 1930s. Communists were involved in these cooperatives, but in spite of the desperate conditions, most people were very supportive of the American free-enterprise system. Considering the massive unemployment and underemployment, Kerr was impressed at how optimistic people were and how they supported the government: most felt that communism was not the answer to this major challenge to capitalism. Grounded in direct observation, Kerr's conclusions from these events would later color his views of people's worries about the threat from communism and the "free speech" controversy that would engulf American campuses.

"Some University of California regents and many California conservatives believed that one or two Communists would destroy our nation, our universities, by corrupting the youth. I always thought this was ridicu-

lous and never really could understand it." And while his direct experience with communist influences during the Depression immunized Kerr
from many of the emotions that seized many people during the fifties,
these same experiences may have led him to discount—or even disre-
gard—concerns of some conservatives during the 1960s. His work as one
of the nation's top arbitrators also reinforced the notion that conflict
leads to conclusions and solutions that might not otherwise ever be
reached.

Kerr met Catherine (Kay) Spaulding through his Stanford roommate
Dean McHenry in 1933 at a meeting where Kerr was speaking. Com-
munist students were trying to take control of the meeting, and the future Mrs. Kerr, who sat next to Kerr on stage, passed him a note asking:
"Are you a communist?" He wrote back: "No, are you?" Kay answered
"No," and this exchange became their first communication. They were
married in December of 1934. McHenry returned to his alma mater
(UCLA) in 1939 to teach political science and might have stayed until
retirement, but his old roommate became president of the University of
California and asked him to be dean of academic planning (and later the
founding chancellor of the University of California at Santa Cruz in
1961). Kay and Clark Kerr traveled widely and often during the following years—first in 1936 to Geneva and London, where Kerr attended the
London School of Economics. In the summer of 1939, a period of great
fear and uncertainty for the world, the young couple bicycled through
Europe, Scandinavia, and parts of Russia. Through his travels Kerr would
be able to experience and reflect on conflict among people and nations
in a broader, international context. He completed his dissertation, nearly
thirteen hundred pages long, in 1939 and began a career as an academic.
Following a year at Stanford as acting assistant professor, the Kerrs moved
to Seattle, where Clark accepted a position as assistant professor at the
University of Washington. He remained there through the war years,
teaching, writing, and continuing his successful career as a labor arbitra-
tor. He did not serve in the military during World War II; his service was
deferred due to his Quaker religious convictions. He did serve in the regional War Labor Board stabilizing wages and settling labor disputes.
Kerr's ability to remain calm and unperturbed in debate and to dissect issues and cut through emotions made him increasingly popular as an ar-
bitrator with both management and labor. His international travel and
study had introduced him to foreign cultures and increasingly enabled
him to translate and understand intellectually the behaviors and actions
of diverse groups.

RETURN TO BERKELEY

In the fall of 1945, the Kerrs returned to Berkeley, and Clark became director of the newly formed northern division of the Institute of Industrial Relations (where he maintained an office until his death in 2003) and associate professor of industrial relations in the School of Business Administration. He continued a prolific scholarly agenda, exploring broader and more universal topics as he matured, from the propensity of interindustry strikes to the "balkanization" of labor markets and, eventually, comparisons of capitalism and communism and the future of industrialism and the information age. The Kerrs purchased five acres in the hills of El Cerrito, just north of Berkeley, with a breathtaking panoramic view of the San Francisco Bay and the Golden Gate. Their house there would become the chancellor's and president's residence from 1952 to 1967, as well as Kerr's primary office throughout his career.

During Kerr's sophomore year at Swarthmore, in 1930, Robert Gordon Sproul had been appointed president of the University of California. Sproul was not an academic but he was the first Cal alumnus to lead the university, serving as president for nearly three decades. He was a remarkable man: tall, with a booming and resonant voice, and an amazing memory for facts and numbers.[9] Admired by legislators for his unusual abilities to deal equally well with external demands and internal academic issues, Sproul transformed Berkeley into a distinguished international center of higher education. During the Depression he saved it from painful budget cuts. He also helped convert UCLA into a major institution, one that would eventually rival Berkeley in national prestige and he mobilized the Berkeley campus to help fight World War II, from cadet training to helping develop the atomic bomb. Sproul, aided by the extraordinary strength of the California economy, raised the university to a level equal to, if not higher than, the Ivy League institutions in the East.

But the transformation of the university was not flawless. Sproul was a vehement anticommunist and his stance on communism often would cause campus problems. One of the major controversies was the faculty uproar in 1949 when the administration demanded faculty members take a loyalty oath, primarily at the encouragement of the university's lobbyist in Sacramento, Comptroller James Corley, who argued for the strengthening of the existing oath to eliminate threats of budget cuts.[10] The story made national headlines and ultimately cost the university a great deal of prestige, but Kerr's mediating role in the struggle would bring him recognition among his colleagues and the university's regents.

The modified oath required all employees to swear that they would support the constitutions of the United States and of California, but it also contained an expanded and more controversial section: "I do not believe in, and I am not a member of, nor do I support any party or organization that believes in . . . the overthrow of the United States Government, by force or by any illegal or unconstitutional methods." The split between faculty and regents widened and led to the involvement of a committee on which Kerr served, the Committee on Privilege and Tenure.[11] Thirty-nine at the time, Kerr was the junior member of the group, which included five other senior faculty. "My selection to that committee perhaps had something to do with my job in industrial relations," Kerr remembered, "but I think they picked my name out of a hat." The chairman, Stuart Daggett, was a reserved individual not inclined to speak publicly and the other members were campus politicians who did not want to make waves. Thus, it would be up to the youngest member of the faculty committee to make the major statement before the regents.

As a compromise, the regents had agreed to a new suggestion providing an alternative to signing the oath, and the faculty committee endorsed it. But then regent John Francis Neylan moved to fire all nonsigners anyway. Kerr instinctively jumped to his feet to defend the committee and began addressing the regents. "I didn't understand how in good faith anyone could vote for the motion that regent Neylan had proposed and I said so. The regents, after all, had themselves voted for this alternative to the signing of the oath." When Kerr rose to speak, the dean of the law school, William Prosser, yanked his coattail hard and tried to pull him back down, but Kerr grabbed the chair in front of him and continued speaking. He referred to the nonsigners as the most "independent spirits" at Berkeley and asked whether, in implementing their policy against communists, the regents would be willing to dismiss these faculty only for their sense of independence. In spite of the impressive appeal of the young professor, the regents fired thirty-one faculty, a decision later reversed by California courts. Despite the firings, Kerr's exposure to the Berkeley community was influential in his becoming a faculty favorite as the first chancellor at Berkeley a few months later. The recurrent themes of conflict, resolution, debate, independence of spirit, and public speaking once again intersected in Kerr's life.

THE FIRST CHANCELLOR AT BERKELEY

While Kerr had gained the respect of his faculty colleagues and that of many regents during the loyalty oath controversy in 1950, the reasons for his selection as Berkeley's first chancellor remain somewhat unclear. His cool behavior and determination in an emotional meeting where thirty-one of the most distinguished Berkeley faculty stood to be fired were to his credit. He was also a superb scholar with obvious gifts in the realms of public speaking, writing, negotiation, and planning. But Kerr also lacked administrative experience and his selection perhaps signaled to some of the regents (themselves uncomfortable with decentralization) that Sproul would continue to run the Berkeley campus and that Kerr would be a "safe" first chancellor posing little threat to the status quo. However, if anyone had ideas about Kerr's docility, his performance as chancellor and his frequent, though always courteous and civil, confrontations with President Sproul would soon dispel them. In any event, Clark Kerr became Berkeley's first chancellor in the fall of 1952, at the age of forty.

Kerr initially had little authority; at first, he didn't even have a proper office. His desk was on the ground floor of Dwinelle Hall, an area once reserved for history department doctoral students. "Everyone in the State of California seemed to report to President Sproul. Even the public relations office at Berkeley reported to him." Initially there were disagreements between Kerr and Sproul about their respective responsibilities, although Kerr's vision of the university gave him sufficient direction to act independently. He focused first on student housing—at the time Berkeley had only two dorms, both privately donated—and construction soon began on twelve high-rise dormitories on land purchased from the City of Berkeley south of the main campus. Chancellor Kerr also worked to increase faculty participation in administration and planning and to involve students in the life of the institution. He continued his prolific writing in industrial relations and economics throughout his chancellorship, and by the end of the 1950s had come to view education as playing a dual role in modern society: education served the function of preserving freedom and choice for individuals in a democratic society while providing the knowledge and skills required in the new "information" age.

Throughout his tenure as chancellor, and later as president, he remained faithful to his faculty responsibilities and to his sense of independence. His highest salary as chancellor was $24,000; there was no chancellor's residence, but he would have turned it down if one had been offered. As president, he continued to live in his private home in El Cerrito and his highest salary was $45,000, always just below that of the governor of California, contrary to the wishes of the regents. He also chose to be part of the same benefit and retirement structures as were other faculty.

> I did not want to become too attached to any perquisites of the office. I never wanted to feel compelled to conform against my will. I wanted to feel independent, to be able to say "no" as well as "yes." I wanted to be willing to mow my own lawn and to enjoy it, to be able to teach my classes, to write my articles. . . . I did not want to build prison walls around myself. Being aware of the perils of the position . . . I viewed myself as a faculty member otherwise engaged for an uncertain period of time.[12]

As California's population exploded and major metropolitan areas developed in southern California and elsewhere, it became increasingly apparent that the governing structure of the statewide university system would have to decentralize; one step was the creation of the jobs of chancellors at UCLA and Berkeley while maintaining a strong central presence in the form of system-wide President Sproul. But the process was neither fast nor easy: Sproul was uncomfortable giving up power, but the California campuses had grown beyond the capacity of the central office to manage them from Berkeley. Perhaps Sproul was so uncomfortable because the Berkeley campus was all he had left to manage: Davis and Riverside reported to the agriculture vice president, and UCLA was controlled by the southern regents, who had even tried to recruit a chancellor without informing Sproul.[13] "I've thought about this and, in hindsight, I should have figured it out [that Sproul felt he was losing control] and been more understanding of President Sproul. It just didn't occur to me then." In any event, even as he admired and respected Sproul for his tremendous record as president, Kerr was convinced that decentralization was needed quickly and this became a top priority on assuming the presidency.

THE UNIVERSITY OF CALIFORNIA PRESIDENCY

Clark Kerr became the twelfth president of the University of California in September of 1958, but he actually began planning for the post in the fall of 1957. He was the faculty committee choice, and the regents, who had seen Kerr in a variety of situations, were also unanimously convinced he was the best choice. His inauguration took nearly three weeks and covered all of California, including a salute from the Cal band at halftime of the 1959 Rose Bowl. As Kerr entered the presidency at forty-seven years of age, the University consisted of seven campuses and centers: Berkeley (19,000 students); UCLA (16,000); Davis, the primary agricultural institution (5,200); Santa Barbara, a liberal arts college north of Los Angeles (3,000); San Francisco Medical Center (1,600); Scripps

Institution of Oceanography at La Jolla (just north of San Diego, with fifty graduate students); and Hastings College of Law (259). The regents had recently approved three new campuses (San Diego, Irvine, and Riverside) and were considering a fourth (Santa Cruz).

Looking ahead, Kerr knew that he had four monumental jobs before his presidency. The first was the day-to-day operation of a complex enterprise that spanned a large geographic region containing several major population centers of tremendous political importance, some of which were larger in population than many individual states. Second, the demographic avalanche known as the "Baby Boom" would arrive soon and a statewide plan for postsecondary education in California was needed, one that addressed the burgeoning institutional aspirations of state colleges. Kerr understood that if this planning problem were not resolved early, he would have to deal with it throughout his presidency, perhaps limiting dramatically what the university could do in the future. Third, Kerr appreciated, perhaps better than most, that decentralization of management was imperative, and that this implied the transfer of three-fourths of the university-wide staff to the various campuses, many of whom had grown accustomed to working in the president's office and did not wish to leave their jobs. Finally, there was the imperative of planning for three, and perhaps four, new universities and of dealing with the "only child" syndrome of the campus at Berkeley, which saw resources being spread among more competitors.

The administrative restructuring would serve the university well, but Kerr understood it would not be sufficient to ensure the continued excellence of Berkeley and the other university campuses. Coordinating growth among the different postsecondary sectors—university, state colleges, community colleges, and private colleges and universities—was an even greater challenge. As was the case in other states, the junior and baccalaureate-level state colleges were announcing plans to grow and to expand their curricula. Following Sputnik, there was a national need for more degrees in science and engineering, and many state colleges wanted to become research universities. The universities, on the other hand, wanted to retain sole control of the ability to award the Ph.D.s and the professional degrees in medicine, law, and dentistry, and veterinary medicine.

Clark Kerr's global approach to problems, perhaps a result of his education as an institutional economist, enabled him to see connections among seemingly unrelated parts of the educational enterprise. Institutional economic studies consider the economic decision-making process against the entire cultural and social context within which it operates;

evolution and conflict, rather than equilibrium and harmony, are seen as the natural conditions for participants in economic decision making. It is a multidisciplinary approach to the study of economic problems, involving of course economics, but also politics, sociology, law, psychology, organizational behavior, and management. Unlike more sequential learners, who tend to be convergent in their thinking, Kerr's ability to synthesize complex problems and to understand in a comprehensive way the "big picture" explains to a notable degree the success of the University of California. In orchestrating the development of the Master Plan for Higher Education in California (1960), Kerr understood the social and political connections, as well as the economic forces affecting the various segments of education in the state.

The Master Plan clarified and defined the roles of the various sectors. The junior colleges would enroll any high school graduate. The state colleges would accept any high school graduate in the top one-third of the college preparatory curriculum and would offer bachelor's and master's degrees. The university would accept students from the top eighth (12.5 percent) of high school graduating classes. More importantly, the university would continue to be solely responsible for doctoral and first professional education and research. Through its three-tier system the plan guaranteed a low-cost college education for every high school graduate in the state. Charles Reed, who has been president of the California State University system and of the Florida system, understood what Kerr accomplished:

> Clark Kerr was brilliant in guiding the process of the Master Plan. He understood before anyone else that the key to developing the University of California beyond Berkeley and Los Angeles centered on keeping doctoral and professional education within the university. This would permanently close the door for any state college to offer Ph.D. degrees. It made the junior colleges happy because their students were guaranteed a spot in a four-year institution. The private colleges also benefited from the better definitions of mission. But the big winner in terms of prestige and funding was the University of California.

Charles Young, who headed UCLA for three decades and who worked as a staff member with Kerr, agrees:

> Working through Dean [McHenry, academic assistant to Kerr as well as his former roommate at Stanford], he managed the proceedings from beginning to end, ultimately developing a consensus where

none had seemed possible among a group composed of representatives of the public-university systems and a member chosen by the private universities, and chaired by Arthur G. Coons, then president of Occidental College. . . . At the 11th hour, however, all seemed lost. Then we met with Clark late at night in his seldom-used office to hear the compromise he had devised (it involved establishing a joint doctoral program to be offered by the university- and state-college systems). It saved the day.[14]

DECENTRALIZATION OF POWER

Despite the development of the California Master Plan, Kerr sensed that demographics, economics, and politics in California would determine the direction if the university did not act clearly and quickly. The expected growth in enrollment, in the research enterprise, and in faculty numbers could not continue to be managed centrally: decentralization was necessary and unavoidable. Thus, even as the Master Plan was being negotiated, Kerr moved to reorganize the university administration and further decentralize administrative duties, something he could not have accomplished if he did not have the institutional knowledge (or "organizational memory") that he acquired working under Sproul as Berkeley's first chancellor and as a faculty member before that. Within a year of becoming president, Kerr appointed Harry R. Wellman as vice president of the university, and the very first chancellors at Davis, Santa Barbara, and Riverside were also named. By 1962, the statewide administrative staff had declined by three-fourths, from more than 1,000 to 275, although many of these cuts were reassignments from the central staff to regional campus positions.

The decentralization of authority from the center—the regents and the president—to the chancellors and the local campuses, was not universally well received, particularly by those directly affected. The changes did not come easily, nor did staffers accustomed to working in the president's office easily accept them. Nearly all eventually found jobs on the various campuses and no one was reduced in pay. However, as UCLA and the other campuses gained in independence, UC-Berkeley would regard itself as the main loser all around. But Kerr may have been the real loser: UCLA blamed him for not having enough resources compared to Berkeley and wanted even more independence from the center; the Berkeley campus with its "only child" syndrome felt betrayed by its own colleague (Kerr) as the San Diego, Los Angeles, and Santa Barbara campuses gained in reputation and resources.

In fact, Berkeley could not fill the demand by itself, but this did not seem to matter to critics of decentralization. In the early 1960s enrollment in the university was just over 50,000; forecasts predicted 215,000 by the year 2000 (actual headcount enrollment in 2000 in the nine campuses was just under 180,000). The California population was growing at the rate of 500,000 people each year, the economy was booming, and southern cities had strong political advocates and supporters. There was also a ceiling at Berkeley of 25,000 students. A campus much bigger than this wouldn't have been manageable; faculty in the same departments wouldn't even know each other. The regents had to agree with the new direction, and half of the board came from southern California anyway and those members were predisposed to assist Los Angeles and San Diego. The university academic senate also agreed, but some Berkeley faculty later forgot this, according to Kerr.

Thus, UCLA would receive treatment equal to that of Berkeley. The first thing to improve was UCLA's library. Salary scales were equalized and so-called "over-scale" hiring was permitted at UC–San Diego, where they were able to hire several superstars during this early period. Arguably, few other individuals could have done what Kerr did for the growing campuses in San Diego and Los Angeles and Santa Barbara because few others were as closely associated with Berkeley and its faculty. But many faculty unfairly, and unrealistically, believed Kerr was failing to treat Berkeley as the flagship, and this perception would cost him as the free speech movement at Berkeley played itself out.

During these years, there were issues of personality and of "turf," although Kerr seemed to be sensitive to them; he had played second or even third fiddle to the system president a few years before. Chancellor Franklin Murphy, a distinguished educator and a medical doctor who had been president of the autonomous University of Kansas (from 1951 to 1960) prior to taking the chancellorship at UCLA (serving from 1960 to 1968), favored even greater control by chancellors. Murphy left Kansas following a rather spectacular, three-year controversy with Kansas Governor George Lawrence Docking, but he was a savvy administrator who brought a great deal of experience to UCLA. He clearly felt that the president had too much authority and that decentralization was proceeding far too slowly. Kerr recalled one incident with Murphy:

> [Murphy] was incensed about the role of the president relative to that of the chancellor. Several times he proposed to me that the president should have the permission of the chancellor prior to going on his campus. I pointed out how unusual it would be for only one person

in the entire state of California to be singled out in this fashion, particularly when that person was the president of the university. But I
finally told him that I would take his concern to the regents if he
would make a formal request. I never heard from him again.

Some years later, in late 1966, shortly before Reagan would lead the regents in firing Kerr, Murphy was approached by Ronald Reagan representatives and asked if he would take the presidency after Kerr was gone.[15]
    The selection of sites for the new campuses was an interesting exer-
cise in leadership and persuasion. The locations of several UC campuses—Berkeley, L.A., Davis, Santa Barbara, Riverside—were already
established. For the new ones—San Diego, Irvine, and Santa Cruz—location and physical layout remained unresolved. The site of the Irvine
campus, somewhere within the hundred-thousand-acre Irvine Ranch,
south and east of Los Angeles and close to the Pacific Ocean, was fairly
straightforward. The site for the Santa Cruz campus was also easily decided when regents arrived at the Cowell Ranch in the redwood-covered
hills west of the town overlooking Monterey Bay. Other sites were either
on earthquake faults or were unbearably hot and smoggy, or involved too
many separately owned pieces of land.
    But the San Diego site was much more controversial and the location
episode would later affect Kerr's presidency. It underscores the variety and
role of stakeholders associated with a complex enterprise like the multi-
versity. A powerful regent, Edwin Pauley of Los Angeles (after whom
Pauley Pavillion at UCLA is named), was opposed to the most logical
site, a twelve-hundred-acre hillside above the location of the Scripps Institution of Oceanography. Pauley wanted instead to buy part of Balboa
Park and also argued that airplane noise from the nearby Miramar Naval
Air Base would be a major problem. He took regents to visit a Hawaiian
island he owned near Oahu where planes from a military base would fly
overhead and annoy him. "The debate over the site became quite bitter,
particularly between Pauley and Roger Revelle, the director of the
Scripps Institution, and Pauley never really forgave me for siding with
Revelle on the alternate site at La Jolla." Eight years later, Pauley would
join thirteen other regents, including H. R. Haldeman of Watergate fame
and Governor Ronald Reagan, in voting to fire Kerr.

MANAGEMENT STYLE

    According to Kerr, getting anything major accomplished at the Uni-
versity of California required going through many different groups; the
president has to face many directions at once. This takes conviction and

considerable personal energy, both of which Kerr possessed. Several of his associates agreed that Kerr was blessed with an extraordinary memory and could assimilate a great deal of information and recall it later with exact figures and dates. Berkeley students attending fall receptions would go through the receiving line twice as a game and Kerr would recognize them from among the hundreds of others; he would play along and say to them: "It's nice to see you, again."[16]

He had a tremendous capacity for work, often putting in eighty-hour weeks and was a prolific scholar who continued to produce high-quality (and widely quoted) articles and books in his discipline. He generally scheduled appointments in his office only one or two days a week. Harry Wellman, one of his vice presidents, recalled that on the days Kerr had appointments, they would be scheduled from nine o'clock through the noon hour with sandwiches at his desk (which was a round table) until seven or eight o'clock in the evening.[17] In spite of his busy schedule, Kerr saved Sundays for his wife Kay and his three children; Sunday without exception was for the family. He played soccer or football with the kids, and with some of the neighborhood kids as well. Later in life, he was glad that he had done so. He also devoted about two hours every Sunday to garden and to working with his hands, weeding and planting new things. "The tall weeds were regents," he smiled. "The short ones were faculty. Sometimes they even had names as I pulled them."

When he didn't have appointments, Kerr worked at home in El Cerrito, but he was always prompt in replying to requests and in making decisions. Each afternoon, his assistant, Gloria Copeland, would deliver to his home the materials and documents that had come in that day that needed his attention. On her way to the office the following morning, she would stop by the Kerr residence in El Cerrito and pick up the material he had gone over. Marian Gade, a long-time associate, noted that Kerr was not "one of those people who worked on his speech in the airplane on his way to a meeting. He would always be ready. He was a great manager of his time."

Kerr became known for his short, nearly illegible comments made in green ink with a very small handwriting. This personal distance in part reflected Kerr's intellectual and rational approach to understanding the world; it characterized his presidency as much as his emphasis on the practical side of things. Like the Quakers who influenced him in his early years, he distrusted irrational thinking. This style had its drawbacks. Personal or face-to-face contact with colleagues was absent much of the time. Eugene Lee, a long-time Berkeley professor and senior administrator who worked closely with Kerr since the 1950s, recalls a typical day with Kerr:

> He would not come in until afternoon, because in the morning he
> would have worked through all the files that had been brought to
> him the night before, or the day before. He was very much a man
> who worked with the written word, and I would go days without see-
> ing him. But we would be in daily contact through memos and notes.
> He would very promptly get back to you. The comments would come
> back in green ink, with his amazingly indecipherable handwriting.
> I'm not sure it appealed to the other VPs as much as it did me. In
> my particular situation, it worked out beautifully, and it got so I could
> draft letters, send them out to him, and they'd come back, "OK, CK"
> or "Good job," or "I disagree, let's go with this." But all of it was very
> much in this written style of work.

When Kerr did have to work face-to-face with his colleagues, he liked
to have a clear agenda. His style was not conducive to easygoing meetings with lots of give-and-take. At chancellor or vice president meetings,
Kerr would present a new policy or make some policy statement, and
"everybody would sit there motionless. A favorite statement of his was 'I
see by the nodding of heads that you're all in agreement.' He liked things
written down in advance, which he would then discuss, as opposed to
completely open-ended discussions." But other associates noted he was
not a good delegator, a trait that sometimes led to confusion about lines
of responsibility, and that the "men around Clark Kerr do not bloom."[18]
Kerr's relations with the Board of Regents were generally solid (until Reagan was elected). Lee recalled:

> Kerr was very good with the board and never got an opposition vote,
> as I remember it. It was a great source of pride with him that he al-
> ways had unanimous votes from the board; if he wasn't quite sure
> about the outcome on a particular issue, we would pull the item from
> the agenda and we'd work on it for another month; he wanted to
> make sure there were no surprises for him at the board meetings.

Kerr's preference for an intellectual, impersonal style, for sending comments to associates with his green ink pen, and, more generally, his absence from the office except when meetings were absolutely necessary,
would be one source of the problems he would face during the student
protests that would soon plague Berkeley.

FREE SPEECH MOVEMENT AND THE STUDENT RIOTS

"Hey, Johnny, what are you rebelling against?"
"Whadda ya got?"
                                    —Marlon Brando in *The Wild One* (1953)

The San Francisco Bay area, and the University at Berkeley in particular, were magnets for political activists and social radicals during the
early 1960s. The Bay area was the center of counterculture, and the
Berkeley campus, labeled as the "best-balanced distinguished university
in the United States," attracted some of the brightest young professors
and students in America.[19] But despite their publicity, the Berkeley
protests of 1964—unlike those across the nation during the late 1960s
and early 1970s protesting the Vietnam War—were quite localized geo-
graphically, and its leaders had no clear idea of how social change would
take place. What took place in fact can be seen as an incoherent series
of emotional spasms that ultimately antagonized and separated. As
breathlessly described by a then nineteen-year-old participant:

> The next day, October 1, the whole campus was hot to trot. That
> was the day of Jack Weinberg and the police car; the most dramatic,
> wonderful thing I'd ever seen in my entire life. It was like being in
> Valhalla, in a war where nobody got killed. I was rid of the burden
> of going to school, and simultaneously an incredible, exciting, won-
> derful new world was opening up.[20]

On the other hand, original members of the "movement" believe the
1964 events profoundly changed American society and were highly influential in the civil rights and women's liberation causes.[21] However, it
seems difficult to argue that the civil rights movement benefited from the
Berkeley riots. In fact, the benefits seemed to flow in the other direction,
as many of the Berkeley protesters had participated earlier that summer
(1964) in the Mississippi Summer Project, a voter registration activity
that brought white civil rights workers into the South. Thus, Berkeley
protest leaders had been toughened and radicalized by clashes with Mississippi state police and even the KKK; university administrators and
campus police would not easily dissuade or intimidate them.

There is also evidence that Berkeley's free speech movement (FSM)
had little interest in women's rights: "The common perception of women
in the FSM . . . was that they were helpmeet, solace and reward . . . The
boys quite correctly perceived this revolution within the revolution [the
women's movement] as a serious threat to what had been for the preceding half-decade the biggest free lunch of all time, and greeted it with
something less than loud hosannas."[22] During one of the early protests,
"money was collected to buy food and by 5 PM women students in the
crowd were preparing sandwiches for dinner."[23]

The principal student protagonist in the FSM episode was Mario
Savio, a wild-haired, articulate, and charismatic philosophy junior who

transferred to Berkeley from New York after deciding that "Berkeley was the place to be" when it came to political activism.[24] A few weeks before the Berkeley protests would begin, Savio and other protest leaders had been marching in Mississippi. But in spite of their energy, the student and other non-student leaders had no clear or coherent idea of what they were trying ultimately to accomplish. Indeed, Savio's most quoted statement, screamed out in front of Sproul Hall on December 2, 1964, indicated a basic misunderstanding of what Clark Kerr had written in *The Uses of the University* about the coming of the "information age" and the role of the university in it.[25]

There were in fact many ironies, both great and small, associated with the Berkeley student protests of 1964:

- that Clark Kerr, one of the great American liberals and free speech advocates, would see his stellar career partly derailed by a so-called "free speech" movement;
- that the actions of liberal, left-wing students, a liberal president, and a liberal university would propel one of America's great right-wing conservatives into statewide office and power;
- that many of Kerr's own actions and university initiatives, such as increased student housing on campus, decentralization of power from the president to the campuses, and the strengthening of the newer UC campuses, would in the end cause him to lose control, influence, and power;
- that one of the nation's most accomplished labor negotiators would not be able to negotiate a resolution to a controversy that affected him directly; and
- that a relatively trivial campus issue—where students could put up tables to publicize various events and candidates—would spark the infamous controversy.

Two months after the December, 1964, protests, Kerr would admit to mistakes. "We fumbled, we floundered, and the worst thing is I still don't know how we should have handled it."[26] But it is not clear that anyone, particularly anyone with so much going on in other areas and with the independent and personally detached leadership style of Clark Kerr, could have remained unscathed by this chain of events.

The "free speech movement," a clever name for a more complicated issue, was never about free speech—Berkeley had free speech in the sense that anyone could come to the campus to speak. The ban in question prohibited "advocacy" on campus property; it was a long-standing policy widely popular among regents, the public, and legislators in Sacramento. At the time, the ban on advocacy was considered constitutional as well, although later the U.S. Supreme Court would clarify the First Amendment freedoms of direct action long after Kerr had left the presidency. In fact, the regents would not have reversed the ban on advocacy in 1964, even if Kerr had asked for it.[27] As far as free speech goes, when Kerr was Chancellor at Berkeley, he had to inform Adlai Stevenson, who was running for president in 1952, that he could not speak at Berkeley because it would violate existing regulations and, at Kerr's insistence, regulations prohibiting speakers like Stevenson were changed. After the Stevenson embarrassment, Kerr found out that there were even more regulations prohibiting communist speakers, and he convinced the regents to change those policies as well. So Kerr did a great deal for free speech on the Berkeley campus.

> The advocacy thing was a campus mess-up, which, for very complicated reasons, including my being the "father" of decentralization and of greater campus autonomy, I did not fix. As my friend Ted Hesburgh might say: "Mea culpa." Maybe I should have acted and tried to reverse the decision of Chancellor [Edward] Strong that prohibited students from setting up their tables.

Kerr failed to grasp the flow of the conflict soon enough, in part because he had been in Eastern Europe, Hong Kong, and Tokyo on vacation and to attend conferences and inaugurate "Education Abroad" offices for most of the summer, from the middle of July to the middle of September of 1964. While he was gone, the Republican Party held its national convention in San Francisco, nominating Barry Goldwater, U.S. Senator from Arizona, for president. Former actor Ronald Reagan gained national recognition as Goldwater's campaign manager.

Kerr perhaps underestimated the effects of the civil rights movements and the power of civil disobedience as a tool in conflict. He did not appreciate the attraction that Berkeley held for liberal students and others who had been radicalized by civil rights protests and demonstrations. He also misunderstood the powerful right-wing conservatives in California; he did not communicate with Ronald Reagan until after his election as governor, and he never met him one-on-one. Perhaps it is unreasonable to expect a university president who was a well-known liberal to get to know a deeply conservative gubernatorial candidate. At the same time, however, the University of California presidency is certainly a highly political job with ties through its regents to all political elements in California. In any event, it would have been quite difficult for any one person to comprehend the complicated spiral of conflict that began in 1964, but ultimately would cost Kerr his job in 1967. Of course, otherwise very effective leaders can sometimes underestimate or misunderstand conditions and situations, and additionally, Machiavelli's *fortuna*, or luck, can play a deciding role in the outcome of important events. In Kerr's defense, it is noted that he had an extremely full agenda already, but the events in California also clearly highlight the amazing diversity and interests of a large public university and how quickly things can get out of control for its leaders.

The thing that sparked the Free Speech Movement was, according to Kerr, "a [UC-Berkeley] campus mess-up." On September 14, 1964, the day before Kerr would return from Japan, the UC-Berkeley administration announced that a twenty-six-by-forty-foot strip of land outside of the Sather Gate (a main pedestrian entrance to campus) at Bancroft Way and Telegraph Avenue was subject to university rules because it was still owned by the university. The Berkeley students for some time had conducted activities there outside of the rules that prevailed on campus property. Five years earlier, in 1959, Kerr had convinced the regents to turn over the strip to the city of Berkeley, but the land was never deeded to the city because one opposing regent had asked the secretary to the regents and the Berkeley campus Chancellor Glenn Seaborg to "sit on it," and Kerr was never informed. Students learned about the ruling through their student newspaper (*The Daily Californian*) on September 17, 1964, a day and a half after Kerr returned from his two-month trip.

Kerr returned from Tokyo on September 15 and on the afternoon of the very next day, September 16, Kerr went to the Berkeley campus to meet with Chancellor Edward Strong and others to discuss the Sather Gate ruling. This was the only time in Kerr's nine years as University of California president that he went onto a campus to tell its chancellor that he was wrong. He recalled he was the only one to speak in opposition to Chancellor Strong's ruling at the meeting and he had immediate second thoughts about his subsequent decision not to reverse this campus directive. He knew that the ruling was unwise, and he wouldn't have gone to the Berkeley campus the same day he heard about it "if I hadn't known it was a horrible thing to have done. But I figured I could work it out later in a few weeks and save Strong's face on campus. After all, I had been the father of decentralization in the university."

But Kerr didn't have a few weeks, or even a few days. On September 21, scores of students held a vigil the Sproul Hall steps, and the situation escalated quickly from there. On September 30, two weeks after

Kerr's return from the Far East, eight students, including philosophy major and spokesman Mario Savio, were indefinitely suspended for occupying Sproul Hall. This suspension began yet another series of crises, all spinning downward with dizzying rapidity. Three decades later, it would be facile to blame one or another party for the events that transpired during these few weeks in 1964. It is useful to remember that California led the nation in political protest, as it did in many other areas like universal access to higher education, traffic congestion, and hot tubs. No other university president and no other university trustees had yet dealt with civil disobedience on this scale of participation, with itchy governors and legislators intent on their election showing their decisive support of "law and order."

Chancellor Strong's opposition to any liberalization of policies was a central element in the hardening of positions. Some regents did not wish to repudiate Strong, which complicated Kerr's attempts at a resolution. By early December, FSM protesters were demanding that disciplinary actions against their leaders be dropped. When no reply came, students took over all of Sproul Hall on December 2, 1964. While student leader Mario Savio addressed the sit-in in Sproul, several regents were meeting with Kerr across the bay in Burlingame at the San Francisco airport. They agreed to support Kerr in his efforts to work out a peaceful solution. Kerr then contacted Governor Edmund G. (Pat) Brown, who agreed to join Kerr in discussing the situation with students the following morning. Kerr proceeded to call Chancellor Strong at Berkeley and told him "not to move."[28] But within hours the governor had changed his mind: he called Kerr and told him he had decided to remove the students from Sproul Hall. Governor Brown would three years later recollect: "In the early morning of December 3 [, 1964]—and on the request of University Chancellor Edward W. Strong—I ordered 600 officers of the Highway Patrol onto the campus to assist local police in ending the sit-in at Sproul Hall."[29]

At 3:00 AM that day, Chancellor Strong asked students to leave and the police began removing and arresting students. The students went limp in the style of civil disobedience, and they were dragged down the stairs and out of the building, their feet and ankles bouncing against the steps. Television cameras would record the removal for viewers all over California and the world to see. It took the police twelve hours—they were still at it the following afternoon—to haul eight hundred limp people (many of whom were not students) out of Sproul, and this gave the media ample opportunity to record the events in great detail. The exposure turned many students who had not been so active before into hard-core activists. It was a disaster for Kerr and a success for the student activists who were diligently endeavoring to provoke such an outcome.

Nonetheless, the regents still supported Kerr and his attempts at negotiation. By December 7, when Kerr appeared in the Greek Theatre to speak before 6,000 students, faculty, and staff, things had apparently improved. After Kerr's talk, a rousing standing ovation was suddenly transformed into mass confusion and shock as Savio approached the microphone to speak and two university police officers grabbed him and yanked him forcefully away from the rostrum. Kerr was visibly shaken and was almost knocked over by the rushing police.[30] Within an hour, 10,000 people jammed into the plaza in front of Sproul Hall and rejected, by acclamation, the proposals just announced by President Kerr. It was obvious no one was in charge.

And when the Berkeley department heads had their opportunity, the faculty en masse next took its turn to record its outrage. Kerr met later that same day with the Berkeley Academic Freedom Committee and discussed a resolution drafted by a large group of faculty (the "Committee of 200"). However, the faculty decided the next day, December 8, by a vote of 824 to 115 to support a resolution considerably different and more liberal than the one Kerr had seen earlier. University Vice President Harry Wellman attended the meeting in Kerr's absence and later wrote that the faculty vote was a repudiation of Kerr and a statement "that they had lost confidence in him."[31] The blow to Kerr's leadership forced the regents to enter the controversy in a more direct way to reestablish authority. But before the regents met on December 18, Chancellor Strong was asked to appear at a dinner meeting to give his views. There, perhaps realizing his tenure as chancellor was limited, Strong criticized Kerr for "an undermining of the respect for those campus officers normally responsible for carrying out the policies of the university. Too often there has been the announcement that 'henceforth law and order will prevail,' followed by vacillation, concessions, compromises, and retreats."[32] Strong was replaced by acting chancellor Martin Meyerson on January 2, 1965.[33] The appointment of a new chancellor known to be sympathetic to the issues raised by the students, in conjunction with new pronouncements from the regents about freedom of speech and the hard line likely to be taken with any new demonstrators, signaled the end of the "free speech" movement at Berkeley.

Everyone won except Kerr: the students had gained concessions during the previous three months, mostly in the area of demonstrator immunity; faculty members at UC-Berkeley were rid of their controversial chancellor, Ed Strong; and the university used the student demands to orchestrate a review of undergraduate education at Berkeley by the edu-cationally conservative faculty. In addition, Ronald Reagan was able to use the entire episode to further his gubernatorial aspirations. Kerr's abil-ity to act decisively had been weakened by a set of forces that combined during those dramatic weeks in 1964. First, his tolerance of Chancellor Strong's stubbornness (or perhaps insubordination is a more appropriate term) hardened positions and made students much more determined to confront the administration. Second, his travels during the crucial pe-riod of July, August, and September, 1964, just prior to the beginning of the 1964 fall semester, may have made it difficult for Kerr to appreciate the intensity of the situation. Kerr's work habits, including his hand-written notes in green ink and the personal distance from his staff and others, reflected his preference for working alone and for an intellectual approach to understanding and dealing with his world and the people in it. He was not an outgoing extravert like Sproul, and he did not suffer fools gladly. And fairly or not, some students and administrators regarded his personal style and intellectualism as distant and aloof. One writer quotes Kerr's Godkin Lectures speech at Harvard in 1963 as indicative of his attitude toward students:

> One of the most distressing tasks of a university president is to pre-tend that the protest and outrage of each new generation of under-graduates is [sic] really fresh and meaningful. . . . The participants go through a ritual of hackneyed complaints almost as ancient as acad-eme, while believing that what is said is really radical and new.[34]

In addition, his refusal to consider the problem as one involving free speech may have limited his effectiveness in trying to end the contro-versy.[35] Some student leaders would claim the issue was about a larger fear of civil rights. But Kerr had no reservations about free speech; he simply felt the university's name and facilities should not be used as a platform for any kind of advocacy, whether personal, social, or political. This is certainly a reasonable position and one that enjoyed wide sup-port among regents, legislators, and even among many students at Berke-ley. Kerr felt such advocacy would compromise the university's autonomy, an independence that was a prerequisite for free speech. To this Quaker from Pennsylvania, advocacy bordered on ideology, and ideology was "the great rival of logic and freedom." His belief in rational discourse and law-ful negotiation might have also caused him, in his words, to feel trapped between "two equally intolerable alternatives: acceptance of mass viola-tions or enforcement of mass discipline."

FIRED WITH ENTHUSIASM

Kerr left the University of California's presidency on January 20, 1967. At a dedication for a building at UC–Santa Barbara in honor of his friend Thomas Storke several months after he left the university presidency, he said he left just as he had entered the university as a young professor: "fired with enthusiasm." Thirteen regents joined new Governor Ronald Reagan in a vote to fire Kerr, although eight regents, including Storke, opposed Kerr's dismissal. Clark Kerr's ironic sense of humor, always more directed toward commentary than toward comedy, is legendary. Right after he became Berkeley's first chancellor in 1952, the forty-year-old Kerr was at a faculty meeting where he was asked: "What is the chancellor going to do about parking?" This was right after an athletics scandal involving Southern Cal and UCLA, as well as a panty raid by the students at Berkeley that had received much negative publicity. Kerr replied that he had come to the conclusion that there were only three major problems the chancellor is asked to deal with: sex for the students, athletics for the alumni, and parking for the faculty. Then he said he made "a terrible mistake," one that he never lived down, when he added: "This is not only a commentary on my job, but on the average age and consequent interests of the three groups involved." Kerr recalled the reaction: "These older faculty members sitting there in front never really appreciated my humor."

That was Clark Kerr's famous trilogy: sex, athletics, and parking. Ronald Reagan would have a trilogy of his own in the aftermath of the Berkeley protests and the firing of its legendary president: scapegoats for the administration to blame; budget slashes for the faculty; and tuition increases for students. Soon after Kerr's dismissal, Berkeley would quickly recognize that the treatment their extraordinary president had received was totally unwarranted and proceeded to honor and praise him. And in 1986, the Clark Kerr Campus was dedicated at UC-Berkeley, eleven years before the steps in front of Sproul Hall would be named the Mario Savio Steps. Hard work and support from caring communities, advancement of education, the belief that "there was that of good in every person," and the pursuit of peaceful solutions in a world of conflict became the central elements of Clark Kerr's life. His wife Kay, he said, reminded him that he might have lived his life with two great illusions or misperceptions about the world: that there is that of good in every person and that all problems have reasonable and peaceful solutions. But, he added: "I'd rather live with these operational beliefs than with their opposites, and I have been programmed to reject the alternatives: distrust and expectation of failure."

NOTES

1. Mary Clark Stuart, "Clark Kerr: Biography of an Action Intellectual" (Ph.D. diss., University of Michigan at Ann Arbor, 1980).

2. Ibid., 15.

3. Ibid.

4. Clark Kerr, *Academic Triumphs*, Vol. 1 of *The Gold and the Blue: A Personal Memoir of the University of California, 1949–1967* (Berkeley: University of California Press, 2001), 36.

5. Stuart, "Clark Kerr," 1.

6. Ibid., 31.

7. Neil J. Smelser, foreword to Kerr, *Academic Triumphs*, xxvi.

8. Stuart, "Clark Kerr," 21ff. The Swarthmore book on honors, *Reading for Honors at Swarthmore*, written by Robert C. Brooks and published in 1927, remains a splendid blueprint for modern honors programs.

9. Verne Stadtman, *The University of California, 1868–1968* (New York: McGraw-Hill, 1970), 257–258.

10. David Gardner, *The California Oath Controversy* (Berkeley: University of California Press, 1967), 31.

11. Ibid., 25ff.

12. Kerr, *Academic Triumphs*, 13–14.

13. Ibid., 20.

14. Charles E. Young, "Clark Kerr: A Quiet Force," *Chronicle of Higher Education*, December 19, 2003, B10–11.

15. Clark Kerr, *Political Turmoil*, Vol. 2 of *The Gold and the Blue: A Personal Memoir of the University of California, 1949–1967* (Berkeley: University of California Press, 2003), 290.

16. Reported in the *New York Times*, March 11, 1965.

17. Stuart, "Clark Kerr," 166.

18. Ibid., 167.

19. Kerr, *Academic Triumphs*, Chapter 5.

20. David L. Goines, *The Free Speech Movement: Coming of Age in the 1960s* (Berkeley, CA: Ten Speed Press, 1993), 475.

21. *Berkeley in the Sixties*, video directed by Mark Kitchell (First Run Features, 2002).

22. Goines, *Free Speech Movement*, 475–476.

23. Stadtman, *University of California*, 448.

24. David Horowitz, *Radical Son: A Generational Odyssey* (New York: The Free Press, 1997), 113. After dropping out of Berkeley in 1965, Savio worked as a bookstore clerk, tended bar, and taught mathematics, both as a tutor and also in public and private schools, at the junior high and high school level. He received a bachelor's degree, summa cum laude, in 1984 when he was forty-two years old and then a master's degree, both in physics, from San Francisco State University. He taught there and at Modesto Junior College before going to

Sonoma State. Shunning publicity and suffering periodic bouts with depression, Savio taught mathematics and philosophy at Sonoma State, where he joined the faculty in the 1990s. He had a history of heart trouble and died November 8, 1996, at the Columbia Palm Drive Hospital in Sebastopol, California, some thirty miles northeast of Berkeley, after suffering heart failure while moving furniture, at age fifty-three.

25. See Goines, *Free Speech Movement*, 151, 361, for Savio's versions of Kerr's educational philosophy. Savio repeatedly asserted that Kerr referred to the university as a "knowledge factory," but Kerr never uses that term in his famous book *The Uses of the University*. Instead, Kerr analyzes the changes that universities were undergoing; Kerr cites Fritz Machlup (*The Production and Distribution of Knowledge in the United States* [Princeton: Princeton University Press, 1962]), a Princeton professor and one of the most distinguished economists of the twentieth century, who referred to the university as a "city of intellect" and also described the "knowledge industry," a term that today seems commonplace but that in 1964 was unusual and even prophetic.

26. A. H. Raskin, "The Berkeley Affair: Mr. Kerr vs. Mr. Savio & Co," *New York Times Magazine*, February 14, 1965.

27. Kerr, *Academic Triumphs*, 148.

28. Stuart, "Clark Kerr," 212.

29. Edmund G. Brown, *Reagan and Reality: The Two Californias* (New York: Praeger, 1970), 141.

30. "Chronology of Events: Three Months of Crisis," *California Monthly*, February 1965, 67.

31. Harry Wellman, "Teaching, Research, and Administration—1925–1968" (Berkeley: University of California Oral History, Bancroft Library), 156.

32. Edward Strong, "Student Demonstrations at Berkeley: A Report to the Regents," December 16, 1964. Reprinted in Stadtman, *University of California*.

33. Stuart, "Clark Kerr," 218.

34. Garry Wills, *Certain Trumpets* (New York: Simon and Schuster, 1994), 81.

35. Stuart, "Clark Kerr," 220.

CHAPTER 6

The Catcher from Dallas, North Carolina

No society can survive without an institution at its heart dealing with values, teaching the importance of history, and revealing the relationship between man and nature. It's there, in the beating, human heart of the university, where you get sustenance for the soul, where you find out what's making your heart sing, where you are motivated to go against the odds to do something.

—William C. Friday

INTRODUCTION

In the mid-1960s, a ten-year political battle began in North Carolina over the establishment of a medical school at East Carolina University. ECU was a former teacher's college in Greenville with a politically savvy president named Leo Jenkins, an unlikely New Jersey native among the farmers of eastern North Carolina. The disagreement pitted many East Carolina supporters against backers and alumni of the University of North Carolina at Chapel Hill, home to the only public medical school at the time. Vernon White, a former state senator from eastern North Carolina, had been an influential actor in the struggle to create the school, involved in the strategy meetings and the politics on a nearly daily basis. Many years later Senator White recalled the role of William Friday, president of the then six-campus University of North Carolina, who opposed a new medical school and favored instead the creation of Area Health Education Centers (AHECs) to send

William Friday.

doctors from the existing medical schools to regions underserved by physicians.

> Bill Friday is as skilled a politician and tactician as any legislator or governor who has ever served in North Carolina. . . . Here was a man who had opposed us, though always very courteously and politely. But when it was finally all over, he came to the legislature and basically this is what he said: "You know I believed other alternatives were educationally sound. But it's time now for all of us to move on. However, the university will not be associated with anything other than a first-rate medical school, not if I have anything to do with it. We're going to make it as fine a facility as we can for two reasons: first, that's the standard of the university and, second, we need to focus on preparing doctors who really will care for the people in North Carolina. I am here to share with you what this will cost."
>
> That ended it. You could just feel the tension and the politics evaporate from that room. It was at that moment my real admiration for Bill Friday began.

The East Carolina University four-year medical school opened in August of 1977 with twenty-eight students, including fourteen from eastern North Carolina towns and cities. Since its establishment three decades ago, the school has graduated hundreds of medical doctors and is ranked by surveys as one of the nation's best in educating physicians who specialize in family medicine. One of its professors in cardiac surgery, Dr. Randolph Chitwood, won the University of North Carolina's prestigious O. Max Gardner Award in 2004, given to the faculty member in the UNC sixteen-campus family who has made the "greatest contributions to the welfare of the human race." As Friday promised the legislature, the East Carolina medical school has developed as a first-rate institution and has been fully incorporated into the UNC system as one of its most successful achievements. But it is Friday's grace in controversy and, more importantly, his uncanny ability to make supporters out of previous adversaries that defines the essence of this legendary North Carolinian.

EARLY LIFE

In his prize-winning biography of William Friday, Bill Link begins with this sentence: "William Clyde Friday was born on July 13, 1920, in Raphine, Virginia, a Shenandoah Valley village so small that it did not merit mention in that year's federal census as an incorporated town." When Bill Friday opened Link's book for the first time, he paused with that sentence. "With that beginning," he laughed, "I wasn't at all sure that I wanted to read on."

To be sure, Raphine is not much of a metropolis, although two major inventions originated there—James Gibbs' sewing machine and Cyrus McCormick's mechanical reaper. In fact, the word "Raphine" comes from an old Greek word meaning "to stitch or to sew," and the town was so named at Gibbs' insistence in the 1880s.[1] It lies forty miles west of Charlottesville, home to the University of Virginia, and twenty-five miles south of Staunton, the birthplace of another famous university president, Woodrow Wilson. Raphine was the hometown of Friday's mother, Mary Elizabeth (Beth) Rowan; his grandfather, William Henry Rowan, owned one of the local merchandise stores. The Rowans, strict and devoted Presbyterians, were known throughout Rockbridge County for their moral rigor. Grandfather Rowan was a deeply religious influence on the family; the Rowans observed the Sabbath unwaveringly, with no work or play allowed. They were, as Friday noted, "farm people, tithing people," who descended from the Ulster Scots, immigrants during the late 1700s searching for religious freedom and economic security. Grandfather Rowan calculated his precise earnings each week so that later, in accordance to tithing practice, he could contribute exactly one-tenth of it to the church.[2]

At her father's urging, Friday's mother Beth attended Linwood College, a Presbyterian school that used to exist in Gaston County, North Carolina, near the border with South Carolina and about 275 miles to the south and west of Raphine. It was there that Beth met a young World War I veteran, David Lathan ("Lath") Friday, and they eventually married in July of 1919, and they moved to Dallas, North Carolina, also in Gaston County, a small crossroads a half hour west of Charlotte. When Beth became pregnant with their first child, she went back to Raphine to be with her family for the childbirth, as was customary then. Their first son was named after Lath's brother William Clyde, who had died during an influenza outbreak in 1918.

Friday's father was of German and Scots-Irish descent whose ancestors emigrated to America and to the foothills country, in the southwestern part of North Carolina, in the mid-1700s. Lath completed ninth grade at the Dallas High School, the highest grade offered at the school then, and later enrolled in a short education program at the University at Chapel Hill before returning to Gaston County to teach school. Lath's father, or Bill's grandfather, David Franklin Friday, was a big, physically imposing man. He was a "public person," like many others on his father's side, and he worked also as a judge, merchant, and farmer. Lath Friday was a physically forceful man like his father, with "muscle power" derived from years of hard physical labor. He is described in Link's book as a bon vivant, gregarious with a good sense of humor, who loved hunting and fishing and strumming the banjo.[3] Lath progressed through the ranks at the Cocker Machine and Foundry Company in Gastonia: he worked as a skillful and "aggressive" salesman, general manager, vice president, and member of the board of directors. He traveled frequently and was often out of town during Friday's youth. But in spite of his frequent travels, he was, like grandfather Friday, a strong advocate of public service, and he served as alderman and later as mayor of Dallas, where the family home was located directly across the courthouse square.

As is the case with other eventually successful leaders, education was highly valued in Bill Friday's home, extraordinarily so among families in comparable times and economic situations, and children were strongly encouraged to study.[4] Although Lath Friday had a limited education, eventually all his five children—Bill, Dave, Rudd, John, and Betty— would complete college. Three of the sons became attorneys, including John, who served as a superior court judge in North Carolina. The family's educational emphasis stemmed from Lath's work habits: in the Friday home, life was centered around hard work, and the children, particularly the oldest, Bill, were frequently encouraged to excel, study hard, and make something of themselves. From his father, Bill Friday would learn the importance of hard effort and from his mother and her family (Rowan), he would come to appreciate moral responsibility and behavior. But Lath's drive to work hard exacted a "high price" for the family, as the traveling and frequent absences would contribute to family stress. Friday's brother John recalled that the children were able to see Lath "on the weekends, if we were lucky."[5]

Friday's "best memories" of childhood revolved around the three summers he spent in Raphine with his maternal grandparents, where he would cement his personality around the values of thrift, hard work, and Protestantism. During those summers in Raphine his grandfather William would put his ten-year-old grandson to work in his store, which sold every item imaginable, including clothes, shoes, food, and horse tack. Friday accompanied his grandfather when he went out to collect bills and recalled that his grandfather sometimes carried a pistol. When business at the store was slow, Friday was sent to the farm of William's brother, where different work had to be performed, such as picking apples and bagging wool from sheared sheep. Religion was a central aspect of Rowan family life and Bill would attend Bible classes and services at the Old Providence Church, where many of the Rowans are buried.

North Carolina in the late 1920s was a rural, agricultural state, rank-
ing second nationally both in the number of farms and in farm population. As the Depression approached, however, the state was rapidly
becoming industrialized and most of its industrial workers, over 60 percent, were in textile manufacturing. Work in the mills was hard and not
very rewarding: in the mid-1920s, the average annual income was around
$750 and the normal hours of work were six-to-six, five days a week, and
six-to-eleven on Saturday. Over one-third of the workers in these mills
were under nineteen years of age, and families averaging five persons were
usually crowded in four-room houses clustered on the periphery of towns
or along railroad tracks. Great tensions existed between industrialists and
workers regarding working conditions and child labor issues.[6] After the
New England textile strikes of 1928, union organizers from the North
made plans to penetrate the South. They focused on Gaston County,
southwest of Charlotte, concluding that "North Carolina is the key to
the South, Gaston County is the key to North Carolina, and the Loray
Mill is the key to Gaston County."[7]

In 1929 Bill Friday was in the third grade. Decades later he would still
vividly recall the violence in textile-rich Gaston County. The mammoth
Loray Mill was owned by a corporation in Rhode Island whose absentee
owners emphasized productivity and cost controls: within fifteen months
the mill had reduced the workforce from 3,500 to 2,200 without decreasing production. The firings emboldened union organizers, leading to
worker demands and to angry retaliation by mill supervisors unaccus-
tomed to the tactics of northern unions, or even to their "Yankee" ac-
cents. In June of 1929, four months before the October stock market
crash, disturbances at a colony of displaced workers culminated in the
shooting of five people, including the Gastonia chief of police, who died
the next day. Fifteen strikers were indicted for murder and Governor O.
Max Gardner had to send troops to Gastonia to restore order. The issues
were so polarized that newspaper editors throughout North Carolina felt
compelled to insist upon the rights of the accused to fair trials.[8]

Friday's father was strongly anti-union and anticommunist, as were
many others then across North Carolina and the nation. "As we drove
through the Loray Mill area, we saw guns stacked up in the center of the
street. I remember my father telling us that communists had murdered
the police chief." He also recalls the human face of the suffering during
the Depression that ensued shortly thereafter: "Children around dinner
tables were hungry, a true hunger with medical consequences. The desperate circumstances of the economy and their impact on family and on
society had a tremendous impact on your sense of arrogance." His life-

long concern with helping others may be traced to these childhood experiences: "I know how lucky I was to be one of the few to get out and have a successful life. I know many people back home who didn't have the luck I did and who struggled. I went back and I saw them. They never got out. And I also understood that I could have easily gone another way."

But Friday did get out. In elementary and high school photos, Bill Friday always seems to be standing the straightest, with a confident smile and jet-black hair. Wilma Thornburg, the elementary school teacher from Dallas whom Friday would decades later take to a ceremony at UNC Charlotte where a building was being named in his honor, remembered Friday as a boy with a "real gift for making friends," very "dependable" and without any "show" to him. "She was a major influence," Friday remembered, "because her message awakened me: she would say that we all had the ability to make something of ourselves and also that we should make ourselves useful to our fellow citizens. She was a tremendous motivator." In his teens, Friday already exhibited leadership traits: he was class president all four years at the Dallas High School, and contemporaries observed that he possessed exceptional interpersonal skills and leadership abilities.[9]

Friday also matured early in other areas, including public speaking. With the opening of new high schools in North Carolina, competitive declamation, or debating, contests had become a popular activity among many young people. Lath strongly encouraged his son to participate, urging him to work at it five days a week, like an army drill sergeant with a recruit. Friday, who is a natural introvert, would later recall that getting up in front of crowds was very uncomfortable and stressful for him as a teenager. Like Winston Churchill, who as a child memorized the speeches of Cromwell, Burke, Macaulay, and Disraeli to overcome a speech impediment, Bill Friday would be able decades later to recite some of the talks he practiced as a teenager.

It wasn't all declamation. Baseball was a highly popular community activity and most mills had a baseball team; teens that were good athletes gained significant recognition. By the time he was sixteen years old, Friday had developed a reputation as an excellent ballplayer, a catcher with solid skills and a chance for a professional career. The catcher on a baseball team, of course, stands anonymously masked behind the scenes just in front of the home plate umpire. But he is the only one with a view of the entire playing field and is in control of the pitcher. The position suggests a compelling metaphor for Friday's leadership style, which was always typified by his quiet, behind-the-scenes control of events. Young Bill Friday, in fact, played with distinction on a select American Legion team under coach Jack Kiser that toured several counties and cities in the sum-

mer of 1937.[10] His sports participation led to a job in the sports department in the *Gastonia Gazette*, an experience that enabled him to appreciate the work of journalists early in his life, something that would serve
him well later. But as much as he enjoyed baseball, the game was second
to his demanding work schedule: as a sixteen-year-old, Friday worked
forty to fifty hours each week at eighteen cents an hour at the mills. "I
never practiced with the other players. I ran home after work on Saturdays, got my mitt and mask, and went to the games."

A partial rendering of the young Friday thus emerges: a resilient young
person who attracts supportive adults such as his grandparents and teachers because of his engaging personality; assertive, polished, and even
charismatic, as described by contemporaries, Friday was a "smoothie" (to
use a popular North Carolina term). An inclination to work hard and
long was already a pattern, and his family persistently urged him to excel
and to pursue his education. His personality is complex for someone of
his age: open and friendly, but at the same time introspective and
thoughtful, highly sensitive to others, with an intense dislike for the violence he witnessed as a child. The Depression left its mark, as it did on
all who lived through it, and the stresses at home also had an impact. As
Link notes, "marital problems had erupted by the time Friday reached
college age and he was quite aware of the problems as he left home to
attend Wake Forest College." Nonetheless, as a way of coping with the
disagreeableness, he "fought thinking about it" and would speak very affectionately and matter-of-factly of his parents to friends in college.[11] His
resiliency in dealing with serious disappointments and personal challenges is evident in Friday's behavior and responses. Emotional "scar tis-
sue," as Friday termed it, had formed and he would return home
infrequently, plunging into his college work in a way that, according to
Friday, "some people would think abnormal."[12] His life experiences, along
with the mental strength he had developed to cope with the adversity of
his youth, would build his capacity for empathy with the problems of others, a sort of legendary antenna that detected conflict and inner turmoil
without being told, perhaps, as he said, "because I understood what they
were going through." When he arrived at Wake Forest in the fall of 1937,
"I had a physical rejection, almost, for the partying and the fraternities
and so forth." Sounding remarkably like Clark Kerr and Ted Hesburgh,
he added: "I wanted to get things done, to make a difference."

WAKE FOREST AND STATE COLLEGE

As a first generation college student among wealthier students from
larger cities and towns, Friday "felt immensely lonely at first and also out

of place" at Wake Forest College, then located in Wake Forest, North Carolina, a small town a few miles north of Raleigh. Channeling his fear of failure into work, Friday became a "compulsive worker," but he adapted quickly and learned that he could work well with perfect strangers.[13] Wake Forest reinforced in him the sense of service instilled by his family, and by the end of his freshman year he was elected class treasurer. Although Friday would shortly begin making friends and enjoying Wake Forest, Lath continued to insist that his eldest son join him in the textile business and persuaded his reticent oldest son to transfer to NC State and to its School of Textiles.

Moving from Wake Forest to Raleigh in 1938 might have felt like the trip from Athens to Sparta: Wake had a strong liberal arts tradition whereas "State College" was still a technical institution with no Ph.D.s in its administration and limited commitment to the humanities and social sciences. This absence of a liberal arts tradition and its impact on the eighteen-year-old Friday would play a major role several years later when, as president of the University of North Carolina, Friday hired political scientist John T. Caldwell as chancellor of NC State, and Caldwell eventually planned and established a new school offering degrees in the humanities and social sciences at NC State.[14] State College, with two thousand students in 1938, was twice the size of Wake Forest College, and Friday had to readjust to another campus environment with a much different academic orientation. It was clear, however, that the study of textile manufacturing was not for him: he really did not want to return to the mills in any capacity. At the urging of Charles Romeo "Romie" Lefort, assistant dean of students, Friday turned his energies to campus affairs. Lefort, whom Friday regarded as a second father, was a "great humanitarian . . . a beautiful individual . . . who sat under people who didn't have the vision he had and who were afraid to let him loose." Many years later Lefort would observe that he had easily recognized Bill Friday's abilities to communicate effortlessly with all sorts of people and to understand and empathize with their problems.[15]

Friday continued what would be a lifelong association with the media and with college sports, working as a "spotter" at football games and also as sports editor of the school newspaper, *The Technician*. As an undergraduate student at NC State, Friday had a distinctive look, "very neat and very dignified," according to one classmate, and his journalistic connections afforded him an opportunity to develop further his leadership skills: often his columns and articles would criticize "rough stuff" or other unsportsmanlike behavior. Prior to a basketball game with the archrival Tar Heels, Friday exhorted students to treat "our brethren from Chapel

Hill" as guests. His assistant sports editor, Bob Pomerantz, recalled, "I did all the work," while Friday just "had a way of motivating people," appearing to "talk it out" without imposing anything; but he nonetheless "generally had his way."[16] While his classroom performance was average, Friday distinguished himself outside the classroom. He was senior class president, had been elected to all the major honorary leadership and service fraternities on campus, and was the first NC State student chosen to speak at commencement.

WORLD WAR II

News bulletins from Europe during the summer of 1941 were not encouraging, and Winston Churchill was doing all he could to bring the Americans into the fight against the Germans. After graduation Bill Friday took a textiles job with DuPont in Waynesboro, Virginia, a small town just west of Charlottesville, placing him back within 20 miles of Raphine. His work experiences there, perhaps in combination with its nearness to home, decidedly convinced him that he wanted something else. During the summer he applied for a commission in the U.S. Navy, but he also received a call from the NC State dean of students Erdahl Cloyd offering him a job. His mentor Lefort had resigned as assistant dean to work with the ROTC program, and Lefort had urged Cloyd to hire Friday as his replacement. He jumped at the opportunity to leave Waynesboro and went back to Raleigh to await the Navy's response about his commission. The Navy's decision was still pending on December 7, 1941, when he heard about the Japanese attack on Pearl Harbor that Sunday morning on the radio.

The inevitability of the war seemed to speed up life; it made things seems more urgent, more pressing. Bill Friday and Ida Howell, a tall and strikingly beautiful young woman from Lumberton, North Carolina, a small, rural town near the South Carolina border, had met on a blind date in the fall of 1940 during the annual State-Carolina football game. It was not, as Ida recalled, "love at first blush." Friday was not a social hummingbird, at least when it came to dating, and was involved in "so many other things" that he rarely attended dances and parties around west Raleigh. "The truth is I don't think he ever dated anyone else in his entire life, he was such a serious young man," recalled Ida. "I was the first." Friday received his commission from the Navy in the spring of 1942 and the urgency of the war sped up Bill and Ida's romantic timetable. They were married on May 13, 1942, two days after Friday received his commission as a Navy ensign, in the Hayes-Barton Methodist Church in Raleigh, with Ida outfitted in a $30 wedding dress.[17]

Shortly after the wedding, Friday was assigned briefly to South Bend, Indiana, and to the Naval Gun Factory in Washington, D.C. He was then transferred to St. Julien's Creek Naval Ammunition Depot, near Norfolk, Virginia, where he would learn about ordnance, ammunition, and dangerously volatile explosives. The rush of the war was stunning: "If the Nazis had known how disorganized we were, they would have attacked us directly." Perhaps because of his industry experience, a surprised Friday was chosen, at twenty-two years of age (the same age as his father was when he joined the Army for the first world war) as plant manager for the entire ammunition depot. He was on call twenty-four hours a day, responsible for everyone at the place, and the round-the-clock work was stressful and tense, with little tolerance for mistakes: a young woman was killed shortly after his arrival when explosive materials blew up in her face. Friday was among the first to reach her and the event left a deep imprint on Friday's psyche; the constant danger and unremitting tension would remain with him long after the war was over: "I would get very jumpy for years whenever anyone struck a match near me. Just the sound would give me chills."

World War II immediately expanded the world of all whose lives it touched, much like the impact of travel abroad. It required a "translation" across cultures, regions, and ethnicities for young people thrown together with others from very different parts of the nation and with very different backgrounds. The wartime experiences also made Friday more aware of the narrowness of his collegiate preparation and of the chasm in opportunity created by the poverty of the south. Death's reality among young people full of promise is surely a transforming event, and work in the ammunitions depot with the weapons of mass destruction made Friday feel as if he were "killing more people than anybody else." He left the Navy in early 1946 after the reality of war had wrung all romance out of the military. He decided to enroll in law school.

> My generation—Hesburgh, Kerr—is different. I really believe that. We came in with a different perspective, with a sense of purposefulness to get things done. We all went through the Depression, the violence of unions in different areas but in very similar contexts, and also a horrible world war that had a tremendous impact on all of us. Half of my classmates at NC State died in that war and don't think that doesn't stay with you. I struggled with the question of how I could make my life worth something.

The Fridays arrived in Chapel Hill, then a pleasant town of fifteen thousand, in February of 1946, and Bill and Ida would live there uninterruptedly for the remainder of their lives. The college town twenty-five miles west of Raleigh was alive and vibrant and veterans with a sense of purpose were flooding back to campus. But Friday's transition after the war was a personal struggle he shared with other veterans: a combat pilot with two Navy Crosses for gallantry in combat sat in front of Friday in class and unconsciously would tear small strips from the newspaper and encircle himself with them. In law school Friday would become close friends with individuals who later became important actors in the state and the university, including future governor (and U.S. Senator) Terry Sanford, as well as UNC board chairmen Bill Dees and John Jordan.

After passing the North Carolina Bar in 1948, the twenty-eight-year-old Friday hoped to combine his textiles education from NC State with the law, and thought a job with Burlington Industries, the premier textile company in the world at the time, would achieve this goal. Burlington did not offer him a job, but his mentor from NC State, Romie Lefort, had not forgotten him. Every time Lefort saw President Graham, he reminded Dr. Frank about Bill Friday. Lefort, along with others, finally convinced Fred Weaver to offer Friday a job as assistant dean of students at Chapel Hill. So, after another unplanned move, Friday entered a university environment defined by the presence of Frank Porter Graham, leaving behind both a legal career and the textile industry.

EXPOSURE TO THE TOP: EARLY CAREER AT CAROLINA

The administrative atmosphere in South Building shaped Bill Friday's leadership style in significant ways. Although Frank Graham presided over the three-campus system, he was primarily associated with the campus at Chapel Hill. In this sense Graham's role was similar to that of his contemporary Robert Sproul, the president of the five-campus University of California who was associated mainly UC-Berkeley. (During the early part of Friday's tenure as president, the same association would be the common perception. As one faculty member put it: "The common, but mistaken, feeling was that Friday was the head of Carolina [UNC–Chapel Hill] but that he was more loosely related to the other campuses.") Graham was a deeply moral presence. A devout Presbyterian all of his life, his perspective was actually more moral or ethical than it was religious.[18] His concern for people was expressed as a feeling for human rights, for whatever makes it possible for one to be human. The presidency under Graham thus had a spiritual underpinning to its basic

concern for social justice and constitutional equality. Based on his studies at the University of Chicago, he felt the South needed to free itself
from its archaic social systems and from the deepest poverty in America
to meet the social changes that would come. These concerns pulled Graham into the center of controversies, including the textile strikes in that
Bill Friday had witnessed as a child.

Friday was often "lent" as a chauffeur to Frank Graham, who had never
learned to drive. "I would drive him all over the state, literally. Sometimes he would nap, but often we would just talk about the university or
things that were going on in the state." Early exposure to the highest
level of an organization provides a young person with an overarching
view of the enterprise and working in South Building gave Friday an ac-
celerated course on how the university functioned. Gradually Friday
would become fully immersed with the Consolidated University office,
as the headquarters of the three-campus system was then called. When
Fred Weaver took a leave of absence for the fall of 1949, Friday was
named acting dean of students.

In South Building Friday experienced Graham in his presidential
prime and also observed Graham's folksy and gifted administrative team.
Graham was not known for his administrative skills, and he relied heav-
ily on the mellow Robert House for internal operations. Friday learned
from Graham about idealism and ethics in public service, absorbing Graham's personal style of dealing with students and faculty, while the
harmonica-playing Bob House taught him about "the nuts and bolts of
the university's inside operation." The individual with the biggest impact
on Friday was William D. (Billy) Carmichael, whom Friday already knew
from his days at NC State and from whom he learned practical responsiveness, modesty, and deference in dealing with the public and the legislature. Gregarious, funny, and politically savvy, Carmichael connected
with legislators and alumni in ways that the cerebral and idealistic Graham could not, and he also became a good friend and mentor to Friday.
As he drove the group to meetings with legislators or with others making up the power structure of North Carolina, Friday would quietly soak
up their strategic thinking.

A few months after Friday had moved into South Building, in March
of 1949, North Carolina's junior U.S. Senator, J. Melville Broughton,
passed away, and Governor Kerr Scott had to appoint a replacement.
Scott was a liberal Democrat from a powerful political family: his brother
Ralph was an influential state senator and his son, Robert, would fifteen
years later become lieutenant governor and then governor in 1968. For
his own election, Kerr Scott had pulled together an impressive coalition

of factory workers, farmers, and blacks, and after his election he launched a number of populist programs, including the largest rural road-paving program ever undertaken in America. An earthy and engaging leader, Scott had championed the legalization of winemaking by farmers in a largely prohibitionist state, claiming people needed wine for their church communion services.[19] Two weeks after Broughton's death, Graham announced that he would leave the university for the U.S. Senate. Bill Friday was disappointed to learn that Graham would not be taking him to Washington, but Graham's decision spared Friday from the experiences of a bitter primary election in 1950 that has lived in political history as North Carolina's dirtiest campaign. Graham's loss to lawyer Willis Smith in that senatorial primary left Graham a "broken man" and convinced Friday, despite many requests over the years, never to seek elective office. Nonetheless, one of Friday's few professional regrets is that he never took a year off during his presidency to go to Washington "to learn how that place really worked."

Following Graham's departure, the university experienced considerable instability in its leadership. Billy Carmichael served eleven months as acting president, until February of 1950, when the UNC trustees elected Gordon Gray as president, who followed Carmichael's strong recommendation to hire Friday as his assistant. A solid administrator and an unusually hard worker, Gray was the son of Bowman Gray, the CEO of R. J. Reynolds Tobacco Company, and had served as an attorney in private practice and as a state senator. An extremely private person, Gray was a sharp contrast to Frank Graham and also to Bill Friday. Friday provided the warmth and personal touch for the Consolidated University office as he was gaining polish in boardroom rituals, while Gray made progress in formalizing a highly informal administrative structure and clarifying relationships among the three UNC campuses, including the roles of the president and the chancellors who administered the individual campuses.

But succeeding Frank Graham would have been difficult for anyone and Gray seemed frustrated with his inability to make changes in the university's administrative structures. He left the presidency in June of 1955 to become assistant secretary of defense under President Eisenhower. With Billy Carmichael in poor health (high blood pressure would claim his life in 1961), the trustees turned to a former Emory University administrator who was serving as UNC's provost, J. Harris Purks, Jr. But Purks was not well suited for the job either—Friday later described Purks as "a man with lots of nervous energy"—and his interim presidency lasted only nine months. The frequent turnover and the sense that the UNC presidency was adrift had become major concerns among UNC trustees.

THE MATURE LEADER: UNC PRESIDENT

UNC trustees faced a long list of important challenges in the winter of 1956. They had to find a president and create stability in the office. They had to define more clearly the role of the central administration in relation to the campuses. They had to plan for the "baby boom" population that would soon be clamoring for a higher education. They also had to worry about the expansion plans of the regional state colleges, each a distinct legal entity with its own board of trustees and president. With Billy Carmichael still ill, and with no other viable candidate, the trustees turned to Bill Friday and appointed him as acting president. As the secretary of the university during the previous five years, the thirty-five-year-old Friday had developed into a confident administrator with the support of several key members of the executive committee. Within months, however, he confronted the first of several challenges with intercollegiate sports, as well as a faculty uprising at the Woman's College in Greensboro, where a campus committee was preparing to fire the chancellor for a variety of personal and professional transgressions. Friday admitted that he was unprepared for those first few months in office and he benefited greatly from having Billy Carmichael as an advisor.

Friday addressed the Women's College dispute with a set of moves that quintessentially define his leadership style. Following the counsel of Billy Carmichael, he persuaded the committee to disband, pledging to handle the matter himself. He then created a new committee with the authority of the president's office and with the most distinguished university leaders on it, chaired by Billy Carmichael. Within two months Friday had quietly obtained Chancellor Edward Kidder Graham's resignation. His performance during this awkward situation for the university established him as a viable candidate with the trustees. Even faculty who had worried about his lack of scholarly qualifications remarked on his approachability, good judgment, and decisiveness. But in spite of his effectiveness, Friday was still only one of eleven finalists in the fall of 1956. There was disagreement: several trustees felt that Friday was too young. A deadlocked committee finally agreed to offer Friday the presidency if he appointed William De Vane of Yale, another of the eleven finalists, as his "number two" person. When the prearranged deal was presented to Friday, he immediately rejected it and said the issue was not negotiable. In spite of Friday's flat refusal to accept any preconditions, the trustees on October 18, 1956, selected Friday as president. He was thirty-six.

THE ATHLETICS CHALLENGE

It is ironic that Bill Friday, the former gifted athlete and college sports-writer, both began and ended his career trying to maintain a proper balance between the university's main academic purpose and the conduct of intercollegiate sports. As Gordon Gray's assistant, Friday was aware of the serious problems created for university leaders when academic control of college athletics is lacking. In the early 1950s, UNC–Chapel Hill boosters insisted on hiring two big-name coaches, Frank McGuire and Jim Tatum, to head their basketball and football programs, respectively. And in 1954 and again in 1955, NC State's Everett Case had won major recruiting battles against Adolph Rupp's Kentucky Wildcats, only to find the university reported to the NCAA for recruiting violations and placed on major probation for the infractions.

The problems Friday faced in 1956 originated while Gray was president, but the NCAA's announcement came after Friday had become acting president. In addition, another investigation of NC State's basketball program was underway, this time involving Jackie Moreland, a highly recruited six-foot-eight-inch forward from Louisiana. The allegations were typical of NCAA inquiries: excessive reimbursements for transportation expenses, under-the-table cash award promises, money for the education of a girlfriend. The inquiry allegedly was instigated (again) by Kentucky's coach Adolph Rupp; Moreland had actually signed a "letter of intent" to play for Kentucky but he changed his mind at the last minute after a visit by Vic Bubas, an assistant coach and former player at NC State who later went on to coach Duke's basketball teams in the 1960s. NCAA director Walt Byers personally conducted the investigation, and the results were announced on November 13, 1956, just after Friday's appointment as permanent president. One of the stiffest penalties ever meted out in NCAA history was imposed: four years probation with no post-season play.

> I still remember the shock and the scope of the penalty. And to this day, I am bothered by my inability to get to the bottom of what happened there. The NCAA would never tell me what they had found and I never got an answer from the principals at State [assistant coach Vic Bubas and head coach Everett Case]. But I am convinced now that I was lied to. The NCAA official who called to say I was not being told the entire story was also lied to.

Friday's inexperience with college sports was obvious and the inade-quate conclusion of the Moreland episode would haunt him for years. But the UNC trustees, perhaps because many of them felt closer kinship to the Chapel Hill campus and because they also knew Friday was not re-sponsible for the infractions, were not keen on prolonging the agony. So when Friday reported that he could not get any information from the NCAA to make a judgment, the trustees agreed quickly to drop it.

The forces that touch college sports are brought to focus by this episode, except for their much greater commercialization, they remain largely un-changed fifty years later. First, the influence of the NCAA, even with changes made in recent years to involve presidents in its organizational structure, is still quite strong, and its methods of investigation remain highly secretive and even capricious. To a neophyte president trained in the law, such investigatory processes, where the accused does not confront the accusers and where charges are not clearly disclosed or findings re-vealed, seemed bizarre and even illegal. Second, the world of coaches, re-cruiters, and boosters is foreign territory to virtually all college presidents, a situation made even worse by the intensity of the commercial and alumni interests around big-time sports. For many college presidents, deal-ing with big-time college sports is at best a walk down a slippery slope, and their advisors—the athletic administrators and the coaches—typically have significant financial involvements with enterprises such as athletic shoe companies or television networks with major stakes in the outcomes. More importantly, Friday's experiences confirm the value of sufficiently long presidential tenures and of on-the-job learning. Friday was deter-mined that he would deal forcefully and unequivocally with any future in-stitutional control issues. And he wouldn't have to wait long to try out his recently acquired expertise.

BASKETBALL ON TOBACCO ROAD

Friday's next brush with sports would remind him of the advice Claude Teague, the university business manager under Frank Graham, gave him: "Most of the daily problems you'll face are routine and variations of other familiar problems already experienced. But a small fraction will be un-expected and unlike any previous problem. Save your talents for these, because these will test you and will demand your full energies." For a change, the problems this time began in Chapel Hill, with Coach Frank McGuire's basketball program. In the fall of 1960 the NCAA investi-gated UNC's program and placed it on a one-year probation for recruit-ing violations.[20] Chancellor William Aycock of the Chapel Hill campus initially said the penalty was for "errors in judgment rather than for a de-liberate violation of rules." But a few months later, the real nature of the "errors in judgment" would be known: the point-shaving scandals that a decade earlier had plagued Madison Square Garden were being dupli-cated in North Carolina's Research Triangle. Representatives from the District Attorney's office in New York City came to Chapel Hill in March of 1961 to investigate point-shaving allegations and two UNC players eventually would be implicated and suspended. And then in May, 1961, a district solicitor from Wake Country walked into Bill Friday's office and proceeded to relay some shocking information: three more players from NC State had shaved points in a 1960 Dixie Classic game between the Wolfpack and Georgia Tech. The Dixie Classic, held between Christmas and New Year's, was the nation's top holiday event and rivaled the NCAA post-season tournament in popularity and national interest. The point-shaving stories, including visions of enraged gangsters pointing guns at the stomachs of college players, became a daily fixture in the state's newspapers. Coach Case was psychologically and physically de-stroyed by the scandal, but he was responsible for bringing the North Carolina State Bureau of Investigation to investigate after recognizing the erratic play of two Wolfpack players in several games.

Eight days after the district solicitor's revelations, Friday met with the UNC trustees symbolically on the NC State campus. During the previ-ous week, Friday stayed on the phone constantly with trustees, particu-larly those on the executive committee. He had forceful discussions with his two chancellors, Aycock from Chapel Hill and Caldwell from Raleigh, and uncharacteristically refused to speak with reporters until after the board meeting. At the tense May 22, 1961, meeting, Friday read, in his typical conversational style, a seven-page document that reflected what the forty-year-old president had learned during his tenure as presi-dent. He began with a recapitulation of actions taken by the trustees re-garding the governance of athletic programs, making it clear at the outset "where the responsibility for action rests." Friday's statement praised the chancellors for their actions and recounted the history of events leading to the current crises. He then laid out the alternatives, followed by a sen-tence containing Friday's imprimatur: "I, therefore, report the following for your information." By the end of his sixteen-minute statement, Fri-day had detailed the actions already taken by the president. The most controversial recommendation was to eliminate the Dixie Classic, one of the nation's most popular sporting events, which had drawn 713,800 spectators in its dozen years or 25 percent of NC State's total attendance to basketball games. NC State, in fact, had led the nation in basketball attendance during the 1950s, so this was an economically meaningful cancellation of a very popular event.[21]

Friday's decision to bring his actions as "information" to the board was a calculated risk. He knew the actions would be controversial, so their impact on the university's support was on his mind. He had to persuade the chancellors, and particularly NC State's Caldwell, who was worried about the elimination of the Dixie Classic, of the changes.[22] It was likely that members of the board of trustees would question the process, and in fact motions to discuss issues and to delay decisions were made. But coming into the meeting Friday knew that he had the support of both chancellors and of the powerful fifteen-member executive committee, which typically made crucial decisions on behalf of the largely ceremonial hundred-member board. Also in Friday's favor was the fact that the UNC board was dominated by individuals largely associated with Chapel Hill, rather than Raleigh. The Dixie Classic was an NC State event: it was played on the Wolfpack's home court, giving it national exposure among potential basketball recruits, and most of the profits stayed in Raleigh. Thus, Duke, Carolina, and Wake Forest fans were not entirely despondent when it was cancelled.

> The trustees expected direction and we [Friday and the two chancellors] had the authority to act and we did. I knew that any other course of action would have meant long discussions and delays and perhaps total inaction. I was not prepared to accept this. My response to questions from the board was that the rest of the nation was watching what we did or, more importantly, what we did not do.

The state's media was supportive of his actions, reflecting in part Friday's relationships with newspaper editorial staffs and his constant attempts at communication with them: he would unfailingly return phone calls promptly, regardless of what he was doing; he was considerate of reporters "on the budget," on deadline to finish a story. He was attuned to the reactions of commentators and listened while he drove to local talk and sports shows on WPTF-AM and other radio stations. He read the state's newspapers religiously: his office subscribed to all the major newspapers and a secretary would cut out the stories and editorials dealing with the university for him; after he read them, the clippings would be required reading for the senior staff. He often provided "background, off-the-record" comments and information that reporters and editors appreciated.

But Friday underestimated the fury of the reaction from political and other quarters. The episode also highlights the hazards facing leaders of the major universities: the Dixie Classic issue soon made it to the General Assembly. Although the legislation introduced to reestablish the tournament ultimately did not pass, the affair revealed a growing distrust of the university and particularly of the campus in Chapel Hill. Indicative of this mistrust and even disdain, Jesse Helms, another Wake Forest student who later became a conservative local television editorialist and U.S senator, remarked, on the discussion of where to locate the state's zoological park: "They should put a fence around Chapel Hill and call it the zoo."

These circumstances contributed to a loss of political support and resulted in the North Carolina Speaker Ban legislation, which prohibited "known" communists from speaking on public campuses, another serious challenge to Friday's presidency that took several years to resolve.[23]

> In addition to everything else going on, I spent a tremendous amount of time and personal energy trying to survive that period. And I missed Billy [Carmichael] and his relationships with legislators. Even with proper information, it's not clear that we could have reversed the Speaker Ban legislation. There was great public sentiment about communism and civil rights and the legislature was determined to teach the university a lesson. And, yes, the Dixie Classic decision really fed into it, as surprising as that sounds.

The Speaker Ban incident underscored for Friday the terrific diversity in a university's publics, the interest groups that have direct interests in how the organization functions and how it responds to their special concerns. Over a period of several years, Friday forged a compromise that reflected his preference for consensus building, and eventually the federal courts would declare the Speaker Ban unconstitutional. Behind the scenes during most of the process, Friday met privately with the student leaders opposed to the Speaker Ban and even with their attorneys as they plotted litigation against the legislation and against the university itself; he was on top of their every move. He brought the media, the higher education accrediting agencies, and the trustees to the debate in an effort to deflect legislative intrusion into the university's operation.

THE BABY BOOMERS ARRIVE ON CAMPUS

As Friday entered his first year as president in 1956, public higher education in North Carolina included the three-campus University of North Carolina, over which he presided, and nine other colleges (including five historically black colleges, the largest number of such public institutions in the nation) with their own boards with authority to award bachelor's degrees; five of the nine were also authorized to grant master's degrees. In order to coordinate activities among these various campuses, the legislature created in 1955 a Board of Higher Education, which in fact was established at the urging of UNC trustees primarily to curb the expansionary ambitions of the other nine public colleges. UNC-Charlotte was added as a fourth UNC campus in 1965, with plans for its eventual expansion as a doctoral institution, and four years later Wilmington and Asheville were added as the fifth and sixth UNC campuses.

The Board of Higher Education (BHE), under the chairmanship of Watts Hill, Jr., was growing in influence and responsibility. A coalition of the historically black campuses and the other "regional" institutions was also developing; in 1969 these state colleges were designated by the General Assembly as "regional universities," broadening their missions to include the authority to grant doctoral degrees, subject to the Board of Higher Education's approval.[24] Increasing frictions over responsibilities developed between the more prestigious UNC campuses and the remaining ten institutions (the NC School of the Arts in Winston-Salem was added as a public conservatory in 1963). The BHE was accused of a "power grab" by the state's newspapers and by UNC supporters after changing its membership in 1969 to include the governor and six key legislative committee leaders as ex officio members. Thus, UNC forces wanted to remain separate from the political process and independent from further controls while the BHE argued with increasing political effectiveness that the efficient use of the state's resources required that all of higher education come under one umbrella. Friday recalled:

> We did not undertake the comprehensive approach that California did [under the California Master Plan devised by Clark Kerr] and this is in part related to the relative wealth of the two states. Our state couldn't really afford it. We didn't even have the community colleges then and California already had a well-developed system of junior colleges. Also, what works in one state doesn't work in another, and California is pretty different from North Carolina in most respects.

North Carolina in the 1960s was indeed a mostly rural state with its population spread across the state in many relatively small towns and cities (No city would even approach a million in population until the 1980s, and North Carolina ranked in the bottom 25th percentile nationally in per capita income and educational attainment). It also had a disproportionately large number of relatively small private colleges and historically black colleges.

It was within these contexts that Governor Robert (Bob) Scott decided to create a study commission (headed by former state senator Lindsay Warren) to study restructuring and carefully selected its members in consultation with the BHE staff. Scott had developed close ties with the BHE and, as an NC State graduate and a dairy farmer, he was no great fan of Chapel Hill. Felix Joyner, who was Friday's chief budget officer and heir to Billy Carmichael's role as political tactician for UNC, recalled:

> [T]he whole operation had a significant flavor of fellows who had it in for the university. It didn't have a whole lot to do with improving education and had a lot to do with anti-intellectualism. We also knew that any coordinating system [as opposed to a governing system] that would be created would be very complicated and would be really different from the Consolidated University, so that you absolutely didn't know what you would be getting into.

The Warren Commission delivered its findings in May of 1971 and called for a hundred-member coordinating board that would control budgets, programs, and planning for the sixteen public four-year colleges and universities in North Carolina. The BHE faction had held: the plan would disband the highly effective six-campus Consolidated University and put in its place an enhanced version of the BHE.[25] Reaction was both rapid and highly divided. The newspapers loved the divisions and debates but Friday hated the confrontation. "I was uncomfortable with the attitudes. And I also knew that I represented the university and that I should be in the political process but not be a central part of it. Once the trustees became polarized, I knew I had to get out." There is some question about whether Friday took himself out of the controversy or whether he simply went behind the scenes more deeply. It was apparent some change would take place, but it was also evident the governor and the BHE did not have as much support as they thought: in June of 1971, twenty-eight of the fifty state senators signed a statement proposing a delay to restructuring until 1973. The debate continued over the summer of 1971 and it became progressively clear that a central coordinating board, as proposed by the Warren Commission, would leave in place many of the existing problems. Over the summer, Friday began an intensive lobbying within the UNC board to change its position to one of support for a governing board under UNC control, and when Friday orchestrated the appearance of Terry Sanford (former governor and then president of Duke) and of former UNC chancellor William Aycock before the legislature, the issue was settled. The election of Bill Friday as the head of the new system was a foregone conclusion, although he would resist, courteously but firmly (as he had done fifteen years earlier), attempts to elicit commitments from him about hiring certain individuals as part of the deal.

Friday had not been the driving force in the restructuring move; the energy had come from Watts Hill, Jr. and his board of higher education, and later, from the governor and the BHE director Cameron West.[26] Friday was initially reluctant to endorse any restructuring because the outcomes were so uncertain, and he knew how different the other campuses were and how little UNC–Chapel Hill and NC State in particular had in common with them. Publicly Friday remained at great distance from the political battles, especially after positions became polarized, but when he saw that change was inevitable, he took charge of events, confronted his own board of trustees, and directed the outcome. Still, while it is tempting to assert (as does Link), that it is "a testament to Friday's political abilities that most people now regard the sixteen-campus system . . . as his own creation," the system would not really be "created" for several more years.[27] The ongoing East Carolina medical school controversy threatened to rip the system apart just as it was formed. Sixteen very different institutions would have to be consolidated into one highly diverse family. The five historically black universities, along with several of the regional campuses, would have to be significantly strengthened, and their internal management processes restructured, before the system could begin to function properly. Former UNC trustees would have to work with former regional campus trustees. More importantly, the new board would have to take a statewide perspective for the first time. And the sixteen chancellors, some of whom did not know what to expect from Friday or his associates, would have to work as a team. In a real way, therefore, the person who would get the "credit" for the creation of the system would be the person who could make it work. This of course was Bill Friday, but it was the Bill Friday of a decade later, and not the one of 1972.

THE HEW CONTROVERSY

In the middle of this restructuring process—and of a deep recession that affected the university's budget—the former U.S. Department of Health, Education and Welfare (HEW) would force a highly publicized and time-consuming controversy involving the UNC system and "desegregation."[28] The timing, just after the birth of the new university structure, was brutal. And just as restructuring tested Friday's preference for negotiation over confrontation, the new controversy tested the need to

keep the university free from external influences against Friday's inclination for compromise. And from a national public relations perspective,
the HEW battle ironically pitted the University of North Carolina, despite its liberal and progressive image among southern universities,
against the "good guys" who were fighting for civil rights and social justice, including much of the media from the East. According to individuals directly involved with the case, the more radical faction within
HEW, led by Office of Civil Rights (OCR) director David Tatel, was determined to go after UNC and Bill Friday first, since the UNC system
was the largest in the South and offered a legally convenient "one-stop
shopping" situation with its single governing board, its central administration, and its five well-known historically black institutions.[29] The controversy was actually never about desegregation as that term is commonly
applied, but rather, according to Friday, about whether the university
"would determine for itself what shall be taught, where, and by whom it
shall be taught, or whether a regulatory agency in Washington would
make those decisions." The legal process, known officially as *Adams v.
Richardson*, began in 1970, when Kenneth Adams, an African American
parent, was named first in an alphabetical listing of plaintiffs from ten
southern states who sued Elliot Richardson, then secretary of HEW, over
non-compliance with and non-enforcement of Title VI of the Civil
Rights Act; UNC was in fact not a party to the lawsuit.

In K–12 education, black-to-white enrollment ratios and forced busing were the judicial instruments employed, accompanied by an implied
threat to end all federal funding for non-compliance. The existence of
historically black colleges, of which the UNC system had five, the largest
number in the nation, posed a problem for the Office of Civil Rights
(OCR). Their enrollments were overwhelmingly composed of African
American students, and for OCR these institutions represented a legal
history of de jure "segregation." At the same time, enrollment in the
UNC system had been desegregated for years: black students were free to
attend any of the sixteen campuses, and did. Moreover, it was not at all
clear that the five historically black UNC campuses wanted to lose their
racial identities.

But busing of students was not an option in the university context;
university students attend a college of their choice, based on their pref-
erences, financial situations, and levels of academic preparation. So instead of busing students, as in the K–12 model, regulators in Washington
opted for the university analogue: they would "bus" programs from one
university to another and then, they hoped, the students and faculty
members would follow the programs and what they called "desegregation"

would ensue. UNC proponents reasoned that taking the engineering program from UNC-Charlotte and putting it at (historically black) NC
A&T in Greensboro (one of OCR's curricular proposals) would not result in a "desegregation" of the respective institutions. The faculty members probably would not agree to move, and even if they were compelled
to do so somehow, many would opt to leave for other universities. And
the institutional choices of undergraduate students are based on many
factors and considerations, not necessarily whether a law school or an
engineering school is present. Moreover, none of the historically black
campuses wanted to lose their ties to the African American roots from
which they came, although of course they wanted to improve their programs, as did all the other campuses. However, soon after the debate
began, as Link notes, HEW officials realized they were "outclassed by a
formidable array of UNC expertise." David Breneman, then on leave
from the Brookings Institution and working at HEW, was present at several of the meetings: Friday's team, he said, showed that the standards
being considered by HEW were "preposterous, undoable, unmeasurable,
or already accomplished. . . . [W]e were sort of chewed up and spit out."[30]

Throughout the long ordeal, Friday had to contend with media perceptions, with board members committed to a very hard line, and with
his strong personal distaste for controversy. Eventually, after an intense
four-year period, and a longer on-and-off period of nearly ten years, the
issue was settled through a legal consent decree that specified certain enrollment goals by race and that ended the supervision of the university
by the federal government. The national media, particularly the *New
York Times* and the *Washington Post* (civil rights lawyer Joseph Rauh, an
active participant in the Adams case, was a close personal friend of *Washington Post* publisher Kate Graham), howled in protest—after all, the
"good guys" had lost—and the agreement was sharply denounced by the
Times in an editorial on July 11, 1981.[31] A CBS news show ("Sunday
Morning") hosted by UNC graduate Charles Kuralt, a close friend of Friday's, indicated that the UNC settlement would turn back the clock for
civil rights. Friday, who had expected a balanced report, was deeply surprised and hurt; an editorial from the Raleigh *News and Observer* called
reporter Ed Rable's segment a "mugging" of the university, filled as it was
with scenes from the University of Alabama and segregationist governor
George Wallace. CBS later presented a follow-up report that came as
close to an apology as a television network can come, in response to calls
from the governor and Friday himself.[32]

However, by the mid-1980s, more objective evidence would vindicate
the arguments consistently made by UNC. A 1988 study conducted by

the Office of Civil Rights of the ten original "Adams" states showed that the plans of the four states that settled with OCR in 1978–79 (Florida, Georgia, Oklahoma, and Virginia), rather than contesting the program desegregation model of the federal government as North Carolina had done, were ineffective. By contrast, the physical facilities at the five historically black UNC campuses had literally been transformed, and the percentage of faculty members with doctorates at those five campuses had increased dramatically, from about 20 to 80 percent. While the ambitious black enrollment goals at the ten predominantly white UNC campuses had not been met, these ten UNC institutions were found to have led the nation in the increase of black enrollment between 1976 and 1986. And white enrollment at the five historically black UNC campuses increased from 5 percent in 1972 to nearly 20 percent by 1990, exceeding the goal of 15 percent.

MANAGERIAL STYLE AND LIFE CADENCE

In 1972, when he assumed the presidency of the sixteen-campus University of North Carolina, Bill Friday was fifty-two and a national education leader who had advised two U.S. presidents, served on Clark Kerr's prestigious Carnegie Commission, and headed the American Council on Education and the Association of American Universities. Always a disciplined worker, he was productive and efficient and seldom seemed rushed. Unlike Clark Kerr, Ted Hesburgh, and Hanna Gray, Friday was a "morning person." He arrived at his office by 7:15 AM and would begin writing personal notes to a variety of individuals, from staff members to extension workers across the state, in his own handwriting, using personalized five-by-seven-inch embossed cards with "William Friday" printed at the top. On his desk would be the first of several bottles of Tab, the diet soft drink he invariably consumed in the mornings instead of coffee.

On Mondays at 9:00 AM he met in his adjoining conference room with his senior staff to discuss informally the agenda for the coming week. The meetings were relaxed, with banter back and forth among the participants, ending promptly by 10:00 or 10:30, but never until Friday had turned over the meeting to Arnold King, the eminence grise of the administration, for a few words of wisdom. King would typically end the meetings with an appropriately humorous anecdote reflecting his sixty-year relationship with the university. On Saturday mornings, several of the top administrators, including Friday, would come in for a few hours of quiet work. People still telephoned the office, but since there was no receptionist at work then, phone bells would ring in the halls and anyone hearing them could dial "9" and answer them directly. One Saturday morning the phones were particularly active, and Friday, who was always concerned about not being responsive, emerged from his office exasperated at the ringing: "You know, it's a real problem that we don't have anyone working on Saturdays to help us with the phones." "Bishop" King had the perfect retort: "The problem is not that there's no one working the phones on Saturday, Mr. President; the problem is that *you're* working on Saturday." When he did work on Saturdays, he would leave by 10:00 or 11:00 AM and would reserve the rest of the weekend for his family. He seldom attended football or basketball events and played golf exceptionally rarely. "You have to be sensitive to how it all affects your family. It's never easy on them."

Some people remarked that Friday controlled the press and had great influence over what was said about the university, but his policy was to communicate openly and honestly. "People know when you are being manipulative, so it doesn't ever really work over the long term anyway." Friday knew about deadlines and tried to return reporters' calls to meet their schedules. He was easily available and never had a "no comment" in all his years, except for the week-long period during the Dixie Classic scandal. His home phone was—and still is—listed in the Chapel Hill phone book, sending a message of openness vital to a public university. His relations with reporters and editors were the result of Friday's authentic interest in the journalistic profession and the people who worked in it. One reporter put it this way:

> Friday always, always, returned calls, even if you were a reporter fresh out of school. He was always aware of our deadlines. And we would call him automatically whenever we needed a quote for an obituary for anyone remotely associated with the university or for anyone else of any consequence in North Carolina. He would think a few seconds and then ask "Are you ready?" before giving you a thoughtful quote.

Many observers of UNC board meetings would also remark on the apparent unanimity and the lack of debate. The work of the board, however, was behind the scenes, through the work of its committees; Friday typically removed items from the agenda that did not have wide acceptance. Before each meeting, Friday's associates, and Friday himself, traveled to the hometowns of committee chairs to discuss agenda items carefully in their homes or offices. Friday worked diligently to learn about board dynamics: who responded to whom and how they related to one another, studying them carefully and keeping his observations to himself. The nucleus of leaders on the board was well informed, so alternatives and options were clearly understood. "It was always my policy not to surprise any of the men and women in this nucleus. It was also important for me to empower my senior colleagues to speak with all the authority of my voice."

Friday worked extremely hard at listening. "The best thing I had to give to people who came in my office was my time, and I tried to listen carefully to what they wanted to say." Learning to read people, to find out how important an issue is to them, is a valuable skill of Friday's. He scribbled notes on three-by-five-inch white cards he kept in his shirt pocket during conversations as a reminder. "Insincerity is always easily detected—the person in your office has something to tell you that's important to him." He doesn't "talk about the weather" when he meets with someone, but he also does not rush them; he tries to make them feel at ease before getting down to business. And at the annual Christmas gathering held with the entire staff shortly before the holidays, Friday always emphasized above all else his appreciation for the courtesy that the staff showed visitors during the year. "The point is," he added, "your identity gets translated into that of the institution—your grace, your courtesy, your manners, your thoughtfulness."

CONCLUSION

William Friday left his office on February 28, 1986, thirty years after he entered it, as North Carolina's most important citizen of the twentieth century. During the month preceding his departure, there were dozens of editorials and television stories about his retirement and his accomplishments. The *New York Times* called him one of the "most respected leaders of American higher education" and the *Washington Post* referred to him as "one of the three or four most influential figures in postwar American higher education."[33] Just before his retirement, Friday had also been recognized by the American Council on Education for his lifetime achievements and the Council for Advancement and Support of Education had rated him as the most effective public university president in the nation; in 1997 President Clinton awarded him the National Humanities Medal. A speaker at a 2004 building dedication for the alumni association at his alma mater of NC State (for which he had helped to obtain a $5 million gift) referred to him as the "ubiquitous Bill Friday." The preceding day, Friday had been at another building dedication, the William and Ida Friday Center for Educational Leadership, also at NC State. He continued to host his very popular weekly educational television show, *North Carolina People*, gently asking questions of some of the state's and nation's most accomplished individuals—painters, artists, writers, politicians—as he continues to enlarge his circle of friends and contacts. Predictably, he has remained very active after leaving UNC; but also predictably, he has steadfastly refused all invitations to run for public office.

Observers noted that the true test of the North Carolina system would come after Friday's departure, reasoning that Friday's personality alone would keep the system going. But the test would have to wait a bit longer than that because Friday's successor, Dick Spangler, kept the Friday team relatively intact during the first few years of his tenure. The UNC system arguably is the most complex in the nation, and a variety of pressures had been building during Friday's last two years. Signs of discord began to emerge in the early 1990s: UNC–Chapel Hill hired consultants who complained about the level of central control of the system, calling for more flexibility in budgeting and personnel matters. In an audit report conducted for the UNC–Chapel Hill campus, one consultant concluded that she did not understand how Bill Friday "did it;" he must have used mirrors, she said.

But Bill Friday never used mirrors. He used hard work and knowledge and personal humility. He knew people, he knew his state and university, and he knew how the different pieces and actors interacted with one another. Because of his grace and talent, he attracted unusually gifted individuals to work with him and he both empowered and trusted them. He rarely left the state for more than a day or so, and he refused to be paid more than the governor (one year he declined a pay raise for this reason) or to serve for pay on corporate boards. And, as his continuing efforts to help others show, he brought tremendous energy and perseverance to each of his duties.

NOTES

1. See Anne Knox, "James Edward Allen Gibbs," International Sewing Machine Collectors' Society, www.ismacs.net/wg/wg_jeag.html, originally published in the *Virginia Cavalcade* by the Virginia State Library.

2. William A. Link, *William Friday: Power, Purpose, and American Higher Education* (Chapel Hill: University of North Carolina Press, 1995), 5.

3. Ibid., 7.

4. Joyce VanTassel-Baska, "Characteristics of the Developmental Path of Eminent and Gifted Adults," in *Patterns of Influence on Gifted Learners*, edited by J. VanTassel-Baska and P. Olszewski-Kubilius (New York: Teachers College Press, 1989), 146–162.

5. Ibid., 9.

6. See Jennings Rhyne, *Some Southern Cotton Mill Workers and Their Villages* (Chapel Hill: University of North Carolina Press, 1930), 89, and also W. J. Cash, *The Mind of the South* (Garden City, NY: Doubleday, 1954), 270ff.

7. Warren Ashby, *Frank Porter Graham: A Southern Liberal* (Winston-Salem, NC: John F. Blair, 1980), 73.

8. Ibid., 74.

9. Link, *William Friday*, 15.

10. Ibid., 17.

11. Ibid., 20.

12. See also ibid., 20ff.

13. Ibid., 22.

14. Although Friday supported the new school of liberal arts at NC State, he and the UNC trustees initially rejected the school in 1960. After faculty at NC State expressed their concerns, Friday apparently had a change of heart in late 1960 and worked to change board opinions about the school, which ultimately was approved in January 1963, when the first bachelor of arts degrees were authorized. See Alice Elizabeth Reagan, *North Carolina State University: A Narrative History* (Ann Arbor, MI: Edwards Brothers, Inc. 1987), 173–176.

15. Link, *William Friday*, 28.

16. Ibid., 29.

17. Ibid., 46.

18. Ashby, *Frank Porter Graham*.

19. Ibid., 143.

20. Smith Barrier, *On Tobacco Road: Basketball in North Carolina* (New York: Leisure Press, 1983), 83ff.

21. Ibid., 89.

22. Caldwell understood the significance of the Dixie Classic to Wolfpack fans and to North Carolina residents in general, who often gave tickets to the event as valued Christmas presents. He may have been concerned about its elimination, but he also understood that something dramatic had to be done. More importantly, however, the Dixie Classic probably would not have lasted much longer due to the advent of televised games, limitations on the number of contests allowed by the NCAA, and increasing opposition from the other participating North Carolina teams, who felt they did not get the best seats for their own fans or their share of the profits and publicity.

23. Arnold King, *The Multicampus University of North Carolina Comes of Age, 1956–1986* (Chapel Hill: University of North Carolina Press, 1986), Chapter 4.

24. As John Sanders notes, "the General Assembly never intended to vote the funds to make this grand gesture a reality." See J. Sanders, "The University of North Carolina: The Legislative Evolution of Public Higher Education," *Popular Government* 59 (1993): 20–29.

25. Ibid., 26.

26. Ironically, the articulate and handsome Watts Hill, Jr., was the son of a powerful and influential ally of Friday's, George Watts Hill, who was a key member of the rival UNC executive committee.

27. Link, *William Friday*, 185.

28. See ibid., Chapters 10 and 11 (277–327), for a detailed history of the HEW controversy.

29. Peter Lebossi, formerly associated with Cyrus Vance's law firm in New York and an assistant to Joseph Califano, then Secretary of HEW, directly said to Friday in a meeting, "What you have to understand is the HEW wants you."

30. Link, *William Friday*, 290.

31. See Tracy Campbell's *Short of the Glory: The Fall and Redemption of Edward F. Prichard, Jr.* (Lexington: University Press of Kentucky, 1998) for descriptions of the relationship between Phil and Katharine Graham and Joseph Rauh.

32. Link, *William Friday*, 363.

33. Dudley Clendinen, "Chapel Hill Welcomes New President," *New York Times*, October 18, 1986; Jonathan Yardley, "Taking Education a Step Higher," *Washington Post*, March 17, 1986.

Theodore Martin Hesburgh.

CHAPTER 7

God, Country, Notre Dame,
and Father Ted

So now the Hesburgh era has ended and the Hesburgh legend begins.
                                        —*New York Times*, May 22, 1987

He was smoking a cigar, an Aurora "Napoleon," in his office on the
13th floor of the Theodore Martin Hesburgh Library, the building on the University of Notre Dame campus in South Bend, Indiana, that houses the famous mosaic affectionately, if irreverently,
known by American football fans everywhere as "Touchdown Jesus." He
also had a box of "Churchills" from Nicaragua unopened on the credenza
behind his desk. On the floor was a colorful University of Notre Dame
carpet. Father Ted normally speaks with a definite up-state New York accent, but now he was on the phone speaking in Spanish to a wealthy
Notre Dame alumnus from South America. His accent was not native
but the grammar was impeccable. He explained to the former student
that he would do all he could to see whether the university would admit
his son—and that he had received the cigars: "*Yo haré todo lo posible para
que su hijo sea admitido. Si, recibí los puros. Magníficos.*"
    He apologized for the interruption as he continued to discuss the ad-
mission status of the alumnus' son. "They still think," he muttered with
his hand over the phone's mouthpiece, "that I have some clout around
this place. I really don't. All I wish now is that the children of my former students had better grades." Returning to his phone conversation,

Father Hesburgh continued speaking in Spanish, puffing on the cigar, and looking out of the window at the university his leadership built from a small, private Catholic college to one of the most prestigious academic institutions in the world.

THE HESBURGHS OF SYRACUSE

Father Theodore Martin Hesburgh was born May 25, 1917 (four days, as he is wont to say, before John F. Kennedy), in Syracuse, New York, the second of five children of Theodore Bernard Hesburgh, Jr., and Anne Marie Murphy Hesburgh. Hesburgh's ancestors are German and French on his father's side and Irish on his mother's. His paternal great grandfather came from Luxembourg in 1848, part of a large wave of young immigrants fleeing the wars engulfing the Low Countries of Luxembourg and Belgium. The great grandfather came with a daughter (Hesburgh's great aunt Mary) and two sons, one of whom was Father Hesburgh's grandfather, Theodore Bernard Hesburgh, Sr. He was Father Ted's namesake.

Grandfather Hesburgh worked his way through college selling liniments and medicines door-to-door to all sorts of immigrants in New York. In order to do this well, he had to learn Yiddish, Russian, German, French, Italian, and Spanish. He would charm young Ted with demonstrations of how one could say the same thing in many different languages; Hesburgh traces his lifelong interest in foreign languages to his grandfather. A teacher most of his life, Grandfather Hesburgh also wrote columns for New York newspapers and the *New York World* magazine under the pen name of "Knickerbocker." He once chastised the archbishop for suspending a Catholic priest who had endorsed a controversial social program. He was a drama critic, and he wrote on economics, labor, everything he could think of, all in the very florid style of those days. The Hesburghs still have a thick book with many of his articles.

But his grandfather's life was also touched by tragedy. His wife died at age twenty-one giving birth to their third son. The baby died also. Two weeks later, a pharmacist botched a prescription for another son, and the two-year old boy died of poisoning. So, within fourteen days, his wife and two of his three sons had died. He abandoned his faith in God, quit his job, left New York City, and took his remaining three-year-old son, Father Ted's father, to live with Hesburgh relatives on a corn farm in Iowa. But the grandfather was not the same man; he had understandably lost his passion for life. After a while, great aunt Mary came to Iowa, with grandfather's consent, and fetched her motherless nephew, returning him to Staten Island, where she would raise him.

Ted's father's quiet and serious nature probably reflected this difficult period. John O'Connor, a friend and neighbor, said, "He was a very laconic guy, almost dour, not at all like Ted." Daughter Betty speculated, "He felt deeply, but he never quite let you know."[1] Although he traveled quite a bit during the week for his job and was reserved with the children, he was a devout Catholic and a member of the Knights of Columbus. On trips by car they would pray the Rosary together.[2] Still, Hesburgh and his father would never be close. "Jimmy [Hesburgh's younger brother] developed a closeness to my father that I never had." But in spite of all his hard luck, grandfather Hesburgh eventually returned to Brooklyn and to God and started attending Mass regularly. When he grew ill, he was placed in a Catholic hospital, saying the Rosary and going to confession each day, to the great delight of his grandson, who by then was a seminarian studying philosophy and theology in Rome.

His mother's family was Irish. His maternal grandfather was Martin Murphy, "an utterly delightful Irishman whose parents had brought him to this country when he was seven weeks old," says Hesburgh. A plumber who lived with his wife on Franklin Avenue at 167th Street in the Bronx, he was very different from Grandfather Hesburgh. As a young man, according to an oft-told story, Grandfather Murphy once drank so much cider at a country fair that, in front of a large group of people, he made a fool of himself dancing and falling down on his backside. "He was so embarrassed about it that he swore off liquor for life," recounted Hesburgh.

Hesburgh's mother and father used to "pal around together in a large group of young people, and so I suppose their relationship just grew naturally out of their social life." They married February 2, 1913, at the St. Augustine's Church in the Bronx, the parish his mother had grown up in, and they moved to Syracuse. During the early years of the marriage, his father was constantly on the road as a salesman, although he came home on weekends. His mother was the romantic one of the two: "merriment seemed to surround her all the time. She loved being with people." She sang soprano and played the piano while the children would sing. She had the dark, Irish good looks that Ted inherited. Ted's mother was barely over five feet tall and his father was six feet, two inches. "They looked like Mutt and Jeff. But the German side from my father gave me a sense of discipline and order; my Irish side gave me an ability to understand people and get along with them."

Father Ted grew up with three sisters. Mary Monica, his only older sibling, Elizabeth Anne, whom they called Betty, and Anne Marie. Growing up with so many girls, Hesburgh constantly prayed for a brother. He eventually got one, but only after a decade of prayer. Brother Jimmy was born when Ted was sixteen, and as a consequence they didn't grow up together (although they did become close later in life as Jimmy attended Notre Dame when his older brother was already president of the university). Ted had a number of jobs growing up, from delivering newspapers and mowing lawns to working nearly full-time at a gasoline station during his senior year. "We lived modestly," Hesburgh remembered, "but comfortably . . . it was the Great Depression and money was tight."

A special influence in Hesburgh's life, Father Harold Quinn, a priest at Ted's school in Syracuse ("Most Holy Rosary School," which Hesburgh attended from the first grade through his high school graduation), was in charge of the altar boys there. He was in effect the spiritual director for the boys. "My interest in the priesthood had to come from God," Hesburgh said. "I always wanted to be a priest. I told Father Quinn I wanted to be a priest when I was still in grammar school, but both he and my mother insisted that I lead a normal kid's life at least through high school."

When he was eleven or twelve years old, four missionaries who were Holy Cross priests came to the school. Young Ted was taken with them, particularly with Father Thomas Duffy. Duffy suggested to Ted's mother that he should go straight into the priesthood because if he went to high school he might lose his vocation. "I will never forget what she replied: 'Well, Father, if he loses his vocation by going to a Catholic school, after growing up in a Catholic family and going to mass every day, then he didn't really have much of a vocation.' If you knew my mother, you knew there would be no more discussion of that, and I'm glad I didn't go off with them and had a normal high school life." According to Hesburgh, Father Quinn agreed. "I want you to date," Quinn said to him, "I want you to dance, and I want you to go parties and study, especially Latin. Just don't do anything that you would be ashamed of if you ever become a priest."

Hesburgh has always been a voracious reader. "I read like mad when I was young. Still do. Mostly adventure stuff, *Drums Along the Mohawk*, that kind of thing, good books, not too many sports books, because in truth I was never much of a sports fan. I was very interested in geography and the world, and I read a lot about other cultures." The Catholic school provided him an excellent educational foundation and nurtured his diverse interests.

> In the "Most Holy Rosary School" we had an English book about
> four inches thick filled with readings from the Classics. I remember

reading Caesar, Cicero, Virgil. And how's this for a high school curriculum? I had four years of English, four years of Latin, four years of
religion, three years of History, three of French, Chemistry, Art and
Design—I had no artistic talent, though I can admire it—then Phys
Ed and Civics, Algebra and Geometry. I had a bad Algebra teacher
and I never liked it. And at Notre Dame I had to take two years of
Greek, so there's another language.

Father Ted exhibited many early signs of extraordinariness: he won a
statewide contest in geography in the seventh grade, and later he became
editor of the school newspaper, regularly exhorting classmates on various
topics, including reading habits. In April of 1934, during his senior year,
he played the lead part (of Jesus) in a religious play that received significant praise in a regional Catholic publication. On June 24, 1934, he was
the student chosen to speak at his high school graduation; he thought-
fully thanked teachers and parents and also urged his classmates to read
"good books" that were "true to life" and would "satiate your most san-
guinary tastes." He specifically recommended nine books in adventure,
travel, and religion.[3]

After high school he moved on to the Holy Cross Seminary and to the
nearby University of Notre Dame in South Bend, Indiana. His mother
and father and sister Mary drove him from Syracuse to South Bend in
September of 1934. "I was just seventeen and the campus was so different from anything I was used to. It was hard saying goodbye, and I was
pretty homesick for a while. But as I got into the routine at the seminary
and with classes at the university, the loneliness and homesickness quickly
faded." Being a young seminarian among the "regular" Notre Dame students added both to the sense of homesickness and of uniqueness: Ted and
the other young seminarians, dressed in black, must have seemed unusual
to the other students, even at a Catholic university. In addition, Notre
Dame was not a very diverse place in the 1930s. "The student body was
pretty homogeneous and the curriculum was very narrow compared to
what I had expected. But I settled in quickly after that first month."

After Ted's freshman year, he and two dozen other novice seminarians
were sent to Rolling Prairie, Indiana, where the Holy Cross Order had
recently purchased a neglected seven-hundred-acre farm. His tales of
Rolling Prairie recount severe discipline, disagreeable tasks, and incredibly hard work. In fact, his initial training for the priesthood sounds more
like Marine boot camp than indoctrination to a religious vocation. Only
nine of the twenty-nine young men who entered with Hesburgh made it
through Novitiate, and two others dropped out the next year.

The "drill sergeant" at this Catholic version of Parris Island was Brother Seraphim Herrmann. "But," said Hesburgh, "he was no angel." Then in his mid-thirties, Brother Seraphim had served in the German army during the World War I. He would challenge Hesburgh and his fellow seminarians constantly in an attempt to prepare them for the rigors of priesthood. He spoke with a "dramatic, accented English" and watched over the seminarians, always inventing new ways to make tough jobs even tougher. Once, he had Hesburgh and his associates dismantle a fifty-five-foot-high silo, cement block by cement block, and then reassemble it about a mile away. And then they had to paint it. It was Hesburgh's job to hang from a swing fifty feet off the ground with a bucket of white-wash and paint.[4]

"They were really trying to weed us out early," Hesburgh said. "It bothered them when priests left the priesthood after they were ordained." But as difficult as the silo reconstruction and painting proved, it was nothing compared to the sheep delousing episode:

> Brother Seraphim was fiendishly inventive. One time we were putting in a road and a sewer line, working very hard beneath a boiling summer sun, when a thunderstorm came up, complete with lightning and hail. I dropped my pick-ax and made a dash with all the others for the barn. There we sat down, drenched, and grinned at one another in silence: we were safe from the storm and from work. Some of us, no doubt, grinned at Seraphim: What could he possibly find for us to do here? Ah, his eye roamed the barn, and off at the far end he spied a stall with fifty sheep in it. His eyes suddenly lit up. "I want each of you to go get a sheep and bring it back and pick the lice off it." . . . For the next two hours we sat there with sheep on our laps, picking out lice. The sheep stank, and pretty soon we did, too. On top of that, we also became infested with their lice, and had to bathe that night in Lysol.[5]

Thus, at an early age, Father Ted was separated from his family and endured an amazing amount of discipline and rigor. After a summer that often seemed as if it would never end, he returned to the seminary and Notre Dame for his sophomore year. Most of his time was devoted to spiritual and intellectual development, but he still did "grunt" work, such as waiting on tables. "I waited on tables so much during my one year at Moreau [seminary] that I developed a healthy respect for the job and an abiding tolerance for restaurant waiters, no matter how surly or slow they might be. To this day I become upset if anyone is impolite to a waiter or waitress."[6]

THE GREGORIAN UNIVERSITY IN ROME

Twenty-year-old Ted Hesburgh was stunned when he was informed between his sophomore and junior years that he would be going to Rome, Italy, to study for a doctorate in both philosophy and theology. He was also apprehensive: he had not seen his family for two years, and he was being told he would spend eight years in Rome. "When you're twenty years old, eight years is a lot. It's nearly half your life, so I was really distraught," he recalled. Nonetheless, on September 25, 1937, he boarded the S.S. *Champlain* for the seven-day voyage to a continent already worried about the threat of another world war.

In Rome, Ted would encounter Father Georges Sauvage, the superior at their new three-story home on the Via dei Cappuccini, a block from the Piazza Barberini and a fifteen-minute walk from the renowned Pontifical Gregorian University, where he attended classes. The Jesuit-run Gregorian University, according to Hesburgh, is to the Catholic Church what the West Point Academy is to the U.S. Army: the best priests and seminarians from all over the world are sent there to study theology. "The priests who went there ended up running things." Ignatius Loyola originally founded the university as the Roman College to train priests for the missionary Society of Jesus in 1551. It has an imposing presence in the Piazza della Pilotta in the center of Rome, and counted among its alumni are fourteen popes, as well as twenty saints and thirty-nine beatified.

Life in Rome, like that at Rolling Prairie, was dictated by a challenging routine: up at five every morning, followed by prayers, breakfast, classes, chapel, classes, an afternoon walk at 3:00 PM, study, chapel, light supper, recreation, and finally back to the room by 9:00 PM to read, study, and get ready for the next day. In contrast to his experience at Notre Dame, he would have lots of free time to study and work on learning foreign languages and he tackled languages with the same passion he approached every new thing that interested him. He avoided speaking in English.

Father Sauvage required us to speak in French, even to pray in French. My high school classes back in Syracuse had been so good that within a month I had no problem with French at all. Secondly, on my own I learned Italian. We didn't have a newspaper and we couldn't listen to the radio, it was all very strict, but they used to paste the daily *Il Messaggero* (the Roman newspaper) on the walls and so on the way to school I would stop and try to read a couple articles. It's too bad we didn't have any radio, because that would

have been very good for pronunciation. So I picked up Italian on
the street, French in the house, in the University I continued with
Latin, four hours a day, five hours reading very thick books.

He learned Spanish from a Mexican friend at Gregorian. After nine
months in Rome, Hesburgh and his classmates went on vacation to the
Tyrol, in the Alps near the Austrian border just south of the Brenner
Pass, where they spoke in German. He obtained a German high school
book and wrote out every exercise. By the end of that summer, he had
enough German so that, years later, when he had to go to Vienna for the
International Atomic Energy Commission for the Vatican, he got along
fine in his rudimentary German.

Hesburgh thus is a strong believer in the advantages of knowing a foreign language.

> Learning languages helps you understand your fellow man and helps
> to "translate" and communicate across cultures. It certainly helped
> me as I was developing my personality and style. Later I pushed hard
> to include travel for our Notre Dame students as part of their de-
> velopment at the university. And though it was hard for me to be
> so far from my family, traveling abroad at a young age and experi-
> encing different things from those that I had grown up with—differ-
> ent architectures, different histories, different foods, different
> accents and behaviors—made me a more complete person and gave
> me a more rounded and more comprehensive perspective on things.
> I could see things from more angles and this was very useful later on.

The distance from Syracuse to Rome was truly great: in the late 1930s
there were no phones that one could dial or television one could watch
or even radio one could listen to and find out what was happening at
home. Even to get there, one had to travel on a slow boat and then take
a rickety train from Paris to Rome. Things moved much slower before
World War II, and traveling to Rome was like going to another world for
young Ted Hesburgh.

STATESIDE AND BACK TO SOUTH BEND AGAIN

Benito Mussolini lived a couple of blocks from the university, and
from the first floor balcony of the Palazzo Venezia he would exhort the
crowds gathered below in the piazza. His offices were at the Palazzo del
Quirinale, right behind Gregorian. The Nazis invaded Poland on Sep-

tember 1, 1939, and while the academic and religious routines continued on their schedules, the tension was palpable. By the spring of 1940,
conditions in Italy and elsewhere in Europe had deteriorated to the
point that Americans were ordered to leave for their own safety. Thus,
in May of 1940 Hesburgh's planned eight-year stay in Rome at the Gregorian University was cut short after three years. This was not altogether
bad for Hesburgh: he would see his family much sooner than he had anticipated. He also had become disenchanted with the education at Gregorian. "The teaching was rigid and unimaginative and almost rote; the
syllabus and instruction methods had not changed, I think, from the way
things were done when they started the university in 1558 [sic]."[7] Along
with thirty-six hundred other passengers, Hesburgh boarded the USS
Manhattan on June 1 at Genoa for a nine-day voyage to New York,
slightly longer than usual due to the overloading of the ship. One of his
companions was Emmett O'Neill, who had been with him at Gregorian.
He and Hesburgh met daily during the voyage to discuss theology and
"Catholic Action," the new reform movement of the church. As quoted
by O'Brien, Emmett O'Neill recalled his impressions of Hesburgh from
the trip: "You were carried away by his knowledge, by his awareness of
things. You couldn't help but feel that this man [was] destined to be a
leader."[8]

After a two-week vacation spent visiting his family, Hesburgh resumed
his studies, but this time in Washington, D.C., where he would live during all of World War II. He spent the first three years at Holy Cross College, just behind Catholic University. In June of 1943, along with fifteen
others, he was ordained as a priest in the Sacred Heart Church on the
Notre Dame campus. Sacred Heart is one of the oldest churches in the
United States: its altar came from Paris and its stained-glass windows
from Le Mans, France. The dedication above the sculptured east door, in
memory of Notre Dame students who gave their lives in World War I,
reads: "God, Country, and Notre Dame." Father Hesburgh would devote
his life to this trinity as well.

After ordination, Hesburgh proceeded to Catholic University to complete his doctorate in sacred theology, even as he immersed himself in an
amazing number of community activities, including running the large
U.S.O. organization in the D.C. area, doing parish work, and writing
booklets for the military: well over five hundred thousand copies were
printed of Hesburgh's popular "Letters to Servicewomen," a moral and
ethical guide for young women in the military.

"I really wanted to get into the war; I wanted to be a Navy chaplain on an aircraft carrier in the Pacific." So Hesburgh threw himself into his studies so he could complete them quickly. His 590-page dissertation, "The Theology of Catholic Action," was written between October of 1944 and March of 1945. He wanted to graduate that spring, so he worked from seven in the morning to midnight each day so that he could finish by the deadline of March 1; he took three hours off on Christmas. But his dream of joining the Navy would not be fulfilled: thousands of officer candidates were being sent to Notre Dame for training and the university was in desperate need of faculty. Of course, Hesburgh also did not know about the atomic bombs that would be dropped in Hiroshima and Nagasaki, bringing to an end the war in the Pacific in a few months anyway. "It was as if the Lord were saying to me: Your planning is terrible. Leave it up to Me."[9] The twenty-seven-year-old Hesburgh had clear gifts in the realm of interpersonal knowledge, as well as personal charm, extraordinary energy and focus, and excellent communication skills, but nothing in his return to South Bend would foretell his future as one of America's most distinguished and influential citizens.

NOTRE DAME AND BEYOND

During the first half of the twentieth century, Notre Dame had earned a well-deserved reputation as a "football factory." Knute Rockne, the son of a Norwegian emigrant and a former Notre Dame student and an end on its football team, was the legendary football coach for the Fighting Irish during the late 1910s and 1920s. He essentially invented the forward pass and coached Notre Dame to its 13-7 upset victory over a strong Army team in the October 1924 game mythologized by sports writer Grantland Rice:

> Outlined against the blue-gray October sky, the Four Horsemen rode again. In dramatic lore they are know as Famine, Pestilence, Destruction, and Death. These are only aliases. Their real names are Stuhldreher, Miller, Crowley, and Layden. They formed the crest of the cyclone before which another fighting Army football team was swept over the precipice of the Polo Grounds yesterday afternoon.

But as Elvis Presley once said, the myth is one thing and the man is another. Rockne was brilliant as a coach and motivator, and hypnotic as an orator. However, Underwood adds that "he was also a shameless huckster who played loose with the truth, and there is more than casual evidence that his dedication to the academic side of his players' lives was less than rigorous."[10] Jim Crowley, one of the surviving Four Horsemen, once observed: "Rock wanted us to go to class, but he didn't make a big deal out of it."[11]

The end of the war ushered a flood of GIs into American universities, many of them returning to finish their studies and others to begin them. Hesburgh established a veteran's organization on campus and became its advisor and chaplain; the Vet Club was so large it contained almost three of every four students at Notre Dame. The club and the problems of its members—housing for married students, baby care, marital problems— became a learning laboratory on campus challenges and politics for young Father Hesburgh. He found himself operating as a realtor, a marriage counselor, and a curriculum developer: "[T]here was so much I didn't know about this stuff. I figured they needed a course on marriage at the university. So I got all the books I could on the subject and, with the permission of the dean, started teaching a class: Marriage and Family."

Father John Cavanaugh, the president of the University of Notre Dame between 1946 and 1952, had been a young executive at Studebaker Corporation with a promising career trajectory when he decided to take up the priesthood. A strong priest-executive, he began Notre Dame's ascendancy into the ranks of elite academic institutions. Father Cavanaugh recognized Hesburgh's talent, as well as his potential to be his successor as president of Notre Dame. He said as much to several people, including Edmund Stephan, an attorney and Notre Dame board chairman with whom Hesburgh would have a long and close working relationship: "Keep your eye on that fellow," Cavanaugh said referring to Hesburgh. "He's going to be president of the university one day."[12] Later, Cavanaugh would say that one would "have to be blind not to spot his talents."[13]

Hesburgh was of course a bright student who was articulate, hardworking, and a quick study. But, according to O'Brien, it was his "graciousness" that led many of his superiors to single him out. His courtesy and thoughtfulness with others, which continued throughout the rest of his life, were both genuine and unusual for someone his age. For example, in 1940 Hesburgh wrote his superior at Notre Dame about the war and the advantages of life in America:

> We never appreciated so much the freedom of America until we saw
> the results of the lack of liberty in Europe. It really is sickening to
> see the lives of so many people ruined, their hopes frustrated, their
> families disrupted, merely because a dictator thinks he won them

body and soul. We can't pray too much for war-torn Europe, and
heart-broken Europeans.[14]

In fact, according to Hesburgh, Cavanaugh had approached him once
and asked him to consider working in the administration, three years
after Father Hesburgh's return to Notre Dame. But Hesburgh told him
he enjoyed being a teacher and counselor to students, and he had no particular interest in administration. A year later, Cavanaugh was still not
dissuaded and asked him again to join the administration, eventually
making Father Ted the chairman of the Religion Department, with about
forty faculty under his supervision. A year after that, in June of 1949, he
had another chance meeting with Father Cavanaugh on the way to receive their "obediences," or their work assignments, for the coming
school year. Cavanaugh informed Hesburgh as they were entering the
meeting that he would be appointed vice president. Cavanaugh had quietly restructured the university's organization and had created several new
positions, such as vice president for academic affairs, finance, public relations, and student affairs. As the names of the new vice presidents were
announced, Hesburgh exhaled in relief:

> By the time [Father] Mehling [the Holy Cross principal] reached the
> fourth new vice presidency, I relaxed, convinced that Cavanaugh
> had been pulling my leg. There was no vice presidency left for me.
> There wasn't anything to be vice president of. But obediences were
> handed out according to house age or when you had joined the order.
> He had not yet worked his way down to the youngest priest sitting
> in that chapel. Finally he did, announcing: "Ted Hesburgh, execu-
> tive vice president." I was stunned, just as I had been twelve years
> earlier when Father Burns told me so matter-of-factly that I was
> going to Rome.[15]

His first job was to prepare job descriptions for the new vice presidents.
When he asked Cavanaugh what the executive vice president was sup-
posed to do, Cavanaugh replied that he was the vice president in charge
of the other ones. Hesburgh had read Machiavelli's *The Prince* and he
was especially aware of Machiavelli's warning that the most dangerous
thing a prince can attempt is to try to change the order of things, in part
because there are usually more people who stand to lose from change
than there are people who will benefit from it. Hesburgh, being the
youngest of all of the new appointees, was not looking forward to changing around all the university departments and, least of all, the athletics
enterprise. The Notre Dame Fighting Irish football team was coached by

Frank Leahy, a former player under Rockne and nearly as successful as his legendary mentor: Leahy's teams won eighty-seven games and lost only eleven (with nine ties), including three national championships and an unbeaten winning streak of thirty-nine games that ended in 1950. But Leahy's obsession with winning also brought significant criticism from rival coaches, and the ensuing publicity perpetuated Notre Dame's image of a football school. Leahy's teams would engage in tactics that would so enrage Big Ten coaches that they threatened to stop playing the Irish. According to Underwood: "In one game three Notre Dame players went down at the same time, faking injury to kill the clock. It looked like a battle scene from Warner Brothers."[16]

Cavanaugh wanted to begin the process of changing the football factory image by reorganizing athletics and bringing it under the clear control of the university. At the same time, the thirty-two-year-old Hesburgh was quite certain that the powerful and intense coach would not take kindly to any new administrative rules. Nonetheless, with Cavanaugh's total support, Hesburgh would rein in all of the problem areas in the summer of 1949: he curbed the widespread distribution of complementary tickets, granted absolute authority to the team physician over the playing status of injured athletes, cut back on the number of players who went on game trips (traveling squads), and created a new position of athletic director reporting to the executive vice president. But even as he imposed new limits on long-standing practices, Hesburgh also showed support for Leahy and the team. He proposed, for example, that teams fly to distant games (the "long train rides were making the players sluggish and also keeping them out of school for long periods"), and he defended the coach publicly on several occasions.

Father Cavanaugh proved to be a splendid mentor for Hesburgh. The reorganization of departments was part of an intensive three-year apprenticeship for Hesburgh during which he was also introduced to the world of big-time college sports and benefactor relations. As executive vice president, he traveled with the football teams; Cavanaugh would give him the names of Notre Dame graduates and friends for him to meet at the games. He inherited the responsibility for buildings and new construction, and with that came exposure to contractors, architects, design and function, finance, materials, and deadlines. Increasingly, Cavanaugh would pile more and more responsibility on his thirty-two-year-old protégé, with an unbounded confidence in Hesburgh's ability to get things done well. Finally, in June of 1952, Cavanaugh's six-year term was coming to an end (as required by the then-existing canon law) and the Holy Cross Order had decided that Hesburgh would be the next president.

"That's the way it was done in 1952. No ceremony or speeches or any of that stuff. Still, when Father Mehling said, 'Ted Hesburgh, president,' at the obediences, my stomach did a few turns."

THE PRESIDENCY

Hesburgh became president on June 27, 1952, one month after turning thirty-five, and from the start, he would display evidence of his clear vision and of a lucid and comprehensive understanding of the challenges facing Notre Dame. At his first off-campus press conference as president, he was asked to pose with a football for photographers. "Would you ask the president of Yale to do that?" he asked sharply.[17] He was also especially clear about the challenges and opportunities of religious responsibilities on the one hand and secular changes necessary to improve the quality of the university on the other. "We do not hold that piety is a substitute for competence, but it should not be divorced from competence," he told a reporter in 1952. "If a man is responsible to God he will be responsible to his neighbors, his family, and his country. Our emphasis on religion isn't something that is tacked on to the program, but a fiber running through our entire educational structure."[18]

Hesburgh came to the presidency with the benefit of a long history at Notre Dame. His familiarity with school and its culture informed his plans. More importantly, he understood the university needed to improve in three main areas before it could become a top institution: faculty, facilities, and endowment. There was a good, dedicated faculty, Hesburgh said, but "they weren't the most outstanding faculty in the world. The highest paid faculty member was Frank O'Malley, who taught literature and was paid $5,600 a year (and he had to teach summer school). Of course, we didn't have a single endowed faculty chair." They also needed major improvements in the physical plant, but Hesburgh realized that the first step was to strengthen the faculty.

In accomplishing these changes, Hesburgh had to make tough personnel decisions. Many of the administrators and residence hall supervisors were ineffective and lacked the passion for their jobs that Hesburgh had for his. At one point early on, the dean of the School of Commerce remarked to his faculty that "[W]e've had two bad presidents in a row. We can't stand a third. But we probably won't have to worry about that because we'll outlast Hesburgh." The dean was summarily removed from the administration and given another position at the same pay.[19]

The best illustration of the campus building deficiencies was the existing library, a crammed place with just 250,000 books in 1952. The first thing Hesburgh wanted to build when he had some money was the library. "When it came time to do the library, the architects would ask: 'Do you want to double the size of the one you have now? Quadruple it?' I said I wanted it twelve times the size. I had a deal going with the Ford Foundation: if we could raise $8 million, they'd give us four. We built the library and dedicated it in 1964, and the first month it was open we had five times the students in there that we had in a month in the old library." Today, the Hesburgh library has 3 million volumes, amazing collections, even a sports collection. "And in the basement they put the badly needed faculty offices, secretarial pools, phones, none of which the faculty ever had."

Hesburgh likes to point out that the library is the most expensive building on the campus. This was an important distinction as he endeavored to move Notre Dame into the top ranks of academic institutions and deemphasize the "football factory" image. For several years, while he struggled to find construction funds, he would emphasize the need for a new library above all other potential buildings, including a new athletic facility (which was also badly needed). But it was not until the library was in the planning stages that he allowed his colleagues to begin planning for the new athletic building. Even so, he had set out two prerequisites before planning for the new athletics complex could begin: Hesburgh said he personally would not "raise a nickel for it"; and the new athletic facility had to cost "considerably less than the library." The Father Ned Joyce Athletic and Convocation Center (named after Hesburgh's longtime colleague) cost $9.5 million, three million less than the library. Similarly, Hesburgh resisted pressures to modernize the football stadium, which had been built during the Depression during Rockne's time.

> But at a crucial time in our academic resurgence, when we were working very hard to improve our curriculum and faculty salaries, I was concerned that a new or bigger stadium would send out the wrong message. I feared it would reinforce the widely held misconception that Notre Dame was emphasizing athletics at the expense of academics. I was not about to do anything that would send this message.[20]

But the third thing, and perhaps the most important thing, Notre Dame needed was an endowment, a corpus of funds that would generate returns or interest used to strengthen and supplement such things as fac-

ulty salaries, student financial aid, and library acquisitions. When Hesburgh became President the university had an endowment of about $7
million, with no endowed faculty chairs and very few scholarships. By
the time he left Notre Dame, the institution was ranked among the top
fifteen in the size of the endowment. Hesburgh thus might have been
one of the pioneer university presidents in the area of fund-raising, but
he never enjoyed it. "I used to think that I did it too much, that my
friends would turn around and run when they saw me coming. I relied
on James Frick in this area, he was quite good at raising money." But
Frick agreed with Hesburgh: "He really, truly hates to ask people for
money," said Frick.[21] Hesburgh would "create the environment in which
Frick could operate," and Frick and his colleagues would close the deals.[22]
In all of these activities, Hesburgh learned a lot from watching other
presidents.

THE ALTER EGO

Hesburgh chose colleagues who complemented his strengths, but none
was more important than his long-time right-hand, executive vice president Father Ned Joyce. The tall, blue-eyed Spartanburg, South Carolina,
native was comfortable in his role as the highly visible Number Two man
to Hesburgh. For thirty-five years he played an "inside-outside" game with
Hesburgh, bringing his conventional conservatism to balance Hesburgh's
charismatic and free-wheeling style. "He kept Hesburgh from bankrupt-
ing the place," remembered a former administrator.

A graduate of Notre Dame, Joyce returned to South Carolina after finishing his bachelor's degree and worked as a CPA for five years, training
that would equip him to work a few years later as the university's chief
finance officer. With the war breaking out in Europe, Joyce had tried to
get a commission in the Navy, but the initial eye test showed he was
color-blind. A few months later, during a physical for the draft, they
found a heart murmur, which made him ineligible to be drafted. Unde-
terred, and still trying to do his share in the war, he applied to the FBI,
but by the time the FBI finished doing background checks on him nine
months later, he had already decided to become a priest. (In fact, on his
first day back at Notre Dame for seminary training, Joyce received a
telegram from J. Edgar Hoover appointing him as a special agent.) He
was ordained in 1949 and appointed to head the university's finances after
the vice president of business affairs had fallen ill and had been sent to
Arizona to recuperate.

Hesburgh explained their relationship:

Every guy I picked [as vice president] was older than I was, and that wasn't hard to do because I had just turned thirty-five. They were all smarter, as far as their own areas went, and they were all guys I could live with—the chemistry was OK. Joyce and I were in fact quite opposite. I'm a Yankee; he's from South Carolina. He's terrific with numbers, figures, business, and I never cared much for business. He is very conservative, and I am quite liberal. He is a good athlete; I have two left feet. He's a sharp dresser; I'm a bit of a slob. Impressively, I'd say we never had a fight, though we had disagreements. I gave in half the time, and looking back, he was right most of those times. If it was one of those things he was good at, I'd defer to him; if it was one of the things I was good at, he'd defer to me. Ned would put up with me, I've got to say that. And when we left in 1987, we decided we'd leave together. He was, I think, a little reluctant to leave at first, but I said, "No, if I get out of here, you'd better get out, too, because we're identified as a single team. Let the new guys take over.

THE STUDENT PROTESTS OF THE SIXTIES

The 1960s started, as John F. Kennedy said in his inaugural address, with the torch being passed to a new generation of Americans, "born in this century." The decade ended with the imbroglio of Vietnam; the assassinations of President Kennedy, his brother Bobby Kennedy, and Martin Luther King, Jr.; the refusal by President Johnson to run for reelection; and unprecedented student protests that led to the resignation or firing of a large number of university presidents. Hesburgh, who kept a yellow piece of paper with the names of deposed university presidents, could only recall six contemporary presidents of the major universities who survived the protests (although surely there were others): Bill Friday at North Carolina, Terry Sanford at Duke, Bob Goheen at Princeton, King Brewster at Yale, Ed Levi at Chicago, and himself. Many others, like Clark Kerr at California and Jim Perkins at Cornell, did not outlast the student revolts. In highly publicized events at Columbia University, students took over the office of the president, Grayson Kirk, barricaded themselves and proceeded to ransack his files and destroy his offices. Although Hesburgh's offices were never attacked, Notre Dame did survive a real threat to burn down its ROTC building.

Three factors were important to Hesburgh's "survival" during this period. One was Notre Dame's size and origins, another was the national and even international image and reputation that Hesburgh had achieved by this time, and the third was Hesburgh's interpersonal skills.

Notre Dame was then—and remains today—a relatively small university, and Father Hesburgh was well known to the entire community. He was a congenial president, but he also was clearly in charge. He had unquestioned authority, and the relatively small number of stakeholders to whom he was responsible was unified behind him. (Notre Dame was a Catholic university, of course, then owned and controlled by the Holy Cross.) But these conditions would not suffice to survive the intense protests: Father Hesburgh by this point in his career had served on several presidential commissions and had won the admiration of many people all over the world for his moral stands on difficult social problems of the day. In particular, his distinguished service as chairman of the U.S. Commission on Civil Rights established Hesburgh as one of moral leaders of America and a larger-than-life figure for most Notre Dame students and faculty. The Commission had a daunting set of challenges and met with vigorous opposition at every turn: Senator Strom Thurmond of South Carolina filibustered for over twenty-four hours to try to prevent its establishment and Alabama Circuit Judge George C. Wallace impounded voter registration files to prevent the Commission from seeing them.[23] From his new pulpit, the forty-year-old Hesburgh gave speeches and interviews promoting the Commission's work, recognizing that publicity could add to the force of its findings and recommendations. Hesburgh added a widely quoted personal statement to the Commission's 1961 report. "Personally," he wrote, "I don't care if the United States gets the first man on the moon, if while this is happening on a crash basis we dawdle along here on our corner of the earth, nursing our prejudices, flouting our magnificent Constitution, ignoring the central moral problem of our times, and appearing hypocrites to all the world."[24] Both the *New York Times* and *Time* magazine quoted this and other excerpts from his appended personal statement. "Father Hesburgh," said a *New York Times* editorial, "has done more than write a footnote to another government report. He has pointed a glowing road toward human betterment and decency."[25]

Hesburgh was also in close touch with people and events, an extension of his interpersonal behavior. During most of his tenure, Hesburgh would work late, often as late as two or three in the morning. He was not a "morning person." One effect of his work habits was that students would see the lights on in his office; they always knew he would be in his office late at night, and that his door, or his window by the fire escape, would always be open. "There was a joke on campus," Hesburgh recounted, "that was frequently repeated: 'What's the difference between Hesburgh and God?' And the answer, which reflected the popular, though not entirely accurate, perception of the amount of time I spent serving on various presidential commissions and the like, was: 'God is everywhere, but Hesburgh is everywhere but Notre Dame.'" But, in fact, Hesburgh would go to out-of-town meetings and return to campus from the airport in the afternoons and would then work in his office until late each night. Unlike his predecessor, Father Cavanaugh, Hesburgh did not socialize in South Bend at all; he didn't play golf or bridge or go out to dinners. This late-night open-door (or "open-window") policy worked well with most students, who typically were night owls themselves. It provided Hesburgh with vital "intelligence" about student activities and would enable him to stay appraised of planned activities and protests. However, despite Hesburgh's best efforts, students at Notre Dame and across the nation became more and more objectionable and violent. The stress took its toll, as he developed angina pectoris and generally showed great signs of strain during this period. "Notre Dame seemed to be consumed in controversy. Here and everywhere students were trying to take over. And the toll was heavy. It seemed to me the time had come to draw the line."[26]

In typical Hesburgh style, he decided to write a statement setting forth clear principles of behavior alongside a cogent overview of the larger moral and ethical issues surrounding the controversy. His guiding principle, he said, was civility. But he wrote it only after carefully canvassing the university family—faculty, students, trustees, and alumni—about where exactly to draw that line. Support was not unanimous; while the Academic Council (the highest faculty body) endorsed Hesburgh's statement before he issued it, the Arts and Letters faculty voted not to support it. With broad support behind him, however, he proceeded to draft a letter to be sent to each member of the Notre Dame family. While Hesburgh felt this was "the first of its kind from a university president, the first firm drawing of the line on student protests," in fact many other university presidents had tried the same sort of approach at about the same time.[27] To be sure, Hesburgh's was the only one to be published in its lengthy entirety by the New York Times (on February 17, 1969), but its content clearly benefited from the earlier events in California and elsewhere. For example, he observed correctly that the student demonstrations had been rather formulaic:

> The rhythm is simple: (1) find a cause, any cause, silly or not; (2) in the name of the cause, get a few determined people to abuse the rights and privileges of the community so as to force a confrontation at any cost of boorishness or incivility; (3) once this has occurred,

justified or not, orderly or not, yell police brutality—if it does not happen, provoke it by foul language, physical abuse, whatever, and then count on a larger measure of sympathy from the up-to-now apathetic or passive members of the community. Then call for amnesty, the head of the president on a platter, the complete submission to any and all demands. One beleaguered president has said that these people want to be martyrs thrown to toothless lions. He added, "Who wants to dialogue when they are going for the jugular vein?"

The process was also highly irrational:

Perkins at Cornell got fired because he didn't call the cops, and Nate Pusey at Harvard got fired because he did call the cops. It seemed like irrational improvisation. There were no rules. But I can tell you it was stressful, and there were many times when I wondered why I was doing it, why I was president. You just wondered why any intelligent man would want to be a university administrator.

Hesburgh's contemporaries had been strong supporters of the United States during World War II, and perhaps initially many people had placed the Vietnam conflict in a similar position. But as the conflict raged and the number of casualties rose, support for the escalation of the war in Southeast Asia declined rapidly. Hesburgh was among the more important detractors as the Vietnam war grew, and he made highly visible efforts to express his dissatisfaction. He sympathized with protesters, though he disagreed forcefully with their methods. His style was consistent with Heifetz's notion of adaptive learning. For example, he stated at a press conference in New York: "We might begin by trying to understand what causes the unrest, the protest, the revolt of the young people today."[28] And he obtained significant funding ($125,000) to begin new programs on nonviolence and to create the Robert Kennedy Institute for Social Action at Notre Dame.

VISION AND INSPIRATION

When Hesburgh gave one of his first talks after becoming president, he noted that the university had "an impossibly small library, a not terribly distinguished faculty, a very small endowment, a student body that was dedicated, and a national champion football team." He wanted Notre Dame to be a great university as well as a great Catholic university. The first goal was easier than the second: there are many great universities, but at the time there were no great Catholic ones. His comprehensive plan for a distinguished and more secular institution involved an adaptation of the Princeton model to the Notre Dame setting. Harvard and Yale were too large, he observed, but Princeton was closer in size to Notre Dame. Princeton had a strong undergraduate student body and about fifteen hundred graduate students. It had similar religious roots, Presbyterian in the case of Princeton, strong sports traditions, and an isolated campus. "It also had a great library and a healthy endowment too." But Hesburgh also knew that many changes would be needed if Notre Dame was to become the "Catholic Princeton." Football had been the engine in the past, and huge efforts would be needed on a nearly daily basis to change the football factory perception. Hesburgh knew what it would take and he worked consistently to emphasize academics over athletics at every opportunity. An article in the *Chicago American* observed, "If it seems strange that this story about Notre Dame does not mention football, the reason is that Father Hesburgh had many, many things to say that are more important than anything he might say about a game."[29] Another journalist spoke with Hesburgh for four hours before the topic of sports was mentioned.[30]

In the early years of his presidency, Hesburgh had significant authority and power, often the prerequisites for a strongly charismatic style where the vision and goals are generated by the leader himself with little input from constituents and where the strength of the leader's personality defines that vision. He relied on Father Joyce for "all that football stuff," while he focused on strengthening the academic enterprise at Notre Dame. His notion of Notre Dame becoming the greatest Catholic university was always present. "It is not [just] the words he uses," said Timothy O'Meara, a former provost. "It is the whole way in which he communicates or his presence communicates. He gives people the feeling of being important."[31] A former faculty member remembers a similar presence: "He always gave us the impression that we were doing something terrific here."[32] On difficult decisions involving terminations: "One can be forceful and humane at the same time. But it is not easy."

Hesburgh took a deeply personal interest in people who worked at Notre Dame. He would write them handwritten notes; he remembered their names, and often the names of their spouses and children. He wrote everyone: gardeners, garage mechanics, even a cabby in Manhattan, David Cooper, got a Hesburgh note.[33] People were generally delighted to get such notes, and they were genuine, reflective of Father Ted's strong interpersonal skills and the fact that he has always been a people person.

Several former students also commented on his remarkable memory as he would frequently greet Notre Dame students on campus and ask about their parents by name.

His strength of personality was generally considered an asset, but he also had his detractors. His dominance irritated some subordinates. "His administrative style, while genial, personable, and, indeed, pastoral, was nonetheless always autocratic," recalls Father David Burrell.[34] And maintaining confidentiality was not one of his stronger skills. "Father Ted was the biggest leak on campus. When you had something confidential, he would constantly tell everybody it was confidential, but then he would tell eight or ten other people," recalled another associate.[35] Notre Dame grew amazingly under Hesburgh's thirty-five years of leadership, but the test of presidential power in relation to the faculty would come only after his departure. This is not surprising since the faculty was generally not very distinguished in the early 1950s and it was the larger-than-life Father Ted who strengthened it.

LIFE CADENCE

The frenetic schedule that Father Hesburgh kept during most of his thirty-five-year tenure in South Bend would have been fatal for people of lesser constitutions. He had extraordinary proclivities for hard and concentrated work and a voracious appetite for new things and new friends that kept him constantly on the move. Even with his high levels of energy and his psychological stamina, the student protests wore him out and made him physically ill. He did not exercise regularly ("other than running to and from airplanes"). He smoked Lucky Strikes for twenty-five years, and he continues to enjoy cigars. Still, several routines and rituals helped him renew his spirits and maintain his physical and psychological strengths. His religion is one of the daily constants: he tries to say Mass every day. And he also says his breviary, the daily prayers said by every priest. "They used to be in Latin, *breviare romanum*, now it's English. It's a regular routine. It has readings from the Old Testament and the New Testament, and it's very conducive to reflection and introspection. They take about thirty to forty-five minutes."

The other thing he did regularly was to vacation away from South Bend every Christmas with two Texas Baptist friends, C.R. Smith, founder and president of American Airlines, and Charlie Jones, the president of Richfield Oil. Jones owned a house at a town called Rancho Las Cruces in Baja California, Mexico, where they would stay along with Jones' wife, Jenny. "I got sunshine, exercise, caught lots of marlin, which we either threw back or gave to the villagers for food, shot a few ducks. It was a total break." The house was in the middle of a small village that hadn't had a priest for forty years, so Hesburgh also celebrated Midnight Mass and New Year's Mass.

The Mexican tradition started one fall when Smith, who was on one of the university advisory councils for the College of Business Administration, leaned over at one of the meetings and said to Hesburgh: "You look like hell, you're not going to work at Christmas, are you?" The nonplussed Hesburgh thanked him, and replied that he'd take a little break. Soon after the meeting, Smith sent Hesburgh an airline ticket, along with some money and a note: he was to buy a pair of hunting boots, fly to Los Angeles, and meet him at the Beverly Hills Hotel. Hesburgh had no idea where they would be going from there, but at breakfast the day after getting to Los Angeles, Smith informed him that Jones and his wife Jenny would be joining them and they would fly in Jones' DC-3 to the Baja Peninsula, in Mexico, from the Burbank airport. This mid-year break would go on for three decades, to different places all over the world. They continued going to Las Cruces until Jones passed away in 1970. "We didn't return to Las Cruces again because it was too painful for Smith to return there and be reminded of his old friend." But Hesburgh and Smith would continue to vacation together during Christmas for sixteen more years. Smith, the founder of American Airlines and a major figure in air travel, died in 1990. And right after graduation every year, Hesburgh would head to Land of Lakes, in northern Wisconsin, for two weeks. "I wrote three books up there, stayed in a cabin on the lakes. It was Notre Dame property, given to us as a gift. We've turned it into an ecological study place now, but I could go up there and fish as long as I wanted, and sleep as long as I wanted, fresh air, and the loons crying at night, listen to classical music, and read, and write. I would do this every year, without fail."

CONCLUSION

So it seems John Underwood was wrong when he wrote that "[F]ootball brought Notre Dame to prominence, and then to rewards both educational and financial that were beyond its dreams. If Notre Dame has thus benefited from football, it is not only wrong to deny the credit, it is hypocrisy." The dramatic improvements to the academic side of Notre Dame, and to its endowment and to the distinction of its faculty, would not have taken place without the leadership of Ted Hesburgh. Many institutions have had successful football programs, but they have not been known for much more than that. Notre Dame has taken its place among the elite institutions, a move that was neither accidental nor the result of its gridiron successes. Moreover, the desegregation of college sports that would take place during the 1960s would have, as it in fact has done, balanced out the competition and diminished significantly the Notre Dame domination of earlier times.

Notre Dame was a vastly different university when Father Hesburgh left it than when he first entered it as a seminarian. Among other things, he could be justly proud of helping Notre Dame become a great Catholic university, as well as a great university. Father Hesburgh accomplished these challenging goals through his deep understanding of where Notre Dame was and what it would take to change it as well as through the strength of his personality and talents and with great associates and lots of hard and thoughtful work. He will also add that he did it with God's help.

NOTES

1. Michael O'Brien, *Hesburgh: A Biography* (Washington, DC: Catholic University of America Press, 1998), 7.

2. Ibid., 10.

3. Ibid., 16.

4. Theodore M. Hesburgh, with J. Reedy, *God, Country, Notre Dame* (New York: Doubleday, 1990), 16–17.

5. Ibid., 18.

6. Ibid., 24.

7. Ibid., 33. Later, after returning to the United States, Hesburgh changed his mind and came to appreciate the rigor and quality of Gregorian's education relative to other Catholic universities in Europe and in America.

8. Ibid.

9. Ibid., 46.

10. John Underwood, *Spoiled Sport: A Fan's Notes on the Troubles of Spectator Sports* (Boston: Little, Brown, 1984), 265.

11. Ibid.

12. O'Brien, *Hesburgh*, 47.

13. Ibid.

14. Ibid., 28.

15. Hesburgh, *God, Country*, 57.

16. Underwood, *Spoiled Sport*, 266.

17. Ibid., 243.

18. O'Brien, *Hesburgh*, 53–54.

19. Ibid., 54, and interview with Hesburgh.

20. Hesburgh, *God, Country*, 90.

21. O'Brien, *Hesburgh*, 269.

22. Ibid.

23. Foster R. Dulles, *The Civil Rights Commission, 1957–1965* (East Lansing: Michigan State University Press, 1968), and O'Brien, *Hesburgh*, 72–73.

24. O'Brien, *Hesburgh*, 79.

25. *New York Times*, November 19, 1961.

26. Hesburgh, *God, Country*, 112.

27. Ibid., 113.

28. O'Brien, *Hesburgh*, 116.

29. *Chicago American*, May 24, 1958.

30. O'Brien, *Hesburgh*, 56.

31. Ibid., 262.

32. Ibid.

33. Underwood, *Spoiled Sport*, 236.

34. O'Brien, *Hesburgh*, 264.

35. Ibid., 265.

John Brooks Slaughter.

CHAPTER

Lenny, Lefty, and Chancellor Slaughter

Sticks in a bundle cannot be broken.

—Kenyan proverb

The June 4, 1998, edition of the *Los Angeles Times* announced, "Occidental College President John Brooks Slaughter to Retire." The photo showed a smiling, handsome man. The gray in his mustache belied his youthful appearance, but it was the story's first sentence that bothered him. It described him as "one of the most prominent African-American leaders in higher education." When Charles Young of UCLA announced his retirement the previous year, Slaughter said, "I don't recall his being identified as one of the most prominent *white* leaders in higher education." Then came the ironic but still engaging smile: "Chuck [Young] is a good friend and was great at UCLA, but this is just another example of how far we still have to go."

Before becoming president of Occidental College, John Brooks Slaughter headed the National Science Foundation and then the University of Maryland at College Park. His distinguished government service under U.S. presidents Jimmy Carter and Ronald Reagan and his tenure at College Park could easily have been the capstone of an enviable career. Indeed, his record at the University of Maryland is outstanding in many ways; from the day he took office in late 1982, Slaughter tirelessly advocated scholastic rigor and cultural inclusion on a campus that many thought was not living up to its great potential. Students knew Slaughter as a friendly, sincere leader who welcomed impromptu visits to his office and often stopped by dorms to discuss the concerns of students.[1] He also reorganized Maryland's medley of departments into twelve colleges and two schools, allowing for more effective management. By the time he resigned in 1988, College Park was attracting significantly more federal research grants than ever before, reflecting in part Slaughter's connections with the scientific research world. The university was also accepting unprecedented numbers of minority students and enjoying a resurgence of academic prestige as over a dozen departments placed near the top in national rankings of public and private institutions.[2]

But the negative publicity following the fatal cocaine overdose of star basketball player Leonard (Lenny) Bias in June of 1986 overshadowed Slaughter's accomplishments and highlighted the influence of big-time college sports on American universities and their impact on those who lead them. Ironically, this devoted sports fan and former athlete from Topeka, Kansas, who chaired the NCAA Presidents Commission, would come to dread opening the sports page each morning in the aftermath of the Bias tragedy.

"YOU'VE GOT TO LEARN TO SACRIFICE"

John Brooks Slaughter's story begins at the dawn of the twentieth century when his grandfather, a dissatisfied sharecropper born into slavery, slipped from an Alabama farm late one night in search of a better life for himself and his family. His family's new beginning was to be found in Kansas, where work as a coal miner in a "free" state held much more appeal than the intolerable working conditions and seemingly endless poverty Slaughter's grandfather had known as a sharecropper. Though the walk from Warrior, Alabama, to Topeka was too much for him (he contracted pneumonia after reaching Arkansas and died in Kansas shortly after his sons arranged for him to travel the rest of the way by train), his grandfather's efforts were not in vain. No longer of much use to the Alabama farm owner after Slaughter's grandfather had gone, John's grandmother, father, and uncles were released from indentured servitude and found their own way to Kansas. "My father many years later could vividly recall the night when that Alabama farmer came by their house looking for my grandfather, wondering where he was."

The late 1800s and early 1900s saw a migration of blacks from Tennessee and other states to eastern Kansas. Kansas, admitted into the Union in 1861 as a "free" state, outlawed slavery, unlike the nearby states of Oklahoma, Missouri, Alabama, and Tennessee, and its homestead act offered free land to settlers.³ Although Slaughter's mother was born in Topeka in 1897, her family, from Covington, Tennessee, was part of this exodus that brought an estimated 20,000 African Americans from various southern states to Kansas. In fact, the Kansas community where John attended elementary school was known as "Tennessee Town" because so many of its residents had followed this path. In a time when many did not have the opportunity or daring to seek out a better life, John Slaughter's ancestors were able to leave their familiar, albeit stifling, surroundings to take enormous and costly risks in order to improve their situation. "I think blacks in Kansas might have had a different attitude than did the blacks elsewhere. They had that taste for liberty, freedom, and independence, and more importantly, they were willing to move to find these things." It is tempting to agree with Slaughter's assessment, although many African Americans over the years, both before and after emancipation, have attempted to escape from their situations in the South and elsewhere.⁴ In any event, this family legacy would establish a precedent of sacrifice and self-improvement in John's life. In his excellent book, *Lenny, Lefty, and the Chancellor*, C. Fraser Smith notes that Slaughter's father often told him, "If you want to make anything of yourself, son, you've got to learn to sacrifice."⁵ This advice would shape many of the major decisions that Slaughter would make throughout his life.

John grew up with three sisters in a strong family.⁶ His parents were older: Reuben Brooks Slaughter, John's father, born in 1885, was forty-eight years old when John was born, and his mother was thirty-seven. Reuben had only a third grade education, but Slaughter calls his father "the wisest person I've ever known in my life." Reuben eventually became a coal miner, and was nearly killed in a mine accident that left him with burn scars over much of his body and nearly blind in one eye. No stranger to exceptionally hard work, the elder Slaughter sometimes worked two or three jobs to provide for his wife, his three daughters, and John. Reuben incessantly told his son that he wanted him to have a better life than the one he had. One of his father's W-2 tax forms from the mid-1940s, when he worked while in his early sixties as a custodian at a nearby Air Force base, reported an income of under $2,500. By comparison, in 1950, the average minority family reported an income of $1,859, and the average white family made $3,445.⁷

Kansas was a state in educational and social transition at the time that John Slaughter made his way through grade school. In Topeka, classes from kindergarten through the sixth grade were segregated. So while John began his education at one of four all-black elementary schools in Topeka, he later enrolled in the integrated Topeka High School, where classes were racially mixed but the athletic and social events were still separate. The athletic teams for the white students were called the Trojans; the black teams were called the Ramblers. Slaughter kept his Ramblers "letter" jacket for years to remind him "how things were back then. It's a wonder we [black kids] didn't grow up schizoid. In fact, some of the black kids grew up thinking they were inferior, but I never accepted this. I believe my parents kept me from believing it. These barriers actually made me stronger, more determined at some deeper level to overcome these obstacles." Slaughter's family was the only black one on his block; many local neighborhoods had streets with only all-white, all-black, or all-Hispanic households. If John wanted to see a film at a movie theater in Topeka, he would have to sit in a corner of the balcony, where he could hear the epithets and insults from the white audience seated below. White-owned restaurants and hotels did not admit blacks at all. The U.S. Supreme Court ruling in *Oliver Brown v. Board of Education of Topeka, Kansas*, which decreed that "segregation of white and Negro children in the public schools of a State solely on the basis of race . . . denies to Negro children the equal protection of the laws guaranteed by the Fourteenth Amendment," passed three years after Slaughter's 1951 high school graduation.[8]

In school, Slaughter had two teachers who were important mentors to him as a child and who would stay involved in his life for another fifty years after teaching him in their classrooms. Althea McBrier, Slaughter's second grade teacher, supported Slaughter from the time he learned to use a dictionary as a child until his recognition as Kansan of the Year in 1994; McBrier attended the ceremony while in her early nineties. And while Slaughter was in junior high, from 1945 to 1948, Howard Anderson, a white industrial arts teacher (and Slaughter's homeroom teacher) would be another influential figure. Anderson obviously saw in John the interpersonal capabilities and leadership promise that would later be manifested, encouraging him and taking interest in his success. He too stayed in touch: Anderson attended the funerals of Slaughter's father in 1977 and that of his mother in 1987.

Encouraged by his mother, Slaughter developed a passion for reading, a childhood characteristic that John shared with the other university leaders studied in this book. In junior high, he won a contest at school for reading the most books and writing reports on each one. "I spent as much time in the library as I did anywhere." He found he leaned increasingly toward the technical and the scientific, preferring things to people, though this preference could well have been the result of discrimination: "I never really felt like I had a lot of mentors or role models outside of Anderson and of course my parents." In high school, he gravitated toward publications such as *Popular Mechanics* and *Popular Science*. An active and athletic kid, John also enjoyed reading stories about sports. He competed in baseball and track, and he dreamed of being on the sports pages for his athletic prowess.

From an early age, Slaughter was mechanically inclined. He was always taking things apart to see how they worked, and he made many of his own toys; he had disassembled and reassembled his bicycle more times than he could remember. His father's work selling used furniture produced a number of broken old radios that Slaughter discovered he was able to repair. His father soon realized he had a gold mine on his hands; the radios would go into the barn in poor condition, but once they left young John's hands, they were fit to be sold, providing more income for the family. Slaughter took a radio repair class his tenth-grade year, and then his parents purchased some used radio test equipment. His father even built him a small shop out of some scrap lumber. That was all that was needed to launch his radio repair service; according to John, he could "could fix any radio in Topeka" for four dollars plus parts. This business would eventually help to pay his way through college. With his father's example and encouragement, Slaughter developed a talent for finding opportunity in places where others might see nothing at all.

Slaughter felt almost instinctively that he was to become an electrical engineer. From the time he was in eighth grade, he told anyone who would listen about his dream. But he also recalls that no one believed him; no one was there to provide him with the guidance to make the dream a reality. "My parents didn't know enough about college to advise me." Like all other black students, he was "tracked" into a vocational curriculum that did little to prepare him for admission to Kansas State University or the University of Kansas, the two schools he wanted to attend to study engineering. Slaughter was persistent, even in high school, as his dream of being an engineer was an ambitious one; no black children aspired to be engineers. According to Smith, in Topeka's 1940 census, the city was home to one black electrician (out of 215 total) and one black physician; Slaughter once joked that he was "the first black engineer he'd ever met." But his joke reflects the truth: the school system was designed to send white students in one direction and minorities in another. Slaughter believes that "to a large extent, black students are still being tracked today."

During Slaughter's senior year in 1951, Topeka High School hosted colleges and universities trying to recruit students for their programs. As he spoke with representatives from Kansas State and the University of

Kansas in the gymnasium of Topeka High, he was told that though his grades were good enough, his lack of college preparatory courses prevented them from considering his application: his last math class was in the tenth grade, and his only science course was physics. Slaughter enrolled instead in Washburn College, a small college located on the same street he had lived his whole life. In recognition of his good grades, he was named a Whiting Scholar, receiving $150 a year for school. At Washburn, Slaughter took the science and math courses that he should have been advised to take at Topeka High. But because Washburn did not have engineering programs, he also took a number of liberal arts courses, including world history, English literature, speech, economics, and writing, that students who had gone directly into engineering at Kansas State missed because of rigid technical requirements for engineering majors. Typical of his emblematic "turn-lemons-into-lemonade" approach to life, Slaughter said:

> It's strange how what sometimes appears to be a setback turns out to be a wonderful opportunity. [At Washburn] I had to take a lot of non-engineering courses in the humanities and they became the most important courses I've ever taken in my life. Without them, I could not ever have become the head of the NSF or the chancellor at Maryland or president at Occidental College.

Slaughter would discover early in his life that what seems crucial in the short run is often irrelevant over the longer term. When he transferred to Kansas State, he was a year behind in his mathematics and technical prerequisites compared to those students who had gone directly into engineering. However, he came to realize that "my preparation was so much broader than that of my fellow students who had gone straight into engineering. I could write a lot better than my classmates because I had taken many more literature and English classes and I could speak with more confidence because I'd taken speech classes." A strong liberal arts education was important for Slaughter ten years later when he first entered the world of management, and it served him well as he took on increasingly complex leadership roles. Recognizing his unique background, he says:

> If there's one thing I'm sure of, it's that I'm not a typical engineer. Once when I was in school at Kansas State someone asked me what my major was, and when I said electrical engineering, he looked at me as though I were crazy. I didn't behave in the way that most people thought engineers normally did. Much later I found that I

enjoyed working with people more than I enjoyed working with things.

Slaughter certainly does not fit the "engineer" stereotype: he is not linear in his thinking, and he recognizes that the shortest distance between two points is not always a straight line; he tends to see interconnections among seemingly unrelated elements of a problem and leans toward the larger picture in his explanations and analyses. He tends to be a visual learner, preferring graphs and diagrams and pictures to equations and other verbal forms of gathering and evaluating information. He is also a highly effective communicator whose speech flows logically and smoothly over a story.

But transferring to Kansas State and finally enrolling in electrical engineering did not remove all the barriers Slaughter would face. "There were helpful faculty members at Kansas State, but no one who took me by the hand and said 'Here's what you have to go through,' even though I was a pretty good student." Summer opportunities were inequitable; Slaughter remembers how many of his white classmates headed for internships at companies such as Boeing while he went back home to Topeka to wash cars and fix radios for the summer. At a large, predominantly white institution like Kansas State University, there were few mentoring opportunities for black students regardless of their major. He received his hard-won electrical engineering degree in 1956, and he was pleasantly surprised to learn that employers looked at him differently now that he had a degree. Around this time, the federal government started looking over the shoulder of major corporations in terms of hiring practices; government contracts were being scrutinized to see if the firms being used were hiring minorities. Slaughter suddenly found himself in demand: he recalls one Westinghouse recruiter who wanted him to "be the 'Jackie Robinson of Westinghouse,' but that was enough to scare me away from them."

EARLY CAREER

On June 8, 1956, just over five years after the college recruiters had come to his high school and told him that he was not admissible to an engineering program, John Slaughter started his first engineering job at the Convair Division of the aircraft manufacturer General Dynamics Astronautics. Slaughter had been looking for a job in San Diego so that he could join his fiancée, Bernice, who had been recruited to teach there. Bernice and John had met in 1954 at a Christmas party at Pittsburg State

Teachers College in Pittsburg, Kansas, where Bernice was studying while John attended Kansas State. The two married in August of 1956, and they would remain in San Diego for nearly twenty years. Later, while Slaughter was chancellor at the University of Maryland, Bernice worked as a counselor with the Montgomery County Public Schools in Maryland; Bernice was, according to Slaughter, his "principal source of strength during the Bias situation."

Like many other companies, General Dynamics in the 1950s presented a social and professional challenge for a young black man; the company had hired its first black engineer only a year earlier. One day, Slaughter forgot his ID badge and walked up to the security desk to get a replacement. With complete impunity and without reservation, the security guard on duty yelled out to one of his associates, "The nigger left his badge at home. . . . Get him a temporary badge!" Although this was not Slaughter's first encounter with blatant racism, the fact that this occurred where he was employed as a professional left him understandably upset. He shook his head in silence as he relived this moment four decades later, still obviously a painful memory.

Slaughter taught part-time for California Western and San Diego State during the early and mid-sixties as his engineering career progressed. In 1960, hoping to move into the promising field of electronics, he accepted a job with the Navy in the Naval Electronics Laboratory Center (NELC), but he was hired at a lower level than had been advertised; his new boss very straightforwardly explained, "Some people in the organization [would not] take kindly to working for a black man." The two men had a good relationship, and a short time later Slaughter told his boss that while he could have sued him for making such a statement, he instead chose to prove through work and effort his qualification for the job.

In fact, a quiet, dignified, and forceful determination to overcome impediments in his way typified Slaughter's responses over the years to racial slights and injustices. Clear manifestations of Slaughter's style and personality were already evident: he was an engaging and thoughtful young man, quiet and deliberate in his approach to challenges and problems, with an easy smile and an open personality, but also with a realistic assessment of discrimination in American society honed by years of personal and often bitter experiences. Slaughter seemed incapable of direct confrontation, preferring instead a philosophical but determined approach based on logical alternatives and solutions, perhaps a reflection of being raised by older, more mature and loving parents. He was already a gifted communicator, an exceptional listener, and decidedly positive in his approach to problems.

In 1961, Slaughter completed his M.S. in engineering by taking night classes at the University of California at Los Angeles, studying subjects such as digital controls for tactical shipboard weapons. Knowing that he needed a Ph.D. to achieve his goal of winning a promotion to department head, Slaughter approached Charles Manning, his departmental head, for help in 1965, telling him that eventually he aspired to his (Manning's) job; Manning advised him to take the Ph.D. at the University of California–San Diego, where he enrolled part-time while he continued to work. In addition to working and pursuing graduate degrees, Slaughter was also active in his community, serving in leadership roles on a variety of boards and commissions. When Slaughter announced in 1969 that he needed to spend a year in residency to complete his research for the degree, Manning secured him a Navy fellowship to cover his expenses. In 1971, six years after he started the Ph.D., and fifteen years after receiving his baccalaureate degree from Kansas State, Slaughter finally received his doctorate in engineering, at the age of thirty-seven. He defended his thesis in the morning and later that day the Navy interviewed him and awarded him the vacated position of head of the information systems technology department—Manning's former post. This initiation into the world of administration, coupled with the exciting engineering work Slaughter accomplished for the Navy, made his years at the Naval Electronics Laboratory the most productive of his technical career. An inveterate goal-setter, Slaughter had once again reached one of his ambitions, even if it did take him a bit longer than average to accomplish it.

YOU CAN'T SAY NO TO THE PRESIDENT

Slaughter remained at the Naval Electronics Laboratory Center until 1975, when he moved to the University of Washington-Seattle's Applied Physics Laboratory, which he headed until 1977. This was also a Navy lab, and he was doing basically the same kind of work in Seattle that he performed in San Diego. He also held the title of professor of electrical engineering. It was there that he fell in love with academic life and became interested in being a college president. However, Frank Press, President Carter's science advisor, who was familiar with Slaughter's work in engineering, asked him to be the assistant director for Astronomical, Atmospheric, Earth, and Ocean Sciences at the National Science Foundation (NSF) in 1977. Seeing an opportunity to continue his growth in the world of management, as well as the potential to use the position to continue to aid minorities in the sciences, Slaughter moved with Bernice and their two children to Washington, D.C.

But Washington did not agree with the Slaughters. Uncomfortable with the position of assistant director after two years, mostly for reasons of bureaucracy and politics, Slaughter returned to academic life in 1979 as academic vice president and provost at the Pullman campus of Washington State University. Slaughter and his family enjoyed Washington State, and he was on track to become the university's president. The family preferred the West Coast, and Slaughter would often drive to the Snake River for some fishing. However, Frank Press surfaced once again in his life, asking if he would return to Washington, this time to replace Dick Atkinson as head of the NSF. Slaughter was not so easily convinced this time, so Press had President Carter call him about the NSF post. Despite his own reservations, Slaughter assented to the offer because "you just can't say 'no' to the President of the United States." The fact that he would now be the head of government efforts to direct and support scientific research and study throughout the country was important to his decision. In addition, he would be the first black director of the National Science Foundation, an important consideration for someone whose life had been devoted to opening doors for blacks in science and engineering, and, more generally, in education. However, besides the personal sacrifice he was making to his family's lifestyle, the post presented an immediate economic problem: "We were basically broke and we were moving to an expensive region of the nation. Picture the nation's top science administrator driving cross-country in a rented U-Haul truck pulling a small car that had as passengers a dog and a cat."

Slaughter was the last Carter nominee to win U.S. Senate approval before Ronald Reagan took office in 1981; his earlier work in the NSF with Republican leaders such as Utah Senator Orrin Hatch facilitated the approval. However, disagreements with the Reagan administration over values and policies placed Slaughter in a difficult position, and his first year was a tumultuous one. The new Republican administration was mandating huge cutbacks to the scientific research activities of the nation, and Slaughter was caught between loyalty to a new administration and his personal commitment to improve scientific education. Senator Ted Kennedy, a Democrat from Massachusetts, chastised him at a Senate hearing for abandoning the nation's obligation to develop young scientists. Orrin Hatch, a Republican from Utah, tried to soften the criticism of the Reagan administration by suggesting to Slaughter that his appearance at the hearing was an honor that he might have skipped. The NSF director, though clearly frustrated with the Reagan cutbacks, replied: "Not at all, Senator. I'm not always taken to task by such distinguished critics."

THE UNIVERSITY OF MARYLAND PRESIDENCY

John Toll, a physicist well connected in national scientific circles, was president of the University System of Maryland during the late 1970s and early 1980s. He and Slaughter had met during Slaughter's first tour of duty at the NSF. The University of Maryland system then consisted of five institutions: College Park, Baltimore, Baltimore County, Eastern Shore, and University College, which is the worldwide extension institution headquartered in Adelphi, Maryland; the system now consists of those five original University of Maryland campuses plus six other state colleges and two research centers. In 1980 Toll had asked Slaughter to consider the position of chancellor at Maryland. Slaughter wrote Toll a letter explaining that he did not wish to leave the NSF, in part because he had been in office only a few months but also because he did not wish to appear openly disloyal to the new Republican administration. But by early 1982, after two years of "Reaganomics" and conflicts with Reagan's budget director, David Stockman, Slaughter was ready to go.

In May of 1982, Slaughter was commencement speaker at the Cole Field House in College Park, the cavernous, rectangular gym where Lenny Bias would later display his terrific basketball skills. He stood against a wall in the basement of the basketball arena before the ceremony, speaking quietly with Peter O'Malley, a millionaire lawyer and president of the university's board of regents. O'Malley was active in the Democratic Party and had close ties to the Maryland legislature and with various governors; he saw Slaughter as the person who could steer the university in the direction he and many others were hoping it would move. The university, although located in a demographically diverse region just north of Washington, D.C., did not exactly enjoy a progressive image when it came to race relations: a former president and football coach, Harry "Curley" Byrd, after whom Maryland's Byrd Stadium is named, was known to the state's black community as the "George Wallace of Maryland."[9] In College Park one could occasionally see Confederate flags displayed on pickup trucks, and one of Slaughter's first acts as chancellor would be to end a halftime ritual at football games where a student ran onto the field with the Stars and Bars.[10] So after learning that Slaughter was considering returning to Washington State, O'Malley appealed to the quiet but passionate civil rights activist in him: "If you go back [to Washington]," he said to Slaughter, "you'll probably be comfortable, but you'll be as far as you can be from the problems you should have an impact on." Along with Clarence Mitchell, Jr., another influential university regent and a prominent member of the black community, O'Malley persuaded Slaughter to reconsider. Mitchell, a civil rights activist who had himself been barred from attending the university, told Slaughter that he could have a significant impact on race relations and social justice. Once again, Slaughter couldn't say no.

A fortuitous series of events thus connected Slaughter with the Maryland presidency. Slaughter's 1980 letter to Toll stating that he did not wish to be considered for the Maryland job had in fact never arrived on campus, and the search committee had continued to follow up on his candidacy. (Slaughter later learned that his letter had been sent by mistake to one of the University of Maryland's study-abroad offices in Europe, though it had been properly addressed.) His unplanned conversation with the chairman of the Maryland regents in the basement of Cole Field House was also a crucial factor, as the regents up to that point had been leaning toward William "Brit" Kirwan, the acting chancellor, as their choice. Like his promotion to department head in the Navy ten years earlier, things moved quickly, and Slaughter received notice of his appointment the same day he interviewed for the chancellorship. "There were no visits to the campus, no real formal interviews. No search firm was involved. The entire thing was handled quickly by the system staff headed by Toll." He was forty-eight years old when he became chancellor at Maryland, a university he could not have legally attended thirty years earlier, when he was of college age.

THE CHANCELLOR

When he arrived in College Park in the summer of 1982, Slaughter had clear notions of where he wanted to take the university, both academically and socially. His 1983 inaugural address, entitled "Making a Difference," outlined several important objectives. He lauded the research accomplishments of the university but asked the faculty "not to be diverted from our teaching mission." Slaughter also proclaimed the importance of having a strong undergraduate program as a source of pride and development for the state of Maryland. He spoke of the importance of each graduate having a broad base of basic abilities and knowledge in technology, literacy, math, physical health, history, the arts, and their own cultural heritage. He promoted "the exchange of ideas . . . not just the dissemination of information."[11]

Slaughter's rather ambitious inaugural statement made reference to plans for a redesign of the organizational structure, a risky endeavor even for a well-established president. He also explained the importance of reaching out to minority student groups such as those over the age of twenty-five, part-time students, blacks, and Hispanics. He foresaw much of the criticism he would receive in his attempts to increase Maryland's diversity by stressing that "excellence and elitism are *not* synonymous . . . [and] equality and quality are not mutually exclusive." Over the course of his tenure at Maryland, Slaughter would come to realize his goals, despite the basketball scandal that would overshadow much of his work. The academic policies he established began to take effect by the spring of 1986; the University of Maryland enjoyed higher average SAT scores (up to 1050 from 960 in 1982), over a dozen nationally ranked graduate departments, and thriving research programs. Slaughter's presence turned around the image of the institution, as Maryland's undergraduate population grew more diverse than ever before.

One of his internal challenges was to restructure a convoluted and inefficient administrative organization. When Slaughter arrived, the academic hierarchy consisted of five provosts and an academic vice chancellor. Rather inexplicably, the five provosts reported directly to the chancellor, while the deans and department heads were immediately under the provosts; this meant, for example, that the dean of engineering reported to the same person as the head of the math department. According to Kirwan, then the academic vice chancellor (and later chancellor at Maryland and president at Ohio State), Slaughter immediately felt the system was too decentralized and not sufficiently hierarchical. His new structure contained thirteen deans and one provost to whom each dean reported. Kirwan, a popular and bright mathematician who had progressed through the academic ranks at Maryland, assumed the position of provost, and he and Slaughter would develop a close and trusting relationship. Though the restructuring met resistance from the five provosts, who were essentially being demoted, the faculty approved.

By the mid-1980s, toward the end of Slaughter's tenure, Maryland was the sixth most populous university in the nation, with nearly forty thousand students and a budget of $350 million. A case to reduce enrollment at College Park was built around the notions that the university had gotten too big for the resources available to it and that some of the other campuses in the Maryland university system were being underutilized. It made sense to make College Park smaller and more selective, and in the process better utilize the other resources of the state. Slaughter and his associates managed the difficult task of balancing his plans for increased diversity with a need for a more selective admissions process in order to decrease the size of the school. Financially, this was feasible because the Maryland legislature was willing (after much consideration) to replace the tuition that was lost by downsizing. After Slaughter left, however, and perhaps in part as a result of the barrage of negative publicity following the Lenny Bias incident, the legislature reneged on its agreement and Maryland suffered significant budget cuts that Kirwan, the next chancellor, had to address.

LENNY, LEFTY, AND CONTROVERSY

Three tragedies are nested within the story of the Lenny Bias episode. The principal one of course is Bias' death from a lethal combination of very pure cocaine, alcohol, and bad luck. The second and more complex tragedy involves the damage done to the reputation of a great American university and the derailment of its president, who was diverted from the work he could have done in the name of social justice and quality in higher education. The third, however, is the relative lack of consequence this highly publicized episode had on either academic standards for athletes or the unbridled commercialization of college sports, and the NCAA's tacit sanction of it all. Two decades after Slaughter's resignation, college sports are much bigger business than ever, and academics continue to take a back seat in big-time athletic departments.

Slaughter's troubles with the University of Maryland's athletic department began years before Bias' death. Shortly after arriving at College Park in the fall of 1982, Slaughter received a complaint regarding basketball player Herman Veal, who had been suspended from play due to an alleged act of sexual misconduct several months earlier. Apparently concerned that Veal would be unable to play in several upcoming games, Coach Charles Grice "Lefty" Driesell called the woman in question and tried to convince her to dismiss the complaint. Driesell's arrogant remarks afterward only made an embarrassing situation worse: when questioned about the phone call, he remarked that Veal was the "victim" of the affair; Driesell said, "I've got some clout on this campus. We'll see just how much."[12] Athletic director Richard Dull, who had the authority to intervene in the escalating affair, later admitted that he felt intimidated and incapable of restraining the coach.[13] Thus, it was left to Slaughter to chastise Driesell publicly for his behavior, following an official inquiry. But Slaughter's perceived lack of forcefulness in the matter drew heavy criticism, a portent of future troubles for Slaughter and his involvement with athletics.[14]

The national reform movement in big-time college athletics in the mid-1980s, led in large part by the organization that Slaughter himself chaired at the time—the NCAA Presidents Commission—was attempting to reverse serious academic declines (such as dismally low graduation rates for athletes) that had plagued college sports during most of the 1970s and early 1980s. It was not uncommon for the major public universities that competed in the NCAA's Division I to admit most students with SATs well below 700 points (combined) to play in their football or men's basketball teams, contrasted with averages in the 1100–1200 range for other students.[15] The initiative known as Proposition 48, calling for a 2.0 GPA in high school and a total of 700 on the SAT for student-athletes entering in the fall of 1986, began to cause universities and athletic conferences to reexamine their own admission and eligibility standards and procedures for athletes. Several months before Bias' death in June of 1986, Slaughter, like most other presidents, had begun to look closely at the admission standards of his university's athletics department in order to comply with the new regulations. He was also in favor of making freshmen ineligible to compete in varsity sports, but the freshman ineligibility rule was unpopular with most coaches, and university presidents themselves were split on the issue.

Had it not been for the modest impetus given the reform movement by the Presidents Commission, Slaughter and other presidents could not, or perhaps would not, have addressed these issues unilaterally. If Slaughter had tried to deal with them, he would have faced a mostly hostile, or at best indifferent, audience. With the Maryland Terrapins men's basketball team coming off one of the most successful seasons in its history, and with the men's football team excelling as well, Maryland athletics seemed hotter than ever. Operating on a budget of about $6.5 million, the Terrapins posted almost $8 million in revenue during 1985–1986, a striking turn of fortune for a department that commonly ran large deficits.[16] Football coach Bobby Ross finally saw his recruiting efforts paying off with invitations to four bowl games.

THE LENNY BIAS TRAGEDY

Crucial to the success of Driesell's basketball team was Lenny Bias, a first-team All-American and the 1986 Atlantic Coast Conference (ACC) Player of the Year. An amazing athlete with a gregarious personality, Bias was by most accounts the embodiment of confident, if unbridled, youth. Lenny led the ACC in scoring in 1986 and appeared poised for an extremely profitable professional basketball career.[17] The fabled Boston

Celtics of the National Basketball Association (NBA) made Bias their first pick in the draft on June 17, 1986; newspapers across the nation carried a picture of a smiling Bias with a Celtics hat standing beside the legendary, cigar-smoking "Red" Auerbach of the Celtics organization. A lover of cars, Bias soon replaced his Oldsmobile with a brand-new Nissan 300ZX. For the next two days, Lenny and his father James participated in the fast-paced, flashy world of the NBA, traveling to Boston and New York to meet with NBA officials, attend press conferences, and conclude a deal with Reebok representatives eager to enlist Larry Byrd's newest teammate.[18]

Following almost forty-eight hours of frenetic traveling, Bias briefly returned to his home in Landover at about 11:00 PM on June 18, 1986. By midnight, he was in his dorm room discussing his future and eating crabs with several friends. At about 2:15 AM (June 19), Bias left campus once more, presumably to visit a girlfriend, returning to his room an hour later. His teammates Terry Long and David Gregg, his friend Brian Tribble, a bottle of cognac, and a six-pack of beer were with him. Three hours later, at about 6:30 AM, in the middle of a conversation, Bias suffered a violent seizure and collapsed on the floor. Paramedics arrived shortly thereafter and rushed Bias to Leland Memorial Hospital, where doctors pronounced the twenty-two-year-old dead at 8:50 AM after extended attempts to revive him. An analysis of Bias' urine revealed the presence of cocaine, but thorough investigations of Bias' dorm room that morning yielded no evidence of drug paraphernalia.[19] Bias' exceptional athleticism, his recent and widely publicized signing with the Celtics, and the suddenness and nature of his death combined to fuel an insatiable media interest. For the next several months, Slaughter and the University of Maryland would be at the center of a hurricane of publicity, much of it unpredictable in its timing and increasingly critical in its content.

News of Bias' death elicited a sense of shock and loss not only from his teammates, but also from students at the University of Maryland and from a wider spectrum of people across the nation. Shortly after Bias' death, the University of Maryland reluctantly released his transcript, the first in a series of disclosures that would jar the university and draw John Slaughter fully into the tragedy.[20] In a quickening spiral of events closely duplicated at several other universities during the late 1970s and early 1980s, the university found itself in the middle of a limitless examination of admissions and academic practices regarding its athletic department.[21] Shock turned to indignation at Bias' poor academic standing: instead of finishing his senior year just nine hours short of graduation, as Bias himself had claimed, he actually needed twenty-one hours. He also had failed or withdrawn from every class in his spring semester, supposedly because he no longer needed to stay academically eligible to play basketball. Since his frequent basketball games and hectic traveling schedule caused him to miss almost 40 percent of his classes, Lenny stood little chance of earning credit for his courses even if he had not withdrawn from them. Most of Bias' teammates performed at similar levels: five of the seniors on the Maryland men's basketball team would not graduate that spring.

From here until the end, which for Slaughter and Maryland came in painfully slow and highly public steps, starting with Lefty Driesell's departure, then with the hiring of his replacement, Bob Wade, and finally with the departure of John Slaughter for Occidental College in Los Angeles, the Bias aftermath followed a familiar pattern. Viewed in the light of similar scandals, such as those at NC State, Kentucky, Georgia, Florida, SMU, Colorado, or UCLA, the essential elements of the modern college athletic scandal seem almost formulaic: a period of shock and cultured ignorance about the conditions revealed by the episode; self-scrutiny by the university and further revelations and findings, followed by pious commentary from the same media that typically glorifies and always handsomely profits from college sports; negotiations with a departing coach and his prominent attorney; the involvement of the parents of some student-athletes, either vociferously defending coaches or attacking the university; the discontentment and grumbling of the boosters and involvement of headline-grabbing politicians; the inevitable and arcane NCAA investigations and subsequent penalties; the hiring of a replacement coach or coaches and sometimes even a new athletic director; and finally the departure or firing of the university's president. The events and their sequence of course vary somewhat depending on the circumstances, but through it all, the university administration is utterly preoccupied with athletic matters and with little else. And, after a period of decline in the performance of the athletic team or teams, pressures to win begin to build: following an interlude of higher standards, more attention to academic matters, and greater institutional oversight of athletics, things tend eventually to return to the status quo.

During this extended affair, Slaughter would meet with a selected group of advisors every morning at 8:30 AM to decide upon the strategy for responding to the "developments du jour." Of all of Slaughter's actions, the cancellation of the fall basketball schedule in 1986–87 was both the most understandable and the most criticized. By the early fall of 1986, a few months after Bias' death, Slaughter had found that the members of the basketball team were still much too upset by the tragedy to deal with the grueling schedule of games and practices that would come later in the fall and early winter. He also wanted to make a statement about the new priority of academics. Johnny Jones, a guard on the team and a close friend of Lenny's, told Slaughter he had been visiting Bias' gravesite every morning and practicing shots in the afternoon. "Dr. Slaughter," he said, "I can't make any shots. I just see Lenny jumping up and blocking them every time I shoot."

Slaughter came to believe that several team members were not psychologically or academically prepared to play basketball that fall. Moreover, in light of the publicity surrounding academic standards in Terrapin athletics, relaxing the team's schedule appeared to Slaughter and his advisors as the best way to encourage good study habits among the players. However, the NCAA, the ACC, and Maryland fans roundly criticized the chancellor: Slaughter received hate mail, death threats, and menacing phone calls from incensed fans and alumni. An ACC committee headed by professor Ken Pye of Duke University, who later accepted the presidency at scandal-rocked Southern Methodist University, fined the University of Maryland $20,000 for "arbitrarily and capriciously" cancelling a conference game with Wake Forest University in December of 1986. Slaughter was indignant. "Because I had made the kids at Maryland my first priority," Slaughter said, ". . . we were billed $20,000. . . . Of all the things that happened after Lenny died, the threats, the newspaper stories, the personal attacks, this was the most disappointing and, really, the most amazing." He never paid the fine, but it appeared to Slaughter that everything he tried or proposed was immediately second-guessed and roundly criticized.

CONSEQUENCES AND OUTCOMES

It is impossible to consider the Bias episode and not conclude that race played a major role in all of it and in how Slaughter was treated. Throughout the long summer of 1986, Slaughter contended with a media "zoo" that consumed his life. He seemed caught in the center of every issue, opposed by all sides: he stood against many other university presidents who favored Proposition 48 because he felt its minimal provisions affected mostly black students; at the same time he opposed coaches who wanted longer season lengths for their sports and who wanted to play freshmen (Slaughter instead proposed shorter seasons and freshman ineligibility). In addition, the deliberate style that had served him well all his life was now coming under intense scrutiny and criticism in the press. The October 27, 1986, edition of the *Washington Post* profiled Slaughter, noting that his "calculating approach" and "careful attention to detail" often caused him to act too slowly for many of his critics, and that his reliance on committees of experts to suggest action made him seem indecisive.[22]

Criticism also came from unexpected quarters. An emotional James Bias, Lenny's father, strongly criticized both Driesell and Slaughter for their failure to monitor the academic performance and drug abuse on the basketball team.[23] Slaughter's national credibility in the academic reform movement suffered a blow when it was reported that he circumvented standard admissions procedures in 1983 at the behest of Driesell to admit Terry Long, a promising player with a very weak academic record.[24] The university twice suspended Long, but somehow the player found his way back onto the basketball court each time. And Slaughter took further abuse from his own faculty when he ultimately disagreed with a task force chaired by a respected department head, Robert Dorfman, on its admissions recommendations. The university and its chancellor had reached a low point in their credibility and reputation; Slaughter was literally in no-man's land.

The beginning of the end started when Lefty was forced out. On October 29, 1986, four months after Lenny's death, Driesell resigned as basketball coach at College Park. He had coached for seventeen seasons, but he never won an NCAA championship, he never made it to the Final Four, and he won only one ACC championship, in 1984. Maryland never became the "UCLA of the East," as Lefty had promised Terrapin fans when he first arrived, but he was clearly a darling of the press. Lefty departed from Maryland with glowing praise from the media: the Duke University *Chronicle* said Maryland was making Lefty a scapegoat for problems it would have never addressed if Len Bias had not died; the *New York Times* editorialized that Lefty was only doing his job; and the *Washington Post* blathered on about how reporters cried when he left the press conference and about how many people were cheering for him.[25]

Slaughter had run off a popular coach, one with a down-home sense of humor and charisma. Before firing Driesell, Slaughter was decried by his numerous critics in the media and elsewhere as part of a corrupt system that exploited student-athletes and made a charade out of academic standards (even as he was criticized for not understanding college sports). After firing Driesell, Slaughter was amazingly accused of making the coach into the scapegoat. The athletic director, Dick Dull, had already been replaced. Though the student body and outside observers called for swift, drastic reforms, several of Slaughter's counterparts at other institutions praised his composure and supported the prudent, if slow, progress he had made in resolving an extremely complex situation.[26]

Slaughter replaced Lefty with an African American high school coach,

Bob Wade, from perennial powerhouse Dunbar High School in Baltimore. Here was the first black chancellor in the ACC now hiring the
first black basketball coach for the ACC team that had the first black
basketball player back in the 1950s. The news media and the boosters
ganged up on Slaughter: he took four months to fire Lefty, but he hired
a black high school coach in two days, they said; another columnist called
Slaughter "Lightning," a racially pejorative term evocative of the *Amos
'n' Andy* show. A Terrapin Club member was quoted as saying, "I damned
near fell out of my chair."[27]

In fact, however, the time Slaughter took to replace the coach and the
athletic director was not particularly long: when NC State dealt with the
equally complex Jimmy Valvano situation in 1989, Valvano remained as
coach for two seasons after the initial allegations were made and subsequent NCAA investigations began, although the existing chancellor resigned within a year, and this in spite of a local newspaper editor (Claude
Sitton of Raleigh's *News and Observer*) who ran stories criticizing Valvano or his program every day, without interruption, for over three
months during one period. Given the reality of tightly drawn coaching
contracts and the legitimate involvement of multiple parties, ranging
from the governor of the state to the head of the university system to the
various alumni and booster groups, it is unrealistic to believe that anyone can turn around a major athletic scandal in short order. Meanwhile,
the new coach, Bob Wade, had a predictably miserable first season, improved markedly the second, and then was found to be in violation of
NCAA rules during the third, another dismal season in terms of wins
and losses due to the departure of several players. By this time (spring
1989) Slaughter was at Occidental College and Wade was alone. The
coach was fired after his third season and the NCAA penalties followed,
taking the Terrapins out of live television for one season and out of the
NCAA tournament for two.[28]

THE PLEASURES OF DIVISION III

After Lefty Driesell left in the fall of 1986, Slaughter would make another of his emblematic lemonade-out-of-lemons observations: "I
emerged from this episode realizing that I had a thicker skin than I
thought." But he was also a changed man. He shaved his beard, leaving
only the mustache, as if he were trying to hide from the world, to change
his identity. He was tired of reading the sports pages. Before Bias had
died, the Washington chapter of B'nai B'rith had named Slaughter its

"Man of the Year" for 1986. But the dinner at which the award was to be presented was cancelled. It was never rescheduled.

Meanwhile, honors and praise piled up for Coach Driesell: he received fulsome praise in the media; the Maryland House of Delegates and the state senate gave Lefty a certificate of merit; fraternities on campus adored him; he was hired as a network color commentator for ACC games; there was an overflow crowd at a testimonial banquet. "They've got to pay me for eight years," Lefty remarked. "I'm going to collect my money. . . . I went to Duke. I'm not too dumb."[29] Indeed, Lefty had a good contract: because Maryland was committed to pay him $150,000 annually for eight years if he were fired, when James Madison University hired him as their basketball coach for $75,000, the University of Maryland had to pick up the remaining $75,000 as required in his contract.

As the university continued to come under attack, external entities made various inroads into Slaughter's power base: during much of 1987 and 1988, various politicians took advantage of the situation in College Park to propose a plan to modify the university's structure. System head John Toll designed a plan, with the governor's endorsement, to add six state colleges to the five-campus University of Maryland system. Many College Park faculty and administrators were critical of the plan, but the campus leadership was unable to address those concerns effectively because the Bias tragedy had eroded their power. It was time for Slaughter to move on.

In the spring of 1988, Occidental College approached John Slaughter with the alluring offer of a position as president. Richard Gilman, who had been Oxy's president since 1965, had retired, and the institution was seeking a president who understood the importance of a community with different cultures and traditions. For Slaughter, the timing was perfect; not only was he frustrated with the incessantly negative publicity of the last two years, he was also in the midst of wrangling with state education officials over serious funding reductions to the university.[30] An NCAA Division III institution, Occidental is a private liberal arts college in Los Angeles that promised Slaughter an environment free of the intense obsession with athletics and public scrutiny at Maryland. On April 1, 1988, Slaughter announced his plans to resign from his post at Maryland after five and a half years as chancellor.

He brought to Oxy his love for working with people, his resolute belief in inclusion, and his support for scholarship and research; eleven years later, he left the school as one of its most distinguished, praiseworthy leaders. Formerly a mostly white liberal arts school with a primarily white faculty, Occidental now admits freshman classes with almost one-half minority enrollment, and has 32 minority faculty members among a total of 160. Slaughter believes that his policies of diversity might have caused difficult changes at Occidental, but ultimately turned the college into a model for other institutions. Scholarship at Occidental also thrived under Slaughter; Occidental receives more applications than ever before and enjoys unprecedented praise for its academic rigor. Three Rhodes scholars have graduated from Occidental in the past decade, an outstanding record for such a small college. Emphasizing the contrast with College Park, Slaughter notes that at Occidental the policy is "teach or perish, not publish or perish." Walking across campus to the cafeteria for lunch, a visibly upset young woman stopped him to tell him about her car's broken windshield caused by an errant foul ball during an intramural softball game. Slaughter listened patiently and then consoled her and simply said, "Just send me a note and the bill. We'll take care of it." He then turned to his visitor and said, "That's the difference between Oxy and College Park."

MANAGERIAL AND PERSONAL STYLE

Slaughter was the embodiment of many of the changes he and others sought to bring to Maryland. A prominent black scientist who grew up in very modest surroundings, Slaughter possessed a broad range of knowledge in research and the humanities, impressive interpersonal skills, and the ability to communicate clearly and effectively. He had the potential to convince people that quality and equality could, and did, work together. Although he had a range of experiences and traits that prepared him for his new position, Slaughter also faced challenges that no one had faced before at College Park. Here was a man who had been educated in schools the U.S. Supreme Court described as having

> a tendency to [retard] the educational and mental development of Negro children and to deprive them of some of the benefits they would receive in a racial[ly] integrated school system. . . . To separate them from others of similar age and qualifications solely because of their race generates a feeling of inferiority as to their status in the community that may affect their hearts and minds in a way unlikely ever to be undone.

His former boss had told him that white engineers in the Navy would not want to work under him. But now he was the head of a largely white community of fifty thousand and he instinctively knew opposition was inevitable. After Slaughter's appointment, regents' president O'Malley received letters objecting to the university's hiring of a black chancellor, even from residents of Slaughter's own mostly white neighborhood, College Heights. Ted Lewis, president of nearby St. Mary's College, recounted a story of an encounter with a local judge who had graduated from Maryland with both undergraduate and law degrees. The two were at a dinner together, and as they discussed the new chancellor, the judge remarked, "We're on our way down. It's a damn shame."[31]

In spite of living through some trying situations during his life, Slaughter has a widely acknowledged ability to look at things in unusually positive ways. His former provost Brit Kirwan puts it this way:

> John has this wonderful way of looking at the world, a way of looking at things from all angles that says: "It's going to be OK, let's consider it from another perspective." Maybe this comes from being African-American and having the perspective of another culture. He also has a disarmingly warm personality and just after knowing him for a very short time, you feel like he's drawn you in. He makes you feel that he really cares for what you're saying. And he is able, in a very off-the-cuff, spontaneous way, to say useful things. He's very articulate. I'll never forget, very early on in his administration, the faculty members of the college of agriculture were very upset about something. We went to this very contentious meeting and John and I listened at first. He somehow found a way to say things at that meeting that didn't alter the administration's position, but instead put the problems on a different moral level, in a different light. The session ended in a remarkable degree of harmony.

Kirwan also describes Slaughter as "a person with an enormous amount of self-confidence, not in any kind of arrogant . . . way, but in a way that gives him some kind of reserve of inner strength." Slaughter constantly relied on this inner strength and sense of purpose, even in the face of bigotry and insensitivity. The personal style that Slaughter brought to the position of chancellor affected everyone from administrators such as Kirwan to the students and faculty. (Even though Kirwan was on track to become chancellor when Slaughter was hired, he and John became close friends and Slaughter came to rely on the younger Kirwan extensively.) Slaughter's secretary used to dread it when Slaughter would go walking on the campus because he would invite dozens of people to come see him, and they invariably would accept. In conversations, he would smile easily and naturally and would accentuate his remarks by repeating a person's first name, a trait that tends to bring an unusual level of personal warmth to the interaction. Maintaining such an intensely personal style was difficult in a large campus community, but Slaughter seemed determined that no individual would feel that his or her concerns were insignificant. William Thomas, who served as vice chancellor for student affairs under Slaughter, describes him as "a humanist right to the core of his soul."

In dealing with his colleagues, Slaughter was very disposed to delegate, particularly in the area of academics. He trusted Kirwan's judgment in this area implicitly. Charles Sturtz, vice chancellor for administration under Slaughter, describes Slaughter's style as "the most hands-off of any of the two governors and seven presidents I've served under." However, his closest associates also agree that Slaughter had an active interest in both student issues and athletics. If any issue reached his attention in which a student might have been treated improperly, he would take an interest in it. Thomas and Sturtz both cite Slaughter's accomplishments in the area of diversity as his most important work while at Maryland. According to Sturtz, the approaches that had been in place to foster greater diversity "weren't disasters, but they also weren't making a big difference. He took what was working [and built on it to] move us into a posture where the African-American community in this state and in this region accepted us as a legitimate institution trying to do the right thing." Thomas explains: "[Slaughter's] style and manner were absolutely facilitative in that effort. . . . John was so easy-going and comfortable talking about diversity issues that I think it really softened the edges of the issue around campus."

The hands-off style Sturtz describes allowed the vice chancellors to work relatively independently. Slaughter allowed them so much freedom that the four vice chancellors who served under him created what they called the "VP Four," meeting weekly to communicate and serving as a "shadow" cabinet to make routine decisions; in essence, they enacted a structure of their own when Slaughter left them to their own devices. Slaughter believed in trusting the administrators who worked for him, allowing them to carry out the responsibilities delegated to them without constant supervision, and he sought help in areas where he lacked the specific knowledge. Thomas says that "it was easy to work for John because it was an interpersonal kind of relationship . . . he hardly ever had any kind of anxiousness about business." Thomas also notes that Slaughter "was not very much into feedback." Other members of Slaughter's staff described him as "a superb listener, a demanding but compassionate boss, and a man quick to laugh and slow to become angry."[32]

However, several former associates suggest that Slaughter's tendency to delegate, in addition to his many external, off-campus activities, contributed to some of the problems with athletics that surfaced after the death of star basketball player Lenny Bias; athletic director Dick Dull was given a great deal of autonomy, both in academic and athletic policy making. One example was the ten-year contract given to basketball coach Lefty Driesell seven months before Bias died in June of 1986. According to Sturtz, regulations should have required Slaughter's signature on such a contract, but he "supposedly knew nothing about it." This contract caused tremendous problems and great expense when Slaughter forced Driesell to resign from coaching and reassigned him to an assistant athletic director position under an eight-year, $1.1 million contract renegotiated from the coaching contract. However, the new contract was pursuant to Driesell's staying at Maryland, and he left within a year. Reflecting on the contract, Slaughter later conceded, "I should have had a great deal more insight into that picture."[33]

CONCLUSIONS

Slaughter left the University of Maryland a hotly contested and controversial leader. His gifts of thoughtfulness, deliberation, and slow but purposeful action, which had won him accolades elsewhere, exasperated one public demanding swift action (and perhaps more righteous indignation) while another group demanded that the coach stay and the chancellor be fired. In some ways, the Bias episode and Slaughter's saga underscore the explosiveness of modern-day college athletics and the absence of any real options: one either lives the lie or moves on to a college that competes at the NCAA's Division III level, where athletic grants-in-aid do not exist and where the amazing forces of sports commercialism are absent.

In spite of his treatment in comparison to the departing coach, Slaughter could have survived a few more years at College Park. Given more time, Slaughter could probably have overcome the criticism and the stigma of scandal, but the challenge of fighting both racism and the intense NCAA Division I sports culture convinced him to accept the presidency at Occidental College. His effectiveness as a leader and his potential for further improvements to Maryland's culture of inclusion and social justice were ended prematurely by the athletics scandal. He moved on after five and one-half years to fight another day at Occidental and to continue to leave his imprint on education and opportunity for minority students in the sciences in particular. Time has vindicated Slaughter's prudence and restraint; though he was faulted in 1986 and 1987, many observers now praise his deliberate decisions.

His experiences at Maryland transformed his world and also his views about athletics and academia. He still "loves" University of Maryland athletics and follows Terrapin games from Los Angeles, occasionally listening to play-by-play broadcasts on the Internet. But he has changed fundamentally his views about the relationship between intercollegiate sports and access to education. "I have come to reject the idea that a young person with bad grades is given a meaningful opportunity by Division I sports. I just don't believe it anymore, because I have seen the truth of it. If you take kids who are not prepared to compete academically, then you are hurting the university and you are hurting them. Big-time college sports have ruined lots of minority kids under the false promise that athletics was their ticket out of their situations."

NOTES

1. Sue A. Pressley, "U-Md. Crisis Spurs Debate on Slaughter Leadership," *Washington Post*, October 27, 1986, sec. A.

2. "Slaughter Resigns," *Washington Post*, April 2, 1988.

3. Nell I. Painter, *Exodusters: Black Migration to Kansas After Reconstruction* (New York: Alfred A. Knopf, 1977).

4. John Hope Franklin and Loren Schweninger, *Runaway Slaves: Rebels on the Plantation* (New York: Oxford University Press, 1999).

5. C. Fraser Smith, *Lenny, Lefty, and the Chancellor* (Baltimore: Bancroft Press, 1992), 68.

6. One older sister was adopted by the Slaughters' parents.

7. U.S. Department of Commerce, Bureau of the Census, Current Population Reports, Series P-60, *Money Income of Families and Persons in the United States*, nos. 105 and 157; *Money Income of Households, Families, and Persons in the United States*, nos. 162, 174, and 180; and *Money Income and Poverty Status in the United States*, nos. 166 and 168. U.S. Department of Labor, Bureau of Labor Statistics, Consumer Price Index. Information is compiled at http://www.ed.gov/pubs/YouthIndicators/indtab14.html.

8. Clayborne Carson et al., eds., *Eyes on the Prize: America's Civil Rights Years* (New York: Penguin Books, 1987).

9. Smith, *Lenny, Lefty and the Chancellor*, 28. Byrd was once quoted as saying, "If we don't do something about it [integration], we're going to have to accept Negroes at College Park, where our girls are."

10. Ibid.

11. John B. Slaughter, "Making a Difference," Inauguration Speech, University of Maryland at College Park, May 3, 1983.

12. Bill Brubaker and Mark Asher, "Crisis in College Park," *Washington Post*, July 6, 1986, sec. A.

13. Ibid.

14. Mark Asher and Sally Jenkins, "Slaughter Endorses Concept of Task Force Proposals," *Washington Post*, October 22, 1986, sec. D.

15. For example, see UNC Board of Governors, "Intercollegiate Athletics in Fifteen Institutions of the University of North Carolina: Report of the Special Committee on Intercollegiate Athletics," Chapel Hill, October 11, 1985.

16. Barbara Bergmann, "Do Sports Really Make Money for the University?" *Academe* 77, no. 1 (1991): 28–30.

17. "Bias Player of the Year," *Washington Post*, March 6, 1986.

18. Mark Asher, "Dull Tells Driesell: We're All Behind You," *Washington Post*, June 22, 1986, sec. B.

19. Carl Bode, "An All-Out Defense of the University of Maryland," *Washington Post*, June 20, 1986, sec. D.

20. Bill Brubaker, "Bias: Much Pressure, Little Relief," *Washington Post*, June 22, 1986, sec. B; and Asher, "We're All Behind You."

21. Similar events transpired at NC State, Georgia, Florida, Southern Methodist, and Kentucky, for example.

22. Pressley, "U-Md. Crisis."

23. Sally Jenkins, "Chancellor Accepts Criticism," *Washington Post*, August 30, 1986, sec. D.

24. "Slaughter Aided Long's Admission," *Washington Post*, September 7, 1986, sec. D.

25. Smith, *Lenny, Lefty, and the Chancellor*, 221; John Feinstein, "For Lefty, a Sad Farewell," *Washington Post*, November 2, 1986.

26. Pressley, "U-Md. Crisis."

27. Smith, *Lenny, Lefty, and the Chancellor*, 227–228.

28. D. Nakamura and M. Asher, "10 Years Later, Bias' Death Still Resonates," *Washington Post*, June 19, 1996.

29. Smith, *Lenny, Lefty, and the Chancellor*, 238–239.

30. Amy Goldstein, "Slaughter to Quit U-Maryland Post," *Washington Post*, April 2, 1988.

31. Smith, *Lenny, Lefty, and the Chancellor*, 78.

32. Pressley, "U-Md. Crisis."

33. Mark Asher and Sally Jenkins, "Driesell Ousted as Maryland Coach," *Washington Post*, October 30, 1986, sec. A.

William Gordon Bowen. *Photo by Nat Clymer, Kingston, New Jersey.*

CHAPTER 9

Bowen's Beautiful Mind

I had a child at Princeton when Bowen became president; he paid about $7,000 a year. I have a child there when Bowen's leaving; she's paying about $18,000. A boy when he came; a girl when he leaves. That tells the story better than anything else, I think.
—Brendan Byrne, former governor of New Jersey

The College of New Jersey—Princeton University's original name— was initially housed entirely within Nassau Hall. An American Versailles, the three-story Nassau Hall was the largest stone building in the thirteen colonies when it was completed in 1756. And it was in the president's office at 1 Nassau Hall on a Sunday in late summer of 1984 that William Gordon Bowen received a call from his vice president for facilities, Eugene McPartland.[1] McPartland was upset about the delivery of the wrong bricks for the $29 million Lewis Thomas Molecular Biological Laboratories, then in the early stages of construction. Not only had the bricks been delivered late, said McPartland, they were also the wrong color and the wrong surface.

"It was very important for us to get the correct bricks," Bowen recalled, and "we were already behind schedule for other reasons." Unless the building's exterior could be finished before the approaching winter, the work on the inside would be delayed until spring. This delay would have made it more difficult for Princeton to accommodate several distinguished scholars who had been recruited to lead a new molecular biol-

ogy program; the state-of-the-art Thomas Laboratories was a vital in-
centive in attracting these individuals. There were visual and aesthetic
concerns as well, because the architect, Robert Venturi was trying
valiantly to make the boxy, rectangular building look attractive within
severe budgetary and physical site constraints. "The wrong bricks simply
would not work because their color and their shape were important for
the overall look," recalled Bowen.

Somehow the bricks had been obtained from a brick manufacturer located across the country in Salt Lake City, Utah. So Bowen immediately
called John Kenefick, the vice chairman of the Princeton board of
trustees, to see if he could help in his role as head of the Union Pacific
Railroad.

> I just figured right after McPartland's call that John [Kenefick] would
> be able to help us because of his Union Pacific connections and also
> because he was in the West coast and closer to the bricks. Why the
> bricks came from Salt Lake is another story. . . . It turned out that
> Kenefick was watching his niece, Joan Benoit, run the marathon in
> the Los Angeles Olympics, so we had to call all over the place be-
> fore we finally tracked him down. And he was of course immediately
> helpful and then some.

Kenefick tried first to reach the president of the brick company, but he
refused to speak with him and instead had a sales representative call him.
The snub upset Kenefick to no end, but he discovered that the Salt Lake
brick company was in fact owned by a larger holding entity whose chairman he knew well.

"Needless to say, there was a dramatic shift in attitudes as soon as John
spoke with his friend who owned the company; the brick company president was suddenly exceptionally helpful." The manufacturer stopped all
his other projects and fired up a new batch of bricks for the building, the
Thomas Labs, this time the closer to the correct color and texture. But
amazingly, this is not the end of story.

This second batch of bricks was still not quite right: the color contrast between the bricks and the other elements of the building was more
than the architect Bob Venturi was willing to live with. To complicate
matters even further, the architect was vacationing in Geneva, Switzer-
land, at the time, and the Princeton officials had to express mail several
bricks for him to inspect in Europe. As Venturi noted, "I'm sure the custom agents must have wondered what was inside the bricks. The university was on a tight schedule and could have gone ahead. Fortunately,
Princeton is a wise and understanding client."[2] Even with the brick

manufacturer's newly found diligence, making the new bricks still took several more weeks, so Kenefick very helpfully arranged for the speedy delivery of the bricks to the East coast through his train connections. The bricks finally got to New Jersey and the new molecular biology laboratory building was completed fairly close to the original schedule. Bowen still keeps two of the (correct) bricks in his office at the Mellon Foundation. The story illustrates not only Bowen's well-known capacity for amazing hard work but also his careful attention to important details in an organizational environment such as Princeton's where this level of activity is possible.

EARLY LIFE

William Gordon Bowen was born on October 6, 1933, in Cincinnati, Ohio, where he lived until he went to college. He was the only child of Albert A. Bowen of Indianapolis, Indiana, and Bernice Pomert Bowen of South Bend, Indiana. Albert Bowen, a native of Indianapolis, Indiana, was a salesman for the National Cash Register Company (NCR) whose work was centered in Cincinnati. Bowen's mother, Bernice Pomert Bowen, was raised in South Bend, Indiana, and was a homemaker until late in her life when, because of economic necessity, she became a dorm "mother." The Pomerts and the Bowens were mid-westerners of Celtic and German ancestry. Neither of his parents was a college graduate although Albert attended college "for a year or two, but that was about it." Bowen's father sold cash registers to local supermarkets and bars and similar establishments and traveled extensively for his job around Ohio and Indiana when Bill was young; Bill recalls growing up with cash registers in the back of the family car.

Bowen attended public school in Wyoming, Ohio (a suburb of Cincinnati) and excelled as a student and an athlete at a young age. Cincinnati in the early 1950s was a real tennis hotbed, led by native Tony Trabert, who was a local hero to youngsters like Bill Bowen. Trabert, a member of the International Tennis Hall of Fame and winner of titles at all four tennis majors, is easily the greatest sports figure to come out of Cincinnati. The year Bowen finished at Wyoming High School, on Pendery Avenue in the northern suburbs of Cincinnati, Trabert won the NCAA championship in 1951 across town at the University of Cincinnati. Bowen, who was an Ohio Conference tennis champion while at playing for the Big Red of Denison University, has continued to play tennis since those days. While president at Princeton, Bowen enjoyed regular indoor tennis matches for twenty-five years in the bowels of the

Jadwin Gymnasium with Princeton's legendary basketball coach Pete Carril, who coached there from 1967 to 1996; he remains the only Division I coach to record five hundred wins (525–273) without the benefit of athletic scholarships for his players.

Wyoming High School, with unusually small classes for a public school in a large city, provided a supportive faculty and a close-knit student body; Bowen's graduating class in June of 1951 numbered just fifty students, including Bowen's wife-to-be, Mary Ellen Maxwell. The Wyoming school was located in an area known for its excellent schools and consistently ranked among the top five school districts in Ohio. It also had a very diverse student population, with a sizable black population and striking socioeconomic diversity, ranging from lower middle class kids like Bill to the children of Procter and Gamble executives. This school environment perhaps influenced Bowen's lifelong concern with equality of opportunity and affirmative action, as well as his healthy respect for diversity. He speaks very casually, almost uncomfortably, about his academic talents: "I was just a good student . . . it didn't require money, it just required a little work, and it was fun. I liked to learn." Even as a high school student with few ambitions for the future, Bowen discovered that he possessed a capacity for leadership. "I was president of my high school class. I was later also president of student government at Denison. I just had a history of being in charge of things, who knows why. . . . I always enjoyed writing and my debate experiences in high school helped me with my public speaking immensely." His developing skills and talents already showed multiple dimensions: he clearly enjoyed being around people, excelled at tennis, enjoyed debating and the art of persuasion, and he had the capacity and energy to work hard to achieve his goals. Most of all, he seemed to have a very positive outlook, taking setbacks in stride.

His interest in math at Wyoming High intersected with his athletic skills: the school's excellent math teacher was also the school's tennis coach and "he got me started with tennis." Eventually Bowen would be ranked second among high school tennis players in Ohio and his athletic skills, as well as his academic record, caught the eye of a Denison English professor, Tristram Coffin, who doubled as the institution's tennis coach.

> I was very fortunate. A real turning point for me was that I won the Gardner Board and Carton Company Scholarship, provided by a paper company in Cincinnati. It was the only scholarship we had in Cincinnati. It was, by the standards of that time, a pretty generous

award, $500 a year. And it also promised a summer job, so I worked
in the paper mills in the summer. The scholarship, combined with
some help Denison gave me, allowed me to go to Denison. One of
my teachers in high school had been a big fan of Denison. She
thought Denison was a great school, and she had urged me to think
about going to Denison. I was fortunate to have this help from some
excellent teachers because neither of my parents knew very much
about this stuff.

But tragedy also struck in Bowen's senior year of high school (fall of
1950) when his father died of emphysema and left the family with no
source of income. "My father was a big smoker all his life. I watched him
die and I never smoked because I saw what it did to him." In order to survive economically, Bill's mother was forced to take a job as a dorm mother
at the University of Cincinnati. "It was traumatic, a disaster for us. My
family had nothing, no money, zero resources." Bowen continued his education after high school out of his own desire, not because of any pressure at home. Bowen's mother was always supportive, "terrific," but he
recalls that she "never pushed and didn't really understand what I did as
a professor. How could she? She had no experience in any of it. When I
started publishing books, I would give her copies and she would just smile
and say, 'Oh, this is nice.' She had no idea what any of it was about." But
Bernice Bowen was a survivor, and her spirit of perseverance is reflected
in her son's matter-of-fact, unflappable approach to challenges. In spite
of relatively difficult situations growing up, Bowen appears genuinely
comfortable with his lot in life; he also seems comfortable with the ambiguity and uncertainties life presented him. "I never really felt imposed
upon by my circumstances, ever. I always felt I was fortunate and that I'd
been dealt a good hand. The fact that we had fewer resources than most
people never struck me as consequential. It wasn't consequential in my
life." Bowen speaks casually, almost dismissively, about his abilities as a
leader. Yet, a considered examination of Bowen's pre-Princeton years
shows that Bowen exhibited trademarks of gifted leadership even at an
early age. Like the other leaders profiled in this book, Bowen learned early
on to face hardships with poise and grace, developing a resilient personality in the process. He demonstrated unusually advanced personal and
communications skills and formed supportive relationships with excellent
mentors who were attracted to him; and he worked consistently to develop strong communication skills through his debate team activities and
writing skills under the tutelage of good teachers.

COLLEGE IN GRANVILLE, OHIO: DENISON UNIVERSITY

Denison is a small, midwestern college located in Granville, Ohio, about twenty-five miles east of Columbus and two hours northeast of Cincinnati, close enough to Bowen's home so he could maintain close contact with his recently widowed mother. When Bowen arrived for his freshman year in September of 1951 there were some twelve hundred students working toward degrees in a wide variety of strong undergraduate programs. The $500 Gardner Board and Carton Company Scholarship he had won, plus the guaranteed summer job in the paper mills and financial aid from Denison, provided the financial help that enabled Bowen to attend. At Denison Bowen continued to participate in a range of activities. Along with his roommate and lifelong friend David Bayley, later a dean at SUNY-Albany, he was a resident advisor in an undergraduate dorm. "We were responsible for a couple hundred undergraduates during our junior and senior years." He won the Ohio Conference tennis championships and his senior year he was elected president of student government.

Bowen's most important mentor at Denison was economics professor Leland J. Gordon, a well-known consumer economist who taught at Denison for thirty-two years and chaired the economics department while Bowen studied there. He guided Bowen through his first attempt at serious academic research: a four-hundred-page senior thesis on the Council of Economic Advisers that is cited occasionally by scholars interested in the history of the council. Gordon saw exceptional talent in Bowen and encouraged him to consider college teaching as a career. He coaxed him to apply to Princeton, where he knew Richard Lester, one of the nation's most distinguished labor economists. Gordon retired from Denison in 1963, but only after his former students created an endowment in his honor to fund awards for the best honors projects in economics at Denison each year.

Bowen's undergraduate studies were broad and comprehensive, reflecting Bowen's preference for broader perspectives, for a more global way to look at the world: he studied a mix of economics, mathematics, and history. Gordon, like Clark Kerr, was really an institutional economist, and this is essentially what Bowen studied as an undergraduate, an amalgam of economics with a broad base from other disciplines. "Denison was a wonderful environment for me. I liked the academic setting— very flexible yet very demanding—and I was fortunate to have great teachers like Leland Gordon who also had wider contacts in the larger academic community."

A PH.D. FROM PRINCETON

Bill Bowen's enrollment at Princeton in the fall of 1955 was the result, again, of a series of personal connections and unplanned situations that would continue to emerge in his life. Gordon, his Denison mentor, was "best friends with Dick Lester, a very well-known labor economist at that time, who was the head of the Industrial Relations Section at Princeton. And Princeton, then as now, had exceptional strength and resources in labor economics. It had a specially endowed Section; it had excellent faculty and students; it was a major place in industrial relations and labor economics, areas of great interest to me." Princeton and the Ivy League were a long way from Cincinnati and from Denison; all of it required serious adjustment by Bowen. "It was a tremendous change and I wasn't at all sure I was up to it. People from all over the world were there. Everybody else had gone to Harvard and Yale or wherever. . . . But as it turns out I did just fine." Quickly Bowen would realize that Princeton's personable faculty and small student body would offset the intimidation he initially felt. It was a "high-powered place but it was also small"; his entering cohort in the Ph.D. economics program was composed of only twelve students. For the first time in his life, because he held a Woodrow Wilson Fellowship and a Danforth Fellowship, Bowen didn't have to worry about money. He continued dating his hometown girlfriend, Mary Ellen Maxwell, after leaving Denison and they were married a year after Bill entered graduate school, on August 25, 1956. Mary Ellen earned a master's degree in library science at Rutgers and worked as a librarian until their first child was born.

Again, wonderful professors and great mentors became part of his life. Bowen completed his Ph.D. in three years (his dissertation, supervised by Richard Lester, was titled "The Wage-Price Issue: A Theoretical Analysis," published by the Princeton Press in 1960). He worked under the guidance of two of the world's most famous economists, Jacob Viner and William Baumol. Viner was a renowned economic theorist at the University of Chicago, a "Renaissance scholar, if there has ever been one," who had joined the Princeton faculty 1946 and taught there for fourteen years. An exceedingly bright and witty person, Viner was unsparingly willing to give freely of his time to help young people like Bowen do their work. At Princeton, Viner generally taught two classes, both at the graduate level, one on international trade and another on the history of economic doctrines. His "History of Thought" lectures were widely recognized as extraordinary tours de force with amazing scholarly range. The end of the semester arrived much too quickly for students invariably awed by Viner's impeccable scholarship; Bowen recalls being especially interested in how he brought diverse elements from other disciplines to bear upon discussions.

Bill Baumol, Bowen's other academic mentor at Princeton, was also a famous and "simply brilliant" economic theorist and expositor. Jacob Viner would go around saying about Baumol: "I found this genius in the basement of the London School of Economics!" A Brooklyn College graduate, Baumol was born in an area of the Bronx now known as Fort Apache, and had served as president of the American Economic Association. He is easily one of most prolific economic scholars in that discipline, with thirty books and over five hundred articles to his credit. He had a particular influence on Bowen's intellectual development. "He really helped me learn how to focus on the important things, abstract the big issues from all the surrounding shrubbery." Baumol taught economic theory, emphasizing focused, incisive thinking that was based on mastery of fundamental concepts and logical, rational argument.

> It was an incredibly powerful learning experience. He would ask us to go to the blackboard and define a demand curve, beginning with the words "A demand curve is . . ." and you didn't get away from the blackboard until you finished the sentence; or he would ask us to go home and write a four-page paper explaining in layman's language what some paragraph from J.R. Hicks meant. This is the way the course was taught, an incredibly powerful learning experience. We are to this day closest friends.

Baumol and Bowen would later collaborate on a book, *Performing Arts: The Economic Dilemma*, published in 1966.

EARLY CAREER

After finishing his dissertation in the spring of 1958, a time of great shortages of college professors, Bowen received attractive offers to teach at various universities, including MIT and UC-Berkeley, but decided to stay at Princeton because of the close working relationships he had cultivated with professors in the Industrial Relations Section, which presented him an attractive combination of teaching and research. "When I was at Denison, I wanted to be a college teacher, thinking I would teach at a place like Denison. But after experiencing Princeton's culture of scholarship, I knew I wanted to be a university professor. I found out serious research could be fun. I enjoyed the combination of research and writing, as well as the teaching. But the key always is that I had great teachers and great colleagues." Bowen was a creative researcher and a phenomenal writer; between 1960 and 1969, he published ten books on topics ranging from the economics of the performing arts to the economics of major private universities, the latter a project that Clark Kerr had commissioned as part of the Carnegie Commission. During the same period, he also published thirteen articles and fourteen book chapters.[3] Bowen also taught the beginning economics course, Economics 101, which he continued to teach all through his tenure as president.

Given Bowen's traits and emerging talents for leadership—his rapid ascent in the faculty ranks (he was easily among the youngest tenured and youngest full professors in Princeton's history), his interpersonal skills, his distinguished faculty mentors, his personal attitude toward challenges and his perseverance, his abilities in the realm of communication, his physical stamina and gargantuan work ethic, and his increasing familiarity with the workings of the university—it was only a matter of time before he became involved in the Princeton administration through what he calls "an odd series of accidents." In 1962, the leader of the Industrial Relations Section in the department of economics left Princeton on academic leave and then his replacement fell ill, so Bowen was asked to become the acting director of the Section. A year later, the Woodrow Wilson School of Public and International Affairs received a huge gift to create a graduate program in public policy, a tremendous opportunity for that school. Gardner Patterson, another economist and the first director of the Woodrow Wilson School, asked (or as Bowen described it, "dragooned") Bowen to become the director of the graduate program. Then, in 1967, President Bob Goheen decided to create the position of provost, or chief academic officer (and deputy to the president), which Princeton had never had. Even though the young Bowen had only been a member of the faculty for nine years, Goheen tapped him for the job.

Bowen accepted the provost's job reluctantly and only after discussing his reservations with Goheen. In particular, Bowen strongly disagreed with Princeton's male-only admissions policy, and he made his position clear to the president from the start. Bob Goheen was a product of the old Princeton system: his grandfather, an uncle, and his brother had all graduated from Princeton. The son of a Presbyterian medical missionary working in India, where Goheen was born and raised, he attended Princeton during the late 1930s. Goheen was a distinguished student and athlete, winning the M. Taylor Pyne Prize his senior year in 1940, the highest honor conferred upon an undergraduate at Princeton. But in spite of this difference with Bowen, Goheen decided he wanted him anyway, offering Bill the job but at the same time asking that any disagreement about the admissions topic be discussed in private between the two of them. Bowen agreed and recalled that he was greatly impressed at the time that Goheen would actually welcome such diversity of opinion within his administrative team.

> That's an important aspect of leadership: the ability to disagree and to not regard it as personal, and to not have it get in the way of friendship and affection and ability to work together on a host of things. A lesson I learned early, perhaps as far back as high school, was that you could disagree respectfully and for good reasons. If you're surrounded only with people like you and who think like you, you're not going to get a lot done.

Bowen assumed the office of provost at a "pivotal time" in Princeton's development as a university. Coeducation, the enrollment of minority students, the development of the graduate program, the student protests during Vietnam, and the university's antiquated budgeting methods were the principal problems that Bowen had to address during his tenure.

THE PRINCETON BUDGET

Princeton has always been one of the "Big Three" Ivy League schools, the other two of course being Harvard and Yale. But it is also quite different in both tradition and in size. Princeton, for example, does not have the professional schools present at other national universities, like schools of law, medicine, or business. It does have a distinguished engineering program, as well as architecture and public affairs, but these are well integrated into the general arts and sciences. It thus has a single faculty, chaired by the president, and this is a crucial distinction in the coherence of Princeton's organization. (The president also presides at trustee meetings, another important factor contributing to the greater power and control of a private university president.) Bart Giamatti, former president of Yale, described the differences like this: If things go wrong at Harvard, a national committee would be created to discuss why Harvard was not first and how much money was needed to get to the top. At Yale, the faculty would convene; the professors would blame themselves, confess their failing, and vow to work harder. At Princeton, two men would go for a long walk after lunch.[4]

From Princeton's inception until Bowen arrived in Nassau Hall, the notion of a central university budget did not exist because the various divisions and departments made their financial decisions more or less independently. The setting of tuition and fees, for example, was not systematically related to faculty salary needs or other program requirements. To be sure, Princeton's financial condition was relatively solid, the result of an endowment built up over the decades by good financial planners. But the system was still "broken," according to Bowen, and required fixing—the institution had in fact been running small annual deficits when Bowen assumed the presidency. In fact, the need for better financial management was partly behind the selection of Bowen, an economist who had already published several pieces on the economics of universities. One of Bowen's first projects as provost was to impose some order or rationality on the idiosyncratic budgetary process. One early but fundamental problem was that the university's priorities, and the financial means for satisfying them, were unclear. Bowen established (and chaired) a standing Priorities Committee to clarify the university's goals and then to develop and modify the university's budget accordingly. All stakeholders in the budgeting process were represented on this committee—faculty, staff, students, and administrators. "What should we do? What's most important?" These were the questions that Bowen posed to his new committee.

Now something of a fixture at Princeton, the Priorities Committee sparked much discussion both within Princeton and in institutions around the nation when it was first established. In a tribute to Bowen's work, the American Council on Education mailed copies of Princeton's impressive report on finances to all of its member institutions in the United States in 1969. In some settings, the process adopted by Princeton could have led to infighting among diverse claimants of resources. At Princeton, however, the Priorities Committee added transparency and order to a process previously characterized by secrecy and irrationality. Far from being a handicap, the diversity of interests reflected in the committee's membership was, in Bowen's view, its "great virtue." Under the skillful mediation of Richard Spies, later Princeton's financial vice president, all of the university's stakeholders came together, aired their disagreements, and arrived at compromises. The Priorities Committee put into practice what Bowen had learned from Bob Goheen about constructive disagreement. "It forced accommodation and reconciliation, and it worked."

But the nature of universities, their labor intensiveness in particular, means that there are always inexorable forces tending to increase costs.

Even under the most efficient of managerial regimes, it is difficult to
wring out increasingly greater productivity gains in areas of intense
human interaction such as teaching and mentoring. Thus, Bowen
worked, first as provost and five years later as president, to reduce spending in staff positions and trim back on certain operational expenses such
as general maintenance, while at the same time embarking on lucrative
real estate projects such as the Forrestal Center on Route 1 near the main
campus and the sale of Palmer Square. He also became more aggressive
in fund-raising activities.[5] Princeton's endowment was $625 million in
1972, the year he became president, but it more than tripled to over $2
billion by 1987. Annual giving quadrupled during his presidency and,
amazingly, nearly two of every three Princeton graduates donated money
to the university, a ratio that remained unchanged in spite of a significant increase in the total number of alumni. Bowen, with his tireless work
habits, became out of necessity one of the first major president-fundraisers
among college presidents, and the funds he helped raise funded a remarkable number of projects.[6]

RUINING A FINE COUNTRY CLUB, AGAIN

For two centuries, Princeton was all male, even as educational opportunities for women were opening up across the nation in other formerly
all-male institutions. The topic of coeducation at Princeton was not an
easy one to broach. Many influential and conservative Princeton alumni
were bitterly opposed to the idea, but in a front-page article in the student newspaper, The Daily Princetonian, in May of 1967, President Goheen stated the obvious: "It is inevitable that, at some point in the future,
Princeton is going to move into the education of women. The only questions now are those of strategy, priority, and timing."

A faculty committee, headed by Woodrow Wilson School dean and
economics professor Gardner Patterson, was created shortly thereafter to
consider the "desirability and feasibility of Princeton entering significantly into the education of women at the undergraduate level." It fell
to Bill Bowen, as provost, to be the principal representative of the administration on the committee and to integrate the ethical and organizational arguments in favor of coeducation with a research-based analysis
of its financial feasibility. He had the task of convincing some people not
easily convinced at the time "that this could be done both socially and
more importantly, economically, and that coeducation was achievable
and that the university would be helped, not hurt, by the process." The
Patterson Committee published its findings one year later, in September

of 1968, in a report entitled, "The Education of Women at Princeton: A Special Report." Exhaustive in its detail and comprehensive in its scope, the fifty-six-page report analyzed the impact of coeducation from every angle—from the university's reputation, to faculty recruitment, to social life. With Bowen's research on the economics and a Ford Foundation grant, the Patterson Committee concluded that "considerably more undergraduate students can benefit from the presence of more or less the same senior faculty and graduate student populations. . . . Indeed, we believe the addition of 1,000 women undergraduates would . . . confer educational benefits on the undergraduate programs which would far outweigh any disadvantages resulting from the broader sharing of our present strengths."[7] Opening the doors of Princeton to women, a decision that today seems straightforward and obvious, was not so obvious to some of Bowen's colleagues and more than a few trustees and alumni in the late 1960s. While more and more academics at Princeton agreed that women should in theory be included in Princeton's student body, many people expressed concerns that admitting women would necessitate unreasonable increases in the university's endowment. "Nobody was prepared to let the male enrollment go down," recalled Bowen, yet at the same time none of the professors was willing to compromise Princeton's traditional strengths—small class sizes and closely directed senior theses.

Critics were fixated on the average cost per student of admitting women, however. Bowen ultimately won them over with his research by shifting the focus to the marginal economic costs of coeducation—the term economists use for the incremental costs and incremental revenues that the university could expect for each additional student admitted: due to declining average costs, each additional woman student would bring in more revenue than it would cost to educate her. The compelling economics of coeducation had trumped the comforts of tradition and the status quo. Any residual social resistance to coeducation slowly melted away once the first group of female students was admitted. One alumnus, a staunch opponent of Princeton's transition to coeducation, attended a meeting of Princeton's first female cohort and heard some of the women students speak about their dreams and their plans. He turned to Bowen and quietly said: "You know, Mr. Bowen, it was very easy for me to be against coeducation. It's impossible for me to be against Laurie Watson. . . . Once he saw it, not in the abstract, but in terms of the young women who were there, the alumnus gave up."

One hundred forty-eight women, one hundred first year students and forty-eight transfers, began classes at Princeton in September of 1969. Dozens of newspapers and magazines ran stories on what the Princeton women wore or how their first days went, and practically every woman student was featured in her hometown newspaper. A *New York Times* article in December of 1969 reported the inclusion of women in Princeton's formerly all-male-in-drag chorus line, a century-old event that concludes the shows of the Triangle Club, the university's comedy troupe; to dramatize the historical occasion, a photo of Princeton alumnus F. Scott Fitzgerald in drag during a 1914 Triangle Club show was included.[8]

As provost and as president Bowen worked to change the social environment at Princeton and to recruit qualified students from all sorts of backgrounds. For much of the nineteenth and twentieth centuries, Princeton had a great deal in common with the clubby and elitist university caricaturized by Fitzgerald in *This Side of Paradise*. Making Princeton's undergraduate culture more egalitarian was one of Bowen's principal objectives during his tenure. In an important sense, Bowen, a first-generation college student, a Midwesterner who had graduated from a small Ohio college, embodied change. One of the symbolic elements of elitism and exclusivity were Princeton's eating clubs, mostly located on Prospect Street. The eating clubs were closed social circles for elite upperclassmen, originally established in the mid-1800s due to inadequate eating facilities for students on campus. With names like Tower, Ivy, Tiger Inn, and Cap and Gown, over the years the clubs had come to dominate campus life and its social hierarchy, choosing their members through a selective "bicker" process. While it is an exaggeration to say, as an older alumnus remarked, that "you either joined one of the clubs or you ate in your dorm room"—there were always boarding houses and other places where students could eat—the clubs were divisive and hurtful, particularly to those young people not selected in this relatively self-contained, small-campus environment. By the 1960s, however, Princeton students themselves were generating enough pressure to help break the social monopoly of the eating clubs, making many of these organizations "open," meaning that students could select the eating club they would join rather than the other way around. As president, Bowen also created the residential college system for freshmen and sophomores, another step toward democratizing student life at Princeton and breaking its historic social order. Most clubs have changed with the times and today admit women and encourage faculty-student interactions, although a few continue to retain traditional behaviors of selectivity.[9]

A related effort, carried forward in spite of conservative alumni opposition, was Bowen's emphasis on assembling a more diverse student body. Before the 1970s, Princeton admitted mainly white Anglo-Saxon males and virtually no African Americans or women and there were actual quotas for Jewish and Catholic students, as was true in other Ivy League universities. Bowen's sustained commitment to diversity in education, perhaps rooted in his days at Wyoming High School, recently manifested itself in the publication of a book cowritten with former Harvard president Derek Bok, *The Shape of the River*, which was cited prominently in the recent Supreme Court decision upholding the constitutional of affirmative action.[10] Mindful about Princeton's historic affiliation with the Presbyterians, Bowen nonetheless paid close attention to the admission of Jewish students. Bowen, who was neither Jewish nor particularly religious, worked with the dean of the Princeton Chapel and with the Episcopal bishop of Massachusetts to create nondenominational services that would appeal to students of all religious traditions. He was assisted in this effort by Neil L. Rudenstine, who was recruited by president Goheen from Harvard's English department to be dean of students at Princeton; Rudenstine would become Bowen's closest associate in the administration. Later the provost during most of Bowen's presidency and a 1956 Princeton graduate from Connecticut, Rudenstine recalls that the opposition from the Conservative Alumni for Princeton (CAP) group, which was well-organized and even published a newsletter, was intense. "It was at times an all-out battle, and Bill took it head on. But he never raised the stakes or acted in any way that would divide the university. He was always positive and responsive, and, in spite of some heated opposition, was never argumentative or defensive." Throughout his career, Bowen seemed to have a knack for coming up with the right phrase: "We were, in an important sense, united by our differences. This was a recurring theme that I would emphasize, with coeducation, with faculty issues, and with conservative alumni: united by our differences."

INSIDE THE UNIVERSITY:
TWO PRESIDENTS AND TWO PROVOSTS

William Bowen differed from many of his peers at other major universities in the personal attention he devoted to faculty recruitment, a managerial pattern facilitated by Princeton's relatively small scale, the absence of professional schools, and its single faculty chaired by the president, as well as Bowen's almost boundless personal energy. The academic departments, of course, play a critical role in faculty recruitment, but Bowen also recognized that in some cases a department might not be able to attract an outstanding candidate without support from the president's office or presidential promises of funding, personnel, and equipment. The story of Princeton's molecular biology department best

illustrates Bowen's approach to faculty recruitment, as well as his notorious attention to detail.

When Bowen set about looking for a chairman of the university's fledg-
ling molecular biology department in the early 1980s, he personally invited Arnold Levine, an outstanding scientist at SUNY-Stonybrook, to
interview for the position. Bowen became increasingly convinced (and
in hindsight, correctly so) about the central role that biology, and its extensions such as biotechnology, would play in the future of research universities. Levine recalls that Bowen took him out to lunch and spoke
with him for two-and-a-half hours before deciding to hire him. Bowen
also personally interviewed all of the other candidates for the job—something few presidents of major universities will take the time to do. Ultimately, Bowen hired Levine as well as another SUNY-Stonybrook
scientist, Thomas Shenk, because "they had the capacity to identify talent, to attract talent, to keep talent. People wanted to be with them.
That's part of what leadership is, being able to attract other very good
people." Previously, Bowen said, Princeton had hired researchers based
purely on their records, without taking into account their leadership potential. But in hiring Levine, Bowen learned that "good science isn't
enough" to build outstanding programs: "You can have the best scientists
in the world, the best humanists, the best whatever, and if they can't
work together, if they can't build a collective enterprise, they're not going
to succeed. When we finally hired Levine and Shenk, we got good science but we also got more than good science." Neither of these scientists might have come to Princeton had the administration not taken
such an active role in their recruitment, especially when it came to promising Levine and Shenk important resources—mainly a modern research
facility—that could only have been authorized by Bowen and provost
Neil Rudenstine. And Bowen followed through on his commitment, ap-
proving the construction of a $29 million molecular biology laboratory
in 1984 and completing it the following year. True to his penchant for
detail, Bowen saw to it that every aspect of the facility met his expectations (as attested to by the saga of the bricks, which became a campus
legend).

Val Fitch, a Nobel Prize–winning physicist at Princeton in great demand by other universities, once told Bowen that "excellence can't be
bought, but it has to be paid for." For this reason, Bowen was a self-
described "relentless advocate" of salary schedules based on merit, though
as a result Bowen had to resolve disputes between different factions at
the university who felt neglected or spurned. This became more and more
critical as salaries for academics in the sciences and engineering rapidly

began to outpace salaries for professors in the humanities. Just as in the coeducation debate, Bowen resorted to economic analysis to advance his opinions; in Bowen's view, a uniform salary would take away resources needed to draw the best talent in "expensive" technical fields.

Bowen credits the faculty with a great deal of impartiality at the hour of allocating scarce resources among the university's competing needs; the involvement of faculty from all disciplines in the process, and the presence of the president as chair of the Committee on Appointments and Advancements, enforced what Bowen calls a "collegial discipline" through which faculty members learned to compromise and temper their demands. This level of presidential attention to the academic side of the enterprise is not as easy to carry out at a large public university, and Princeton's smaller scale allows the president to oversee the faculty hiring and promotion processes much more carefully.

As president of Princeton, just as he had when he was provost under Goheen, Bill Bowen continued his close collaboration with Rudenstine, his trusted ally in the campus controversies surrounding the Vietnam War. A Renaissance scholar recruited back to Princeton from the Harvard faculty by Goheen, Rudenstine had "impeccable judgment" and uncanny foresight, according to Bowen. "Neil could see around corners when the rest of us couldn't even see the corners." Like Bowen, Rudenstine is a first-generation college student who shared and possibly even exceeded Bowen's extraordinary work ethic. Their relationship during Bowen's tenure was so close, in fact, that faculty joked that Princeton had two presidents and two provosts.

> If he wasn't around and an issue arose in the provost's office, I would deal with it. If I wasn't around and an issue came up in the president's office, he would deal with it. . . . If I were to give the readers of your book a single injunction, I would say that success depends more than anything else on surrounding yourself with all the people who can do what you can't do, and urging them on, and helping them, and letting them help you. And it's the people who are afraid of good people who don't succeed.

In searching for and recruiting new faculty, Bowen always tried to gauge the candidate's appreciation for competence. He always asked himself if they could "go into a department and say, 'Nobody in this department is really up to the standard we ought to have, let's go find somebody better than any of us.'" It was this emphasis on leadership that led him to recruit Arnold Levine and Tom Shenk, who built Princeton's molecular biology program from the ground up.

Rudenstine left Princeton with Bowen in 1988 to work in the Andrew W. Mellon Foundation (and so denied Princeton its best inside candidate to replace Bowen) and afterward became Harvard's president. He was Bowen's alter ego: Rudenstine was the more deliberate, reflective element in the partnership. Nonetheless, Rudenstine says Bowen brought to the presidency a conscious and deliberate decision to raise the quality of the faculty. Aided by Princeton's tradition of a "single" faculty (that is, a faculty unified or located under one administrative unit rather than under various colleges and schools), Bowen chaired the university's tenure committee. During Bowen's presidency, the tenure rate, the percentage of assistant professors in a given entering cohort who actually achieve tenured status some time later, went from 30 percent to about 17 percent during his presidency. By comparison, at Harvard the current rate is about 12–15 percent, which is somewhat higher than it has been historically. Says Rudenstine: "At Harvard we found that in tight job markets, no one really wanted to go work at Harvard as a beginning assistant professor. So what we did was to raise standards for the initial appointments so they have a more reasonable expectation of staying, though it is still relatively low." In making tenure and promotion decisions, Bowen emphasized that the salient question for him always was: "What is this person bringing to the university? We considered the overall contributions and not just whether they had published in this or that journal. A more mature scholar might perhaps publish fewer things but would bring other very important things to the table. Flexibility is very important."

Even though Harvard is considerably larger than Princeton (and most other universities as well, with its $2 billion operating budget, dozens of departments, eight professional schools, 18,500 students, thirteen museums, 120 research centers, and ninety libraries), Rudenstine carried over from Princeton the tradition of deep presidential involvement in academic affairs.[11] At Harvard, as in all major universities, the process of promotion begins locally at the departmental level. But then at Harvard it takes a decidedly external route with reviewers from other universities and comparisons of the individual being considered to the top four or five "best" people in that specialty in the world. Academic deans report directly to the president at Harvard and a committee of members from outside and inside the university (though never from the department of the candidate) meets with the president for most of a day for each potential tenure decision. After this careful and time-consuming process, the case for the candidate's tenure ought to make itself. The point is that it is possible, though time-consuming, for presidents to do everything else such as fundraising and general management and still preside meaning-fully over the academic enterprise. Bowen and Rudenstine both concede this level of presidential involvement in academic issues at Princeton might be harder to duplicate at a large, public research university, al-though one clearly gets the sense that Bowen would figure out, as Ruden-stine did at the much larger and complex Harvard, a way to do it.

In raising faculty quality, however, Princeton never used the "star" sys-tem, whereby senior professors are hired from other universities at very high salaries; Harvard has also refused to follow this path, unlike a num-ber of other universities such as Columbia and Texas, where the salaries of "stars" are often twice or more those of other senior professors in the same departments. "If we ever broke the sense of internal fairness within the institution," said Rudenstine, "then it would destroy the institution, the sense that everyone is treated fairly." Thus, neither Princeton nor Harvard displays the substantial ranges in faculty pay (within a given area or department) that exist at other universities. This is because, as Bowen notes, "salary isn't everything." What really matters, according to the "two presidents," are five things:

1. Overall quality of the institution, the density of quality, and its consis-tency across all departments
2. Quality of the colleagueship, of the faculty in one's own department
3. Quality of the students
4. Quality of the facilities—the library, the laboratories, the classrooms
5. Quality of life in the community, important for family considerations

"Thus, we see at Harvard and at Princeton people making $90,000 who turned down $160,000 for these sorts of reasons," says Rudenstine. So at Princeton Bowen pushed quality upward and made tenure harder to achieve, but he maintained equity within departments and disciplines. "There are other things besides salaries that can be used, such as schol-arly leaves for certain departments, and one can try to keep equity in this fashion even in the face of sizeable market differences among the vari-ous disciplines. An important point about the 'star' system is that when you bring the star into your existing team, often the team's chemistry is upset."

LEADERSHIP STYLE

Bowen was thirty-eight years old in July of 1972 when he moved into the president's office, approximately the same age as Bob Goheen was when he took over the Princeton presidency sixteen years earlier. He was reluctant to take the position at first. "I continued to see myself as a mainline academic," he explained. "I continued to teach, continued to write . . . so I wasn't at all sure that I wanted to take an even larger administrative role." He had observed directly the "variety and intensity of the pressures that beat upon the office and the person holding it," and he tried to convince the faculty and the Princeton trustees to pick someone else, though he eventually relented and agreed to accept. The faculty in particular felt that Bowen would be the best candidate because of his deep connections to the university and his familiarity with its culture. The trustees also had faith in Bowen's proven record of accomplishment, especially his reputation for recruiting good faculty, his work in making Princeton coeducational, and his help to Goheen (along with Rudenstine, who was dean of students at Princeton during this time) in handling of the Vietnam War protests. The pressure for Bowen to take the job came primarily from the faculty; he was the faculty's candidate, and the head of the search committee, Stanley Kelley, Jr., a professor of political science, was especially insistent. But Bowen did not assume the presidency at Princeton without opposition and he was by no means everybody's choice. A group of conservative alumni worried about Bowen, who was not a Princeton undergraduate; instead, he was from the Midwest and he had been a big proponent of coeducation, probably the biggest. They knew that he was not enamored with the eating clubs, and that he had been very involved in opening up Princeton to nontraditional students. But ultimately the will of the trustees and the faculty prevailed.

When Princeton hired Bowen as its seventeenth president, it got a bright academic and an incisive thinker, an extremely hard worker with great physical vigor, and a person deeply familiar with the culture and traditions of the university and its supporters. Princeton trustees and its faculty had observed his work and his behaviors in a number of important and stressful situations over a period of years. His closest associates, like Bill Baumol, his faculty advisor from the old days in graduate school and colleague in the economics department, and Neil Rudenstine, agree with this general assessment. On his recruitment by J. D. Rockefeller III for a book on the economics of the performing arts, Baumol recalled, "I agreed but only if they could recruit this bright young man called Bowen to co-author it with me." He added:

> We tend to be neurotic in the same ways. I had the reputation of turning in exams earlier than anyone else in the department, that

is, until Bowen came to Princeton. Most faculty waited until the last moment and then would hand them to the secretary for typing. The secretaries of course always appreciated getting them sooner rather than later. So one fall I turned my exams in and was quickly informed that I had come in second; Bowen had gotten his in first.

Bowen was also incredibly efficient in conducting empirical work and research. On the book on the performing arts, Bowen drew up an outline of the book. "I've never seen such a meticulous and careful outline. There was nothing for me to do except follow directions. His presidency at Princeton was that way," Baumol said. As an administrator, Baumol recalled that Bowen showed utmost flexibility, utmost responsiveness: "He read everything, made suggestions, he was very careful, energetic, dedicated. His aim was to reach higher levels of quality." Bowen's book with Derek Bok, *The Shape of the River*, is also illustrative of Baumol's remarks. It is meticulous in its attention to detail, based on a data set with over sixty thousand students, but Bowen's pragmatism comes through as well. Like his earlier work on the economics of higher education and the economic analysis of coeducation at Princeton, Bowen's ability to marshal data to support his beliefs moves the debate from the personal to the reasoned and the thoughtful. He is interested in what is right, but he knows the best way to get there is also to answer the question, What works? These two words—pragmatic and democratic—define the essence of Bill Bowen.

His general approach to work and dealing with people is also rooted in reason. "A university is and should be a disciplined place where you give reasons, where you're accountable for giving reasons, and it's not enough just to say, 'We're doing this because this is the way we're doing it.' You've got to explain why." These were the standards Bowen would apply to student protesters during the late 1960s and early 1970s. The radical students would ask him what it would take for him to change his mind and his usual reply would pop out: "Better reasons, better reasons." This philosophy was also the basis for the university-wide committees that he developed to deal with the budget and with reallocation of resources. "If you can't justify with good arguments and solid logic your positions, you wouldn't get very far. I think ultimately this is the truest form of positive leadership: creating a structure, a set of situations where the various contending values and positions are exposed and debated. This is the only thing that lasts."

His great energy and capacity for work are well known if not universally appreciated. "Why did I work hard? I worked hard because it was fun, I enjoyed it and liked what I was doing." One of his associates wrote that Bowen "was an economist by trade, and he was all business. He was unhappy and depressed only when he had no problems to solve, the thornier the better. He took an almost demonic delight in system and in work, and as provost earlier he had devised budgetary programs that worked well."[12] Another remarked that in "twelve hours, he'll do eighteen hours of work."[13] And Bill Baumol remarked that Bowen is "the hardest working person I have ever met." But one administrator also remarked that Bowen's style was to get involved in "minutiae," and that this had led to a centralization of power that was not useful. Likewise, a tenured professor complained that Bowen's "consuming interest" in detail, his emphasis on day-to-day operations, made it difficult to develop a clear sense of the mission of the university.[14] Bowen did work long hours, and he also went to the office on Saturdays; the story of the bricks for Thomas Laboratories shows he was not hesitant to mobilize university resources on a Sunday, either.

Bowen is the only one among the six cases studies who did not seem to have a predictable cadence of work and renewal like Hesburgh or Friday, for example, who took time to decompress and think on a routine basis. "I guess my 'rhythm' came in fifteen-year intervals: I was a standard academic for fifteen, then provost-president for a little more than fifteen or so, and I decided I had another fifteen-year interval left, so now I work here [the Mellon Foundation]." In any event, there is little evidence that the larger, more comprehensive "visionary" goals for Princeton suffered as a result of Bowen's (or Rudenstine's) work ethic. By most reasonable measures, Princeton University was remarkably better off after Bowen's presidency than it was before he arrived.

CONCLUSION

A good friend of Bowen's told him, "Life is what happens to you when you're planning something else. None of the steps that I took were planned, none." His career indeed was an evolutionary process: his original ambition to be a college teacher gradually changed into a desire to do substantive research at a university as a professor, and later it evolved as he discovered his talent for administration. "I found out that I got a certain satisfaction out of accomplishing things. I always liked to get things done." He will forever be thankful for the "fortunate circumstances, terrific teachers, very supportive environment I had. I was also lucky that the things I was good at were well rewarded."

Bowen was president of Princeton for a sufficiently long time to learn from his mistakes and to build upon his experiences. "You need to be president long enough to accomplish things. My first five years were nothing like my last five in terms of how much we accomplished. No comparison." But he also felt he had been president long enough. One measure of his success as president was to have an institution that was strong enough that it could thrive on change, one that could do well under new leadership. When Bowen left Princeton, the university was very well positioned.

> We had a hugely successful capital campaign, the finances were in very good order, we'd had a lot of success with faculty recruitment. All the life signs were very good, and so that's the time to leave. You always want to leave when the band is playing the loudest. And that gives the university the best chance to attract a top person as your successor, which is what you want, so it just seemed right: a good moment, for the university and for me.

When Bowen accepted the presidency of the Andrew Mellon Foundation, his colleagues at Princeton chuckled knowingly. Princeton philosophy professor Paul Benacerraf said: "I don't know how he will turn his new position into a twenty-hour-a-day job, but if anyone can, it's Bill."[15] Bill Baumol told about a bet among his friends: "When he became the president of the Mellon Foundation, the joke around Princeton was about how long it would take Bill to turn that new position into an eighteen-hour-per-day job. The bet was six months, but the answer was two weeks."

NOTES

1. A similar version of this story appeared in the *Princeton Alumni Weekly* in 1987. See David Williamson, "The Bowen Legacy: A Close-up Review of His Vision and Accomplishments," *Princeton Alumni Weekly*, December 23, 1987.

2. Williamson, "Bowen Legacy," 9.

3. For a compendium of Bowen's works, see William G. Bowen, *Ever the Teacher: William G. Bowen's Writings as President of Princeton* (Princeton, NJ: Princeton University Press, 1987).

4. As quoted in Alvin Kernan, *In Plato's Cave* (New Haven, CT: Yale University Press, 1999), 203. Presumably the "two men" would have been Bowen and his longtime associate Neil Rudenstine.

5. Kyle Crichton, "Departing President: William G. Bowen, the Economist Who Taught Princeton Basic Economics," *New York Times*, May 10, 1987. These ventures were not without critics, however. Local officials at the time accused the university of contributing to the overdevelopment of the area through the

sale of Forrestal Center, a charge Bowen denies by noting that development to the previously rural area was inevitable as the population continued to grow.

6. Williamson, "Bowen Legacy," 13.

7. "The Education of Women at Princeton: A Special Report," Princeton University, September 24, 1968, 32.

8. Tom Fernandez, "Going Coed with Guts and Grace," *The Trentonian*, 1969.

9. Information partly based on Alexander Leitch, *A Princeton Companion* (Princeton, NJ: Princeton University Press, 1978).

10. William Bowen and Derek Bok, *The Shape of the River: Long-Term Consequences of Considering Race in College and University Admissions* (Princeton, NJ: Princeton University Press, 1998).

11. Former Harvard president Derek Bok also participated actively in the academic decisions at Harvard during his presidency. See Robert Rosenzweig, *The Political University* (Baltimore: Johns Hopkins University Press, 1998).

12. Kernan, *In Plato's Cave*, 204.

13. Williamson, "Bowen Legacy," 10.

14. Ibid., 10–11.

15. Crichton, "Departing President."

CHAPTER

Hanna Holborn Gray: The Second Woman

Ye shall know the truth, and
the truth shall make you free.
—Mark 8:32, inscribed on a wall of Chicago's Bond Chapel

INTRODUCTION

"The most striking fact about the higher learning in America," wrote Robert Maynard Hutchins in 1936, "is the confusion that besets it." With these audacious words, the University of Chicago's youthful fifth president sparked a national debate in which he attempted to put an end to the perceived confusion—to redefine the aims of education and prescribe the ideal means of achieving these aims. In the end, Hutchins' crusade to revolutionize the American university failed; part of his problem was his inability to sell his ideas to his own university and another part is the fact that there is no such thing as "the" American university.[1] But the public controversy surrounding his work, *The Higher Learning in America* (1936), firmly established the reputation of the University of Chicago as a place where learning and the pursuit of truth are solemn undertakings, where intellectual brinkmanship and an edgy academic climate are encouraged, and where the vaunted scholarly tradition of the past is continually consulted when making groundbreaking strides toward the future.[2] Hutchins—with his precocity, his overpowering personality, his brilliance, and his missionary zeal—embodied in many respects the essential qualities of the university he led.

Hanna Holborn Gray. *Photo by Will Crockett.*

Hanna Holborn Gray assumed the presidency of the University of Chicago three decades after Hutchins left it—and in the process became the second woman president of a major university and the first (and still only) at Chicago—but she inherited much the same culture that Hutchins helped shape.[3] Chicago remains a place where students pitch tents in front of administrative buildings—not to purchase tickets for basketball games, but to register for the university's most popular classes. John Hope Franklin, a noted historian who chaired the history department where Gray and her husband Charles both worked at the beginning of their academic careers, declares that he "just plain love[s] the University of Chicago," and amusedly observes that the busiest day of the year at Chicago's Regenstein Library is the day after Thanksgiving vacation, when students flock to the shelves, hungry for reading material after a few days of deprivation.

Even though the first Heisman Trophy went to a University of Chicago athlete, John "Jay" Berwanger, a six-foot, 190-pound halfback who graduated in 1936, Chicago's president might still be the only major college president in America who does not know when the football coach resigns. Gray only found out her head coach had resigned when the post office returned her Christmas card with the envelope stamped: "Moved, Address Unknown." When she asked the dean of students why she wasn't informed, Gray was told that they did not think she needed to know. ("They were probably right," she says.) After a *New York Times* article reported the story of the missing coach, Gray received several letters from irate alumni. But their indignation was not related to the coach or to the president's unawareness about his departure; they were demanding to know why the University of Chicago was playing football in the first place.

Chicago's intellectual intensity has produced unquestionable results. In the past century, the university has educated or employed some seventy-five Nobel Prize winners, the most of any university in the world except for Cambridge. Nine Nobel Prizes, including two for physics and seven for economics, have been awarded to Chicago faculty members since 1980. Kurt Vonnegut, Jr., Nobel Prize winner Milton Friedman, and Saul Bellow all received their degrees from the University of Chicago, as did Paul Wolfowitz, Deputy United States Secretary of Defense, John Ashcroft, United States Attorney General, cosmologist Edwin Hubble, and the ex-prime minister of Greece. Enrico Fermi, a critical member of the Oppenheimer team in Los Alamos, performed the first controlled nuclear fission reaction at a University of Chicago facility in 1942. Chicago was also responsible for the development of carbon-14 dating and the discovery of the atmospheric jet stream. The University of Chicago Press is the largest university press in the country and publishes *The Chicago Manual of Style*, the definitive guide to American English usage. Since its inception, Chicago has won renown as a place where, as one university administrator once put it, "[one's] thought runs forward."

Yet, one glance at the university's deliberately anachronistic, Gothic-style campus suggests a flipside to this "Chicago spirit" and to another Hutchins legacy: Chicago's steadfast conservatism. The paradox of Hutchins' thesis on education was that he proposed a solution so rooted in the past—the abolition of elective systems in favor of one-size-fits-all liberal education—that it seemed not only conservative but also radical. Half a century after Hutchins, Chicago professor Alan Bloom published a similar book, *The Closing of the American Mind* (1987), in which he condemned the fads and consumerism pervading higher education and argued for a liberal curriculum based on the classics. "The best thing about this university," said Gray in her last year as president, "is that it has remained a place steadfast to its own purposes, rather than a place that has bent to various fashions that from time to time have tilted other institutions one way or another."

Therein lay Hanna Holborn Gray's greatest challenge as the leader of the University of Chicago. For in American higher education, the years from 1978 to 1993—the fifteen years of Gray's tenure—are regarded as some of the leanest and most difficult in recent times. Budget pressures and declining enrollments made change imperative at many institutions, including Chicago. At the same time, Gray had to contend with an institutional culture that demanded high academic standards and that generally refused to bend to outside forces, no matter how compelling. Chicago's notoriously combative and independent faculty only further complicated Gray's tasks but she, as it turned out, excelled at this sort of balancing act. As a former colleague said about her presidency, "She left the University of Chicago more focused, stronger, larger, more confident about itself, and just as self-critical as it always had been."

EARLY LIFE

Hanna Holborn Gray was predestined for a life in the academy. Born in Heidelberg, Germany, on October 25, 1930, to two prominent scholars, Hanna inherited a strong academic inclination that actually originated with her grandfathers, one of whom was a physical chemist and director of Berlin's Imperial Physics Institute, and the other a physician and a respected expert in medicine. Hanna's mother, Annemarie Bettmann, had a Ph.D. in classical philology from the prestigious University of Berlin. Annemarie, though a Christian and a practicing Lutheran, was of Jewish ancestry, from the Rhineland-Pfalz region of Germany, the river valleys created by the Ahr, Lahn, Moselle (Mosel), and Rhine rivers. Her family had converted to Christianity as had many other Jewish families in the region during the last half of the nineteenth century. (The issue of "Jewishness" by race or birth was of course a central element of Hitler's Nazi regime and led to many of his anti-Semitic policies.) Gray's father, Hajo Holborn, was from Berlin and was a distinguished professor of history at the University of Berlin before he migrated to America in 1934. He eventually became Sterling Professor of History at Yale, where he worked for over three decades. Her brother Frederick is a senior adjunct professor of American foreign policy at the Johns Hopkins' Nitze School of Advanced International Studies. He also served as the legislative assistant to then-Senator John F. Kennedy and worked in the White House from 1961 to 1966. Thus, academic life and public service were central elements in her family and in her own personal development.

In January of 1933 Adolph Hitler became Chancellor of Germany and within three months, Hanna's father was dismissed from the University of Berlin by the new government. Much to Hitler's aversion, Hanna's father, a bright and highly visible young professor, was writing a book on the overthrown Weimar Republic. He also held a chair from the Carnegie Corporation in New York, and Hitler would use the presence of this American-funded chair at the most prominent of German universities as evidence of the corrupt intrusion of American capitalism into what should have been a pure Germanic university. In fact, Holborn, who was a well-known historian and international affairs scholar, had attracted many American and British students to Berlin and had in the process developed a network of friends and contacts that would help him after his dismissal from the university.

At the center of this set of connections was Nicholas Murray Butler, the chairman of the Carnegie Corporation and the president of Columbia University in New York. Butler traveled to Berlin in the spring of 1933 and was understandably appalled by what he saw and heard. Upon his return to New York, Butler held a dockside press conference, which was reported in the *New York Times*, to express his concerns about conditions in Germany and his worries about how the Carnegie chair was being attacked. After Hajo's firing, the Carnegie Corporation removed the chair from Berlin and Butler offered to support Hanna's father for three years at the university of his choosing. This generous offer came at the height of the Great Depression, a time when universities everywhere were in dire economic straits. Hajo initially traveled to London, to the Royal Institute for International Affairs, while Hanna and her brother and mother went to Heidelburg to live with Hanna's maternal grandparents. While in London, Hajo worked on his scholarship and on his English. In 1934, his family joined him for a month before moving to the United States. Hajo was invited to work at several universities but eventually chose Yale, in New Haven, Connecticut, where he remained for the rest of his distinguished career until his death in 1969.

The three-year-old Hanna and her family left England aboard the S.S. *Olympic* to settle in New Haven. The ship arrived in New York and docked around midnight, as was the custom then. Her memories of these events were reinforced by family conversations but Gray vividly recalls her powerful emotions of excitement and awe upon seeing the Statue of Liberty as she cruised into New York Harbor. The wind snatched her hat right off her head, sending it into the harbor. "My mother, I clearly remember, was not happy that I lost my hat." Hanna's uncle and three cousins, whom she had never met before, traveled from New Jersey to greet them at the dock. Her brother Frederick had on his "lederhosen," the knee-length, leather trousers that German, Swiss, and Austrian boys wore during the 1920s and 1930s. She also remembers her brother's fear of the men at customs who were opening their bags. "My brother was much more sophisticated about men in uniforms than I was, having been taught to be very suspicious of such people in Germany."

New Haven was a wonderful place for immigrant children, with museums, concerts, and great teachers. Many foreign professors moved there with their families to escape the war and to teach at Yale, giving the town a decidedly international flavor. Hanna's parents wanted the children to preserve their German, so they made a clever deal with Hanna and Frederick: the parents would correct their children's German, but the children had to correct their parents' English. Eventually, English became the household language, although Sunday remained as the designated day for German in the house. One of those Sundays, four-year-old Hanna, who had evidently begun already to develop an independent aspect to her personality, was heard cursing in English and mumbling about yet "another lousy Sunday" as she came down the stairs, to no avail as the Sunday German-only tradition continued for several more years. A few years later, in 1941, Hanna's maternal grandmother came from Europe to live with them in New Haven, providing more opportunities to speak German.

Growing up, Hanna had to contend with the twin challenges of translation and tradition, rather universal experiences for any recent immigrant.[4] As a youngster straddling two different worlds, Hanna lived with one foot in America and in the future, but with the other in the past, in Germany. She had to "translate" American behavior and culture for her parents, but she also had to interpret her own German identity and traditions for her classmates and neighbors, all during a relatively isolationist, conservative era of American history. Compounding challenges of acculturation were the strict boundaries that her family imposed on her behavior; among other things, Hanna could not eat white bread, a food Europeans considered unhealthy, or use pillows to sleep. She wore traditional German clothing and was not permitted to go to the cinema or listen to the radio except for limited times on Sunday (she listened to the Fred Allen and the Edgar Bergen/Charlie McCarthy shows, and for a while she longed to be a radio comedienne) because her parents felt these habits had corrupted American culture. Hanna learned English quickly at school, but her parents insisted that she reserve her new language for the schoolyard.

As if her German traditions did not single her out enough, Hanna also had the influence of a staunchly intellectual family: her parents spoke in classical Greek when they did not want the children to understand what they were discussing. In keeping with the childhood experiences of many leaders, Hanna read considerably as a child, enjoyed her studies, and received significant encouragement from her parents to excel in school. The precocious Hanna thus developed into a very literate and erudite young girl, steeped in German classical writings as well as English works. Since Hajo's many friends and students in Germany and England frequently visited the Holborn household to discuss the shattering events unfolding in Europe, Hanna also absorbed a great deal of knowledge about world affairs as a child.

> Sometimes we felt that school was the only thing that mattered, the only standard upon which we were judged. We would be allowed to sit, very quietly of course, and listen to very exciting conversations about European affairs, fascism, and world politics. I remember vividly the Italian invasion of Ethiopia in 1936, and there probably aren't many people in the US who have that memory from their childhood.

Education and culture thus separated Hanna from certain elements of American life and prevented her from immersing herself completely in her adopted culture, but they also helped her comprehend her radically new surroundings. Her refugee experience enabled her to understand differences among individuals more deeply and perhaps even to tolerate those differences more readily since she and her family had gone through many of the same emotions—separation, fear, uncertainty, excitement, hope, safety, and security. "Like other children born in other countries who migrated here at a young age, I was different and I had to learn to be different. But I think, in hindsight, growing up different was a positive thing for me." A longtime associate of Hanna Gray's speculated that the intellectual demands of the Holborn household also helped her later understand academic life and "the nature and character of [Chicago]."

Research on resilient children stresses the importance of significant grandparents or teachers or coaches who shield and nurture children in difficult or challenging situations. In the case of children transplanted from one culture into a new one, with a different language from the one spoken at home and with different cultural expectations and behaviors, the child's family takes on a crucially important role since there is often an absence of relatives or of adults with whom they can associate or to whom they can personally relate. In other words, if the immediate family is not a source of comfort and support, the child may have few other options to which to turn. The same may apply to minority populations such as Hispanic or African American children. In the case of Hanna and her brother Fred, their parents Hajo and Annemarie provided a steady foundation upon which they could assimilate into the new culture, enabling them to understand their "differentness" and to receive the encouragement and role modeling they needed to succeed. Paradoxically, in the case of "majority" children (i.e., white males), the family may not be as critical since there may be more potential mentors or role models for these youngsters. The cosmopolitan and more understanding atmosphere of New Haven, even though it probably had significant pockets of provincialism and elitism, also buffered the immigrant children as they adapted to their new country.

> We were different and we knew it. There were different expectations. Despite my parents' delight in America—they were extremely pro-American and appreciative for the opportunity America had given them—they continued to have the view that there wasn't much culture in America. We had to learn to be different and how it was OK to be different.

And there were two ways in which this difference was manifested for Hanna: one was through her refugee status, and the other was through her gender.

Hanna's formal education focused her emerging intellectual aspirations and helped her deal with cultural stresses. At the Foote School in New

Haven, which Hanna attended until 1943, she encountered many British students who had come over from Oxford during the war and who could empathize and identify with her transplantation. Many English children came to New Haven during the war, and the school took adopted an unusual mixture of British and American traditions. Its students also benefited greatly from the presence of many exceptionally well-educated wives of Yale professors who taught there. The international flavor of the school likely helped Hanna not feel so out of place, accelerating her "translation" of American culture.

In 1943, Hajo Holborn began working as a postwar planner for the Office of Strategic Services (OSS), the precursor to the Central Intelligence Agency (CIA). He served in the "R&A" (Research and Analysis) branch as the main liaison between OSS and the Department of State. Many academics and German refugees were asked to work in this capacity during the war, all in an effort to obtain as many insights about Germany as possible. Hajo specifically worked on occupation policy for Germany at the end of the war and wrote on the history of military occupations, becoming a dominant figure in the training of post-war Germanists.[5] Hanna enrolled at the Sidwell Friends School in Washington, D.C., the same school First Daughter Chelsey Clinton attended during the 1990s. A Quaker school by origin, Sidwell Friends, like the Foote School, attracted an eclectic mix of students, usually the children of refugees or diplomats who lived in Washington. While at Sidwell, Hanna embraced the Quaker values of individualism, tolerance, and hard work. She studied there for two years, having skipped two grades earlier in her schooling, and by the fall of 1945, at age fifteen, Hanna was ready to attend college.

HIGHER EDUCATION

The "Seven Sisters" is an alternate name for the Pleiades star cluster; in mythology, the Pleiades were the seven daughters of Atlas and Pleione. More recently, the term has been applied to the seven private, female liberal arts schools scattered throughout the Northeast historically allied with various formerly all-male Ivy League universities. They are: Barnard in New York City; Bryn Mawr in Bryn Mawr, Pennsylvania; Mount Holyoke in South Hadley, Massachusetts; Radcliffe in Cambridge, Massachusetts; Smith in Northampton, Massachusetts; Vassar in Poughkeepsie, New York; and Wellesley in Wellesley, Massachusetts. Hajo Holborn and his wife Annemarie had implicitly assumed Hanna would choose to study at one of these colleges, just as it was assumed that Fred would go either to Harvard or Yale (he chose Harvard to avoid the place where his father taught). In moving to America, Annemarie had to defer her own career hopes and aspirations—in Germany she would have been a teacher and scholar—and perhaps placed some of her hopes on her bright daughter. Hanna went along with her parents' desires, but initially preferred Smith College to her parents' choice of Bryn Mawr. Already an independent young woman, Hanna balked at the notion of entering academe and ending up like her parents, who had met in what she called the "decidedly unromantic" setting of a Sanskrit seminar: she wanted to be a foreign correspondent or a famous novelist. She also rebelled at being told what to do, but in the end her parents prevailed. Of the Seven Sisters, only Smith and Bryn Mawr took her application because she was so young, and both schools accepted her. Years later, Hanna admitted that her parents probably understood her needs and interests better than she did at the time; ultimately, Hanna fell in love with Bryn Mawr and its scholarly life, and "received a better education . . . than my brother was getting at Harvard."

In addition to Bryn Mawr's dedication to scholarship and academic rigor, the genial manner in which women and men taught alongside each other on the faculty particularly impressed Hanna. Of the individuals who left their mark on Hanna during this period, Lily Ross Taylor seems to have been one of Hanna's most influential mentors. A classical scholar who wrote about the Roman Republic and taught the works of Lucretius and Tacitus, Taylor became the first woman Fellow of the American Academy in Rome in 1917. She served as dean of the graduate school at Bryn Mawr, while continuing to be a very prominent scholar in the classics field, serving as President of the American Philological Association in 1942.[6] Hanna's most enthusiastic, passionate, and creative teacher at Bryn Mawr, Taylor encouraged hard work and incisive research, but she was sparing in her compliments. On a paper that Hanna had spent a considerable amount of effort, Professor Taylor only remarked: "Your footnotes all checked out." Hanna thought this was not much of a comment after all the time she had spent, but later found out that was Taylor's highest form of praise for a student paper. She corresponded with Hanna after she graduated and took Hanna and her husband Charles Montgomery Gray on a trip to Rome shortly after their marriage. "Imagine having Lily Ross Taylor, who in another life would have been a distinguished professor at a major research university, as a tour guide through the Roman Forum and other parts of ancient Rome."

Gray also mentions Eric Frank, another professor at Bryn Mawr and a Jewish-Catholic, as a devoted scholar who truly lived the values of his profession and Felix Gilbert, a fellow student of Hajo Holborn at the University of Berlin and a life-long friend and associate, who shared Hanna's passion for Renaissance history.[7] Gilbert directed Hanna's senior dissertation and helped her with her work in numerous other ways. Two of these three models, Frank and Gilbert, were part of her father's network of European scholars, and so for Gray there was something familiar and comfortable about it all. Together, they steered her towards the academic career that she seemed destined to pursue and away from her earlier fantasies of becoming a novelist or radio comedienne in the mold of Edgar Bergen.

By her first year of college, Gray's personality traits and career inclinations were increasingly revealed. Bright and independent, she was already a young intellectual who was fluent in two languages and in two cultures and traditions. She was able to flow from one culture to the other and back again, and these "trips" enabled her to comprehend the differences and similarities between the two worlds in which she lived. A gifted and precocious student, Hanna enjoyed academic life and was obviously an excellent student who attracted serious scholars to work with her. Her interest in history and the Renaissance fed her curiosity about the inter-relatedness of events and conditions. She had also absorbed the discussions of history and world affairs in her family's living room while growing up, and these experiences gave her a rich foundation from which to pursue her increasingly academic career interests. For young Hanna, free debate and intelligent discussion were a normal and exciting part of everyday life.

During her sophomore year at Bryn Mawr, finally determining her parents did not have it so bad after all, Hanna reconciled with academe and decided to pursue a major in history and a minor in Latin, specializing in intellectual history. The sixteen-year-old Hanna never imagined she would be best known for her administrative work. After earning her bachelor's degree (summa cum laude) in 1950, at age nineteen, Gray spent the next year at Oxford University as a Fulbright scholar, but while in England she realized that the flexibility and progressiveness of American higher education were its greatest strengths and she turned down the second year there. She returned to the United States in 1952 to begin her Ph.D. at Radcliffe College, Harvard's "sister." Gray graduated in 1957 with a Ph.D. and with a husband, Charles Montgomery Gray, whom she married in 1954. Ironically, they met in much the same way as did her parents: at a scholarly seminar on the middle works of Erasmus. In 2004 the Grays, who do not have children, celebrated their fiftieth wedding anniversary.

THE UNIVERSITY OF CHICAGO

When Charles Gray was offered a position in the department of history at the University of Chicago in 1961, he accepted and Hanna followed him there. The history department at Chicago in the early 1960s was composed of a large and distinguished group of scholars, such as Walter Johnson, John Hope Franklin, and William McNeill, with a commitment to interdisciplinary inquiry and comparative history. Just a few weeks after arriving in Hyde Park, Hanna fell in love with the beautiful campus, its unpredictable faculty, its serious students, and its fervent devotion to scholarship. The city was also a strong attraction: its diversity, resources, museums, Lake Michigan's waterfront, and the ethnic neighborhoods and restaurants made Chicago interesting and livable for the Grays. When the Grays moved to Chicago they rented an apartment in Hyde Park, which in those days was in the process of urban renewal. Although isolated from the city, Hyde Park had its own identity, much like a village within a larger cosmopolitan area. She held a one-year research fellowship at the Newberry Library in Chicago but she expected to assume the traditionally passive role of the "faculty wife" at the University of Chicago even though she had taught in Harvard's history department. Much to her surprise, however, Alan Simpson, an historian and the dean at Chicago who later became president of Vassar, offered Hanna a full time position as an assistant professor in the department of history shortly after her husband began working. In addition to the standard responsibilities of teaching and research, Gray also helped develop a new curriculum as administrator of the undergraduate history program. This radical gesture of trust and respect endeared Chicago to Hanna: even as a faculty member at Harvard, university policy prevented her from using the Lamont Library, in the southeast corner of Harvard Yard, or entering the faculty club through the front door. She was only one of two women on the faculty then. "The treatment of women was just absurd," she sighed.

Being the only woman in the Chicago history department and having a husband as a colleague in the same department caused some initial tension, and the history faculty watched their newest faculty members warily. But Gray gives credit to her department for granting her considerable independence and autonomy even as a young professor. Her insistence on a strictly collegial relationship—she refused even to sit next to Charles at faculty meetings—assuaged any remaining skeptics. Within a couple of years, she had established a strong reputation as an educator and a scholar, largely overcoming any obstacles her gender posed. When discussing the appointment of a female candidate in the mid-1960s with her colleague William McNeill, McNeill groaned, "Oh, just don't pick a woman, they make such difficult colleagues." Upon noticing Hanna's amusement, he quickly apologized, "Well, it's just that I don't really think of you as a woman."

The democratic and open academic atmosphere at Chicago meshed well with Hanna's temperament and interests. Compared to Harvard, Chicago was less rigid and hierarchical. Gray thrived among her famously contentious colleagues and an academic backdrop that she calls "argumentative, but not confrontational." During the 1960s, Hanna witnessed the department of history begin a variety of new courses and undertake many projects that were unheard of at other major institutions. While most conventional history departments dwelled solely on Western culture and history, Chicago's department already had courses on the Near East, Asian culture, and other non-Western topics, areas that it continued to expand and strengthen; its chairman was John Hope Franklin, one of America's most distinguished historians and an Afro-American. By the late 1960s, Gray's reputation led Barnard and Scripps Colleges to approach her about their presidential vacancies, but she declined their overtures because she felt she was too young and inexperienced for the positions. She was in her late 30s then.

INTO THE ADMINISTRATION

When controversy erupted at Chicago in 1969 as part of the burgeoning student protest movement, Hanna suddenly became quite visible. Earlier that year, a faculty review board refused to reappoint Marlene Dixon, an assistant professor of sociology at Chicago, on the grounds that her research fell below the standards expected of Chicago faculty. Believing that gender discrimination and bias against her liberal sociological theories were the real underlying reasons for her dismissal, Dixon loudly protested the decision and in the process used some of the Chicago students to aid her cause. President Edward H. Levi assembled a committee to review the case and recommend a course of action for the institution. He flung Hanna Gray, at the time one of only three tenured women faculty at Chicago, into the front lines of the administration, naming her chair of the committee. The crisis, which included a few other issues in addition to the Dixon controversy, culminated in sixteen-day student occupation of the administration building that ended when the committee made its report. The committee's objective inquiry and its conclusion that prejudice and discrimination were not involved in the non-reappointment decision converted Gray into a highly visible member of the Chicago faculty. Over the course of the investigation, Gray proved she could take a tough, yet intellectually honest, stand, and that she could deal effectively with administration and oversight. While the committee concluded there was no evidence that "the status of women in the University had any bearing on the decision made in Mrs. Dixon's case," they did find "problems for women as faculty members, and our inquiries into Mrs. Dixon's case have highlighted them for us." The report then called for the establishment of a student-faculty group to study employment, pay, and other issues affecting women faculty.[8]

EARLY ADMINISTRATIVE CAREER

Probably as a result of the publicity surrounding the Marlene Dixon episode, Northwestern University invited Gray to be the dean of their College of Arts and Sciences in 1972. By this time, Gray was ready for a change and eager to "use new muscles" as an administrator. She found she liked dealing with problems that required resolution and that she was comfortable leading a group through a process of collegial inquiry. It was also a convenient arrangement for her family, since her husband continued to teach at Chicago during her two years at Northwestern, which is located in Evanston, Illinois, just north and west of Chicago. Although she enjoyed working at Northwestern, there were some clear differences between Northwestern and Chicago. Chicago thinks of itself as a university first, while Northwestern behaved like a loose confederation of feuding colleges with little sense of institutional mission or solidarity. To Gray, this sense of unity is Chicago's greatest strength. It arises from its birth as a whole university dedicated entirely to knowledge for its own sake. On the other hand, Northwestern's development was more disjointed, with separate schools containing different disciplines; it had yet to reconcile the pragmatic ends of education with its intellectual goals. Northwestern however did feature a very supportive, cooperative atmosphere, in contrast to Chicago's edgy, argumentative, and critical air.

In the meantime, Gray was also serving as a member of the Yale governing corporation and was known as a solid administrator who raised good issues and shared an overarching concern for the welfare of the institution. Yale President Kingman Brewster thus was able to observe and work with Hanna closely, and, in 1974, Brewster offered her the provost's position at the school. Hanna of course had strong ties to New Haven, and she had proven herself in administrative areas, but Brewster's offer might have had other undertones. This was also a time of great change in American higher education, and Brewster knew that her presence at Yale would send an unambiguous message about the role of women and about change at a university bastion of privilege and tradition.

This time it would her husband Charles' turn to follow Hanna; he joined Yale as a professor in its history department. "Charles also wanted a change, so it was a good time for both of us to leave Chicago." At Yale Gray worked closely with Brewster, who by then was an international force in higher education and a central member of a network of powerful and upper class liberals that included New York City mayor John Lindsay, presidential advisers McGeorge Bundy and Cyrus Vance, and Elliot Richardson, Nixon's attorney general. Brewster, who graced the cover of *Time* in June of 1967, graduated from Yale in 1941, where he was chairman of the *Yale Daily News*, and later received his law degree from Harvard Law School. After teaching law at Harvard, he served as provost and then, from 1963 to 1977, as president at Yale, until Jimmy Carter appointed him U.S. Ambassador to the Court of St. James (United Kingdom). His presidency was known for improvements in Yale's faculty, curriculum, and admissions policies, as well as for the admission of women as undergraduates and for the adept handling of student protests against the Vietnam War, which Brewster himself opposed as well. (In May of 1970, Brewster flew to Washington and led a large delegation of students, faculty, and members of the Yale Corporation to lobby in Congress against the expanded war in Vietnam.)[9] President George W. Bush, as well as John Kerry and Howard Dean, all attended Brewster's Yale during the 1960s, a time during which Brewster oversaw the conversion of Yale from a preserve for the male children of privilege to a more open institution.[10] Arguably, only someone with the stature and experience of Brewster could have appointed the first female provost in the Ivy League and particularly at Yale.

Hanna Gray served as provost for the next four years, assuming the title of acting president for the final year (1977) following Kingman Brewster's departure as U.S. Ambassador to England. "I was both provost and president at Yale for a year, which certainly made the meetings a lot shorter." Yale gave Hanna a great deal of experience in dealing with difficult administrative issues. One of the most pressing was formulating the annual budget, an especially difficult task in the austere, inflationary years of the 1970s. The budget at Yale was "a mess," and it was complicated by the casual, patchy methods by which the budget was composed. The various autonomous schools at Yale had a great deal of trouble arriving at a consensus on expenditures, perhaps also reflective of Brewster's growing outside interests over the course of his presidency and to the decreasing attention he was devoting to internal university issues. While Gray does not dwell on it, Yale was not exactly a comfortable place for her. She was in the running for the permanent job at Yale, a post that eventually went to Yale's humanities division director, A. Bartlett Giamatti (who later would complain about the treatment he received from some of the alumni and would resign to become Commissioner of Baseball).[11] Whether Gray would have gotten the Yale job is of course not known but she probably was too closely associated with Brewster, and some at Yale were probably glad to see him leave for England. She was also a woman and in spite of growing up in New Haven and of her father's sterling career there, she was not "Old Blue." Said William McNeill, a professor from Chicago who knew Hanna well from their days together in the history department: "Unlike Yale, we've always had the co-ed tradition here, so that was never an issue."[12] And Gray herself admitted to no regrets: "If you were a woman president of Yale, you'd spend half your time being the woman president of Yale—and that's not how I'd like to spend my time."[13]

THE PRESIDENCY OF THE UNIVERSITY OF CHICAGO

President John T. Wilson of the University of Chicago resigned in 1978, allowing Hanna Gray to begin her longest and certainly most challenging assignment, the Chicago presidency, that same year. In spite of facing some daunting problems with finances and image, she would serve the third longest tenure as a Chicago president, behind only Hutchins and Harry Pratt Judson. Gray became Chicago's tenth president at a time when higher education in America—and particularly private higher education—was facing twin crises in finance and identity. Applications to Chicago were declining steadily, inflation was strangling an inadequate endowment, the campus was in disrepair, the latest fundraising drive had fallen embarrassingly short of its relatively modest target, and, in a particularly crushing blow to a university that proudly calls itself "the teacher of teachers," the job market for academics and for liberal arts faculty had collapsed. This last dilemma was of special concern to Hanna Gray as 40 percent of Chicago's alumni held jobs in academe when she took office in 1978.[14] Articles with titles like "Everything's Shrinking in Higher Education" and "The Management of Decline" were commonplace in higher education journals and publications during this period.[15] Nonetheless, Chicago was still an amazingly prestigious school and an outstanding place to learn, but it was also a complex institution with several professional schools (the medical complex was hemorrhaging financially). In an era of rising costs and student vocationalism, its emphasis on a core curriculum and the liberal arts seemed a problem.

Gray brought her various strengths to her new job, and she would need all of them. She owned a solid record of scholarship, which helped her establish a rapport with those under her; in Chicago's institutional culture, only a true scholar could win legitimacy in the eyes of the faculty. Indeed, Gray turned down two presidential offers in the 1970s so she could continue with her writing and research, and even as president of Chicago she would remark occasionally that "being president is no big deal." And in her private life, filled as it was with the meetings and administrative minutiae, Gray took care to dedicate weekends and evenings to reflection, reading, and writing. She was a solid thinker with relevant experience at two other universities. But she was also familiar with the unique institutional culture at Chicago and understood that the university had always been, and probably would always remain, driven by the energy of its distinguished faculty. She readily admits to having a temper and she expected her associates to be well prepared for meetings, just as she always was. One department head said: "If people thought she'd be sweet and gentle because [she is a woman], they got a rude awakening. She's tougher than most of the men around here." However, Gray was clearly inclusive in managerial style and treated faculty as colleagues, encouraging thoughtful and vigorous debate. Her cognitive style, the way she processed information and understood problems, leans toward a global perspective, something her preparation in, and preference for, history reinforced. She was interested in the inter-relationships among different parts of the enterprise and was intellectually motivated by complex situations that needed a comprehensive approach. When asked a question about a particular topic, such as Ph.D. education or fund-raising, she tends to couch it in its broader, historical contexts, from which she draws certain general or overarching principles. In this very nonlinear approach to problems, Gray's mode of understanding and analyzing problems is quite similar to that of the other five individuals studied elsewhere in this book and is based on an "aerial" view of the various pieces of an issue and of how they fit together. And she had the capacity to do a great deal of work. As her husband noted: "Hanna works all day and all night. In that she resembles her father."[16]

Many of the changes needed at Chicago, though necessary for the university's longer-term success, did not resonate well with some of the school's conservative and traditional culture. It is also ironic, or perhaps bizarre, that Gray was initially criticized for being too external, but

toward the end of her tenure as president, some trustees complained that
she did not like fund-raising and did not spend enough time on it. In
fact, however, Hanna Gray was here a victim of sharply raised expectations: there existed no real fund-raising structure at Chicago when Gray
became president but by the end of her presidency annual gifts had
quadrupled and several fund-raising campaigns had been successfully concluded. During her first year, one faculty member (anonymously) complained: "One of the problems is that she isn't here that much. She seems
to see her task as that of largely raising funds. Sooner or later someone
has to watch the store."[17] In fact, Gray took over the Chicago presidency
during an unprecedented period of "stagflation," when both inflation and
unemployment were hitting the economy with both barrels. The university's fund-raising campaign started by the previous president (Wilson)
had come up considerably short of its $80 million goal; the Reagan ad-
ministration was cutting aid to universities and to graduate students in
particular; and the school's 1979–80 budget deficit was nearly $3 million.
In short, the financial situation of the institution was not secure. Thus,
it seems obvious that Gray should have addressed the external and financial concerns first. As one of the deans noted: "If Hanna wasn't preoccupied with finances, and if I had the authority, I'd fire her on the spot.
How these critics think you can have a 'vision' and go broke is weird
kind of talk. She may have a vision, but [the faculty] may not have a job
while she has her vision."[18] In making these changes, Gray was well suited
to deal with the tough-minded Chicago faculty. "She was an unusually
strong presence," said a former associate. "Strong presences usually attract strong feelings over time." A professor at Chicago added: "Cross her,
and you're likely to feel the icy chill of the north."[19]

The University of Chicago has had a tremendous impact on other universities and on world affairs. It probably was the first to create special
committees of professors from various departments to learn from one another; the Committee on Social Thought, which novelist Saul Bellow
once chaired, is one of the best known of such groups. Traditionally,
nearly 80 percent of the faculty historically has lived near campus, and
the institution encourages this sort of collegiality. While there is some
disagreement about the advantages of such an intense environment, the
results are impressive: more Nobel Prizes than any other American university and a body of research that has affected the lives of generations.
For example, William Gray's "Dick, Jane, and Spot" books taught people
all over the world to read, while Nathaniel Kleitman documented the
REM stage of sleep.[20] In the intensity of such an ambience, an indispensable piece of leadership, as the early events and criticisms of Gray's pres-

idency underscore, is the ability to have not only considerable physical stamina, but substantial psychological stamina as well.

During her first months, Gray in fact became engaged in some heated debates. She survived them, but not without criticism. The most notable controversy involved the 1979 decision to bestow a university award (the Pick Award) on Vietnam-era Defense Secretary Robert J. McNamara. Gray was actually unaware of the existence of this new award when she came to Chicago; it had been established the previous year (1978) and she did not know about its existence until a previously appointed faculty committee came forward with its recommendation. A rowdy crowd of two thousand students and faculty carrying signs reading "Keep Imperialist Butcher Off Campus!" and "Horrible Hanna and Murderer Mac" protested a $25,000 award to then World Bank president McNamara for "outstanding contributions to international understanding." One-third of the regular faculty, including thirteen department chairs, signed statements distancing themselves from the event. Gray went ahead with the award, noting that peaceful dissent is part of the tradition of Chicago. Some thought she handled the affair well and many others felt she did not. "It would have been wrong," she recalled, "to have withdrawn the award because the recipient was controversial and because it created problems. . . . It would have been wrong to say that because someone is controversial, one should withdraw an award." However, recognizing that no progress could be made without the thoughtful involvement of the faculty, she appointed a few weeks later a distinguished faculty panel to study the manner in which the university gave out special awards. The episode clearly highlights the brevity of presidential "honeymoons" and the difficulty in predicting when and how the marital bliss will come to an end.

THREE FUNDAMENTAL CHALLENGES

Three more fundamental and important, if less dramatic, challenges faced Gray during the early stages of her presidency. First was graduate education: Chicago traditionally considered itself a graduate institution, and she set up a committee in 1982 to consider whether and how it could remain one. The seventeen-member faculty commission headed by historian Keith Baker proposed major changes in the graduate program that would make the experience more relevant, more stimulating, and more desirable to students. From a low point of about 2,000 graduate students in the various divisions in 1982, enrollment increased to about 2,800 by 1988 and to over 3,100 by 1993, her last year as president. Fundamental reforms were implemented, including: shortening the time to the degree;

developing a graduate course of study that prepared students for jobs in government and industry as well as academe; making long-standing requirements for the doctorate more flexible; providing more reliable student financial aid; and giving career training for Ph.D.'s higher priority. Gray also assembled interdisciplinary workshops where graduate students and faculty advisors could meet to discuss ideas for projects and papers, helping to alleviate the isolation sometimes experienced by graduate students working alone on their dissertations. More importantly, the Baker Commission was substantially different from earlier Chicago committees and faculty study groups. Unlike the Kalven Commission in the 1960s, which dealt with social investments and the relationship of the university to political causes and created more of a "thought piece" than a blueprint for change and action, Gray's commissions were charged to propose solutions to problems that could be implemented. Gray's success with the commissions she charged can be attributed in part to the approach she took with them, which, like the tone of her tenure, was collegial and not confrontational. "I believe until the very end she was highly regarded by the faculty. She was one of them. She respected them. She was not seen to 'use' them, but rather to include them," said another former associate.

A second challenge facing Gray was the undergraduate enterprise. Historically, Chicago has had a small undergraduate college, with intimate classes and majors in fields like Sanskrit. A vintage "Second City" episode in the late 1970s, "Football comes to the University of Chicago," painfully underscored the predicament: one player in the sketch described the shape of the football as a "demipolytetrahedron" while another one confused the left guard with Kierkegaard.[21] The stereotype of the Chicago undergraduate comes from the days of Hutchins, when very young students with excellent academic preparation were enrolled; the image tended to hurt recruiting because people thought only young geniuses could apply. Stories about urban crime in the south Chicago neighborhoods surrounding the university were another hurdle in attracting undergraduates. But Gray was determined to make the university friendlier for undergraduates. "There was a perception that life here was—I won't say gray, that's hard for me—but beige." She decided to increase the size of the undergraduate class and also to reaffirm Chicago's well known two-year common core curriculum, the latter a clever nod toward the conservative faculty while at the same time modernizing other parts of the undergraduate experience. The core curriculum, the centerpiece of Robert Maynard Hutchins' educational scheme, stresses the sciences, the humanities, and the social sciences. While consumerism within the elective framework had eroded many curricula at other schools, Chicago bucked the trend by asserting more strongly that an educated person should follow a rigorous course of study. Gray's decision to endorse the general education curriculum honored Chicago's institutional culture while making the university more distinctive among a field of tough competitors. So as she improved the conditions and atmosphere of student life—renovating recreational facilities, building new student housing, joining a new athletic league (albeit at the Division III level of the NCAA, with institutions like Carnegie Mellon and Johns Hopkins)—Gray also created a group headed by former dean Donald Levine to review the undergraduate curriculum. The faculty committee solidified Chicago's unswerving commitment to general education and affirmed a new, two-year common curriculum for all students, regardless of their major, requiring proficiency in civilizations, social sciences, humanities, a foreign language, and mathematics and natural sciences.

Two different reports, the Bradburn report (after committee chair Norman Bradburn, who later became provost) and the Greenstone report (after David Greenstone, a professor in political science) urged increases in the size of undergraduate enrollments while preserving the traditional character of the institution as a graduate and research university. Whether the efforts to change the image of the undergraduate experience as portrayed in the "Second City" sketch were successful is not entirely clear. Gray and her colleagues made a gallant effort to improve student life and initiated many extracurricular activities and programs, including the introduction of the Kuviasungnerk, a popular winter festival. And the enrollment of undergraduates did increase significantly, both absolutely and relative to the total enrollment: when Gray was inaugurated in 1978, undergraduate enrollment stood at 2,653, but by 1991, undergraduate enrollment had increased by nearly one-third to over 3,400. (In 2003, there were 4,216 students enrolled in the undergraduate college.)

The third issue involved finances. With declining applications at both the graduate and undergraduate levels, and with rising inflation costs and an economy in deep recession, Gray and her colleagues at Chicago faced a highly uncertain economic future. After the fund-raising campaign of her predecessor fell significantly short of its relatively modest $80 million goal, Gray had no choice but to wait several years before a new campaign could be announced. Instead, she sharpened her pencil and set about finding ways to reduce spending. She would benefit from her experiences at Yale, whose budget was "a mess" when Gray arrived there. In comparison to a university like Princeton, which has the largest endowment relative to the size of the program and to enrollments, Yale is very large and very fragmented, with professional schools in areas like music, art, law, and medicine. Among other things, she had to slash the budget of Yale's venerable faculty club. So Gray knew how to bring a sense of discipline and order to complicated enterprises like the University of Chicago.

Hanna had recovered $4 million in facilities expenditures at Chicago by 1984 and administrative costs had also fallen sharply—from 40 percent of total expenditures to about 25 percent.[22] Gray's spartan economic style was embodied in personal behaviors as well: her office was simple, devoid of any personal effects or fancy furniture, and ascetic by the standards of the suites occupied by presidents at Stanford and Yale. The University of Chicago Hospital, which used to neglect even rudimentary bookkeeping, began using more modern methods to keep its records. The hospital also generated most of its own funding, reducing the previous drain on general university resources. For various academic considerations or for lack of student interest, certain programs, such as library science and geography, either disappeared or were absorbed into larger degree programs, a difficult feat given the notorious eternalness of university departments. The faculty has also declined by two hundred members over a period of several years; Gray compelled senior faculty to spend more hours teaching in order to preserve its exceptional seven-to-one student-faculty ratio.

Many universities have a "phantom" deficit that does not show in the bottom line, but instead is reflected in the deferred maintenance for buildings and landscaping. Deciding that the best way to avoid high maintenance costs in the future was to invest in new facilities and to reserve a share of capital funds for scheduled maintenance, Gray initiated an unprecedented building and renovation program accompanied by an equally ambitious plan to raise money for it. Chicago's Science Quadrangle and state of the art technical libraries, its Physics Teaching Center, Court Theatre, Mitchell Hospital, and Irving B. Harris School of Public Policy are all concrete legacies of Gray's tenure, a solid accomplishment given the general austerity of the 1980s. By 1987, Gray had been in office nine years and had successfully completed a fund-raising campaign for the arts and sciences that surpassed its $150 million goal. In addition to the arts and sciences campaign, the medical center, the law school, and the graduate school of business all had exceeded by nearly $10 million their (combined) fund-raising goals of $75 million.[23] And in October of 1991 another five-year campaign for $500 million ("Campaign for the Next Century") was announced; within two years it was closing in on the $300 million mark. Overall, the Chicago endowment increased by over 400 percent, from $250 million to $1.3 billion, during Gray's fifteen-year tenure as president, a compounded rate of increase of 12 percent per year in spite of a prolonged period of "stagflation" and two recessions.

GENDER AND THE PRESIDENCY

Like the University of Maryland's John Slaughter, Hanna Gray is an oft mentioned "first" in the administration of higher education, even though both Slaughter and Gray were actually "seconds" in their respective categories. (Lorene Rogers at Texas-Austin and Clifton Wharton at Michigan State were actually the first woman and the first African American presidents of major research universities.) Gray had the fortune of attending Bryn Mawr, where she saw men and women working as equals and with mutual respect. She went from there to Radcliffe. (Or, as she says, was it Harvard?) Radcliffe, one of the Seven Sisters, had no real existence as a graduate school in the 1950s and early 1960s, but Harvard would not yet admit women as graduate students. She arrived at Harvard the first year women were allowed to sit in the main reading room of the Widener Library. And throughout her entire time at Harvard, as a student and then as one of a handful of women faculty, Gray was not allowed to enter Lamont Library, the undergraduate library at one corner of Harvard Yard, even though men from Harvard were allowed to enter the Radcliffe library. In addition, women faculty members were not meant to go through the front door of Harvard's faculty club, although Gray would walk through the front door whenever her department held a meeting there. "No one ever dared say anything to me, although the rest of the time I would go in through the back."

She became president at a time when American society was creating new opportunities for women and when there was a new momentum to create those opportunities. Perhaps, she acknowledges, as a woman she was in the right place at the right time for her jobs at Northwestern and Yale. After all, more women were being appointed as provosts and deans during this period. Perhaps Chicago was also more willing to buck trends and to reaffirm its iconoclastic image. But in spite of the fact that there were few women in administration in the 1970s, it remains undeniable Gray had a unique set of skills, talents, and professional connections that would make her stand out regardless of gender. In particular, her fit with Chicago's culture is undeniable. When asked about intercollegiate athletics, for example, she immediately proclaims it as corrupt: "Chicago is so lucky we don't have it." And as far as physical education requirements go, Gray is equally absolute: "Required P. E. is for the birds. I don't believe in educating the whole person, I believe in educating their minds."

Gray considers herself a "Bryn Mawr feminist," as opposed to some of "the newer and more radical forms" of feminism, and believes that some segments of the women's rights movement have been rather humorless and focused on things not fundamentally important. "I don't mind men standing up when I come in a room or opening doors for me; these are courtesies that are charming aspects of civilized living. So I think you can remain true to your principles about professional opportunities for women and not have to act like a man." But regardless of her gender, Hanna Gray was tough and what she said is what she meant. There was no hypocrisy or disinformation in what she said or did, according to associates. She was intense and could even be described as a workaholic: she was not morning person, but she rarely left the office before 7:00 or 8:00 PM, unless she had an evening meeting or social occasion. Indicative of Gray's physical energy was her significant juggling act between 1965 and 1972 when she was mixing career with travel back to the East to take care of her parents and grandparents. Her office door was open most of the time and she welcomed discussion about the issues. She used every lunch she could to meet with faculty or staff or downtown with trustees or donors. But society also treats tough women differently, and perhaps less charitably, than it does tough male CEOs or presidents. According to Kleinbard, who worked closely with Gray during most of her tenure:

> She was not one to let you off the hook mercifully, if you were silly, inarticulate, lacked the kind of information that should inform a decision, or otherwise did not perform to her expectations. If Mr. CEO is this way, we attribute it to testosterone. If Ms. CEO does it, we are unforgiving. She did not play golf with the boys or do those other things that the guys do. I am sure that this had some impact on how she was seen by some members of the Chicago community, some faculty, and some students.

While Gray has obviously dealt quite successfully with obstacles facing professional women, she clearly prefers to focus on how much progress has been made and how rapidly change has occurred. She also understands the importance of role models: "I was very conscious of how fast things changed once there began to be women on the faculty or entering through the 'front door.'" But in spite of this progress and of dozens of women presidents, only one major American university, the University of Pennsylvania, has replaced a woman president with another woman.[24] And choices are still important, although Gray believes it is possible to have a family and a career (in her case, cancer prevented her from having children: "I didn't make a choice; it was made for me"[25]), just as she believes young women should feel free to choose the option *not* to have a career.

A fascinating and largely neglected aspect of the female presidency is the role of the president's spouse. Traditionally, the female spouse of a male president devotes a significant amount of time to the "regal" functions of the job: hosting parties, standing at reception lines, meeting with women groups, and the like. A few universities provide a budget and even an assistant for the spouse to handle these duties. In recent times, due to the dramatic movement of women into the labor markets, the female spouse of the male president has perhaps distanced herself from such activities, but the societal expectations about gender roles in such cases remain relatively unchanged. Less is known about the male spouse of the female president, as was the case with Hanna and Charles Gray.

"You have to understand Charles Gray," said Hanna, "to know that this role was not an issue for him. He's a scholar and that's what he did." Charles was regarded as an outstanding teacher who cared for his students and who enjoyed a competitive game of squash, but played no role in the administration of the university. What this means is that the female president typically has to pull "double duty." One of Hanna's close associates put it this way:

> It is very difficult for women to maintain a marriage or close relationship when they are in senior positions of this type, especially if they must arrange the social occasions, supervise events, maintain a home, go to theatre or concerts, as though they had loads of time to do all those things in addition to their work responsibilities. Mrs. Gray did not have a social secretary. She had to accomplish these tasks herself. The level of expectation on our part is very high and must generate a lot of anxiety. Perhaps this is changing, but I haven't seen it.

CONCLUSION

The University of Chicago presented Hanna Holborn Gray with a set of unique challenges. Her task may have been eased slightly by the university's relatively small size (compared to a major public research university) and by its private funding, which reduced the number of constituencies she had to respond to and allowed her to build more personal relationships with faculty. But at the same time, the Chicago cul-

ture—a curious mixture of ambition, innovation and conservatism—
coupled with the financial problems that plagued American higher education during the 1980s, made Hanna's tenure arguably more complicated
than the presidency at most other institutions. Because of fundamental
changes in graduate education, in the economy, and in how private universities were financed, universities had to turn toward private fund-
raising with unprecedented vigor. Hanna Gray was one of the pioneer
university presidents in the area of fund-raising, devoting a much larger
percentage of her time to outside fund-raising than her predecessors.
However, perhaps the biggest challenge of her presidency was bringing a
sense energy and optimism to the university community at a time when
there was a great deal of uncertainty and even pessimism about its future.

Under Gray's leadership, the University of Chicago survived, grew, and
prospered during the 1980s and early 1990s, even as she became known
nationally for her leadership in broader university activities such as her
chairmanship of the prestigious Association of American Universities.
Hanna's way of managing business at Chicago—inclusive and collegial,
but always professional and goal-oriented—proved successful both in addressing the institution's desire to retain its preeminence and in honor-
ing its traditional respect for debate and collegiality. If Gray's leadership
style could be faulted, it would be that she was too businesslike and thus
came across to some people as brusque and unfeeling. Her personality
may have particularly grated some faculty members with more traditional
gender expectations.

At the same time, it is unarguable that Gray successfully reconciled
the pressing demands of her times with the unique and intense institutional culture at the University of Chicago. Hanna Gray has by a wide
margin served the longest tenure as president of the Chicago in the last
fifty years, second only to Pratt and Hutchins, both of whom of course
began their presidencies in the 1930s or before. Longevity aside, Gray
left the University of Chicago much stronger than when she first arrived
as president in 1978. Raised as an emigrant and as an academic, she was
accustomed to being different and thinking independently. This gave her
an intuitive understanding of the concerns of those who followed her and
a clear program for restoring the preeminence of Chicago. In her style,
Hanna Gray recognized, as Machiavelli did also five hundred years ago,
that change is among the most difficult things a leader can undertake; if
it is not based upon a broad consensus, it does not tend to last, and it is
much harder to achieve. So Gray reached out to the faculty across the
campus. "New things had to be done and these colleagues came up with

thoughtful ways to do them. Creating new things became not only possible but also more lasting and widely accepted."

NOTES

1. To many of Hutchins' critics, "confusion" was quite different from diversity or freedom to choose. University of Chicago economist Harry Gideonse published *The Higher Learning in a Democracy: A Reply to President Hutchins' Critique of the American University* (New York: Farrar and Rinehart, 1937) a year after Hutchins published his book and attacked the basic ideas that Hutchins was advocating. In particular, Gideonse argued that Hutchins' thesis was elitist and antidemocratic and that there were many ways to study the world: "Unity imposed by authority," wrote Gideonse, "is only another term for uniformity."

2. John Maynard Hutchins, *The Higher Learning in America* (New Haven, CT: Yale University Press, 1936).

3. Dr. Lorene Rogers actually was the first woman president of a major American research university and Hanna Gray was second, even if one considers Gray's interim presidency at Yale during 1977. Rogers was named president *ad interim* of the University of Texas at Austin in 1974. The following year she was appointed president and served in that capacity until August 1979. While the University of Chicago is generally considered to be more prestigious, Texas is of course also highly regarded and has a much bigger budget and a wider range of programs. The Lorene Rogers Scholar-Athlete Award is presented annually to the senior student-athlete at UT-Austin with the highest overall grade point average.

4. Gustavo Pérez Firmat, for example, describes these challenges for Cuban Americans and other immigrants in his *Life on the Hyphen: The Cuban-American Way* (Austin: University of Texas Press, 1994).

5. See Robin Winks, *Cloak and Gown: Scholars in the Secret War, 1939–1961* (New York: William Morrow, 1987). The book Hanna Gray's father wrote while at the OSS is Hajo Holborn, *American Military Government: Its Organization and Policies* (Washington, DC: Infantry Journal Press, 1947).

6. See "Biography of Lily Ross Taylor (1886–1969)," http://www.brynmawr.edu/classics/taylor.html.

7. See Hartmut Lehman, ed., *Felix Gilbert as Scholar and Teacher*, German Historical Institute, Occasional Paper No. 6., Washington, DC, 1992.

8. Report of the Faculty Committee to Review the Decision with Regard to the Reappointment of Assistant Professor Marlene Dixon, University of Chicago, 1969.

9. Francine du Plessix Gray, "The Panthers at Yale," *New York Review of Books* 14, no. 11 (June 4, 1970).

10. Geoffrey Kabaservice, *The Guardians: Kingman Brewster, His Circle, and the Rise of the Liberal Establishment* (New York: Henry Holt and Co., 2004).

11. See A. Bartlett Giamatti, *A Free and Ordered Space: The Real World of the University* (New York: W. W. Norton, 1988).

12. Clifford Terry, "The Dawn of Gray at the University of Chicago," *Chicago Tribune Magazine*, October 14, 1979, 26.

13. Grant Pick, "Headstrong Hanna: U of C Soars Under Gray, but Critics Remain," *Crain's Chicago Business*, October 28–November 3, 1991, 60.

14. Paul Galloway, "UC Prexy's Goal? 'A Little More Fun,'" *Chicago Sunday Sun-Times*, July 16, 1978.

15. See, for instance, Kenneth E. Boulding, "The Management of Decline," *Change* 7 (June 1975): 8–9, 64.

16. Pick, "Headstrong Hanna," 60.

17. Terry, "Dawn of Gray," 30.

18. Ibid., 33.

19. Pick, "Headstrong Hanna," 60.

20. Connie Leslie, with Todd Barrett, "A Rock and a Hard Place," *Newsweek*, October 7, 1991, 57.

21. Terry, "Dawn of Gray," 30.

22. Peter Osterlund, "A Life in Academe," *University of Chicago Magazine* 86 (June 1993): 25.

23. Leslie M. Werner, "The Gray Presidency: The First Ten Years," *University of Chicago Magazine* 81 (Fall 1988): 13.

24. At the University of Pennsylvania, F. Sheldon Hackney, formerly provost at Princeton, was succeeded in late 1993 by a female interim president, Claire Fagin, who served for a few months until Hackney's permanent replacement, Judith Seitz Rodin, was chosen. When Rodin retired in 2004, she was replaced by another woman, Amy Gutmann, another former provost from Princeton.

25. Werner, "Gray Presidency," 13.

CHAPTER 11

Lessons, Conclusions, and Implications

Adde parvum parvo magnus acervit erit.

—Ovid

A REPRISE

In this concluding chapter I go from the individual to the general, from the patterns in each of the six case studies to more systematic themes found in leadership and followership writ large. I begin with a recapitulation of the main premises before proceeding to specific conclusions gleaned from the six cases studies viewed as an ensemble. Toward the end of the chapter I focus on the issues that will benefit from greater consideration and study.

The university is one of the more enduring and complex enterprises in the long history of human organizations; it thus provides a useful vehicle through which to study the phenomenon of leadership in all of its human expressions. Two of the university's defining qualities as an organization are the vast variety of stakeholders or publics that depend upon it and the employment relationships with its main employees, the faculty. There are other features contributing to the intricacies of the university, but these two present singular challenges to their leaders and managers. It is very much like a business in some areas like its financial operations or its physical plant, but it is also not at all like a business in its academic activities—its classrooms, research initiatives, public service efforts—and in its student affairs areas. The contours of the factors that enable the process of leadership and followership—the biological origins of humans, the early lives of future leaders and the stimuli to which they were exposed while growing up, formal education and significant mentors, and the qualities of the mature leader, particularly in interpersonal relations and communication—intersect with the organizational situations and environments to define styles of leadership. This is the framework and these are the contexts within which the six cases have been presented and analyzed.

BROAD STROKES OF LEADERSHIP AND FOLLOWERSHIP

Leadership might be a fundamental and universal aspect of the human condition and of what it means to be human. But leadership is also never simple or easy. Leading organizations that are at their hearts complex and complicated places, as are universities, is even more difficult, for their greater intricacy imposes real limitations on the power of leaders and demands superior skills of persuasion, motivation, and communication. Leading is not without its rewards but it is not without substantial risk: history has shown that in extreme cases, leaders are deposed or even killed by followers and, more commonly, their health or their families and friends often pay a heavy price as relationships and circumstances inevitably change. The popular metaphor of the leader as a strong and solitary figure at the head of the troops, of the warrior on the white horse, is a fiction that reinforces the isolation of leadership. Under this familiar but ultimately misguided view of leadership and followership, power is transferred from followers to leaders, and when problems are not solved, as inevitably happens, the leader is then blamed and made into the scapegoat. It is thus increasingly obvious that leadership is not about power or domination or control, although these are often important factors within leadership, but rather about persuasion and helping organizations expose problems and work toward their resolution. As Heifetz puts it, the "strategic challenge is to give the [organizational] work back to people without abandoning them."[1]

An initial element toward a comprehension of leadership and followership revolves around the evolutionary roots of authority in humans and around the flow of images, symbols, trends, and experiences of a child at the home. The family and its social, political, and cultural environments are leadership systems, and their influences are long-lasting and indelibly scored in people's behaviors and tendencies. Intriguing indicators of future leadership involve the young leader's resiliency and the ability to deal with adverse situations at an early age. Former U.S. President Bill Clinton discusses in his autobiography what he terms the "parallel lives" he learned to live while dealing with the alcoholism and violence he experienced in his home as a child.[2] It gave him a basis, a "mental muscle," for compartmentalizing issues at an early age, enabling him to learn how to lock some problems behind a door while turning his full energies to others. The importance of mentors throughout childhood and during the period of formal education in various domains—the notion of social and professional "networking" and of the things that make networking and mentoring possible—is closely linked aspects of leadership development, as are travel during young adulthood and exposure to different cultures and traditions.

A global, all-encompassing view of the organizational environment, the capacity to climb on a metaphorical helicopter and see it all detachedly from above, is apparently useful in identifying organizational challenges and recognizing the work that must be done and the problems that are emerging. This bird's-eye view emerges as a leadership pattern in the analysis of the six case studies in this book, as all six individuals can be categorized as "global," as opposed to sequential, thinkers: they are good "synthesizers" of information and creative in their approaches to solving problems. They can identify complex solutions quickly, often without being able to describe in much detail how they arrived at the answers; they can see the relationships among seemingly unrelated events and situations and describe problems in ways that emphasize the interrelatedness of various components.

Neil Smelser, in discussing Clark Kerr, refers to a trait he calls "objectification," the facility to remove oneself from events even as they are occurring and to analyze those events unemotionally and objectively.[3] While Smelser's objectification and the global view discussed earlier are not identical notions, they are close relatives. Leadership has important elements of both passive reflection and active participation; possession of a peripheral vision like Larry Bird's or Wayne Gretzky's, who played their respective team sports of basketball and hockey as if they were in the game and simultaneously above it, appears to be a crucial advantage. Whether this manner of viewing the world is innate or learned is of course not easily answered, but there appears to be a relationship between academic preparation in certain disciplines and a tendency toward more comprehensive approaches. For example, Clark Kerr and Bill Bowen both were trained essentially as institutional economists, emphasizing a multidisciplinary approach and the overall connection between and among institutions. Hanna Gray has a decidedly historical perspective, as does Father Hesburgh, which brings a depth of perspective and a longer view to problems not commonly found. Friday's training in the law was broad and John Slaughter considers himself, correctly so, as a "not very typical engineer." Friday, Hesburgh, and Slaughter are also recognized widely for their unusual interpersonal gravitational pull, indicative of their interests in broader human connections.

Closely linked to a capacity for overarching observation are two other factors. The first is a profound connectedness to the organization and to its history and cultural behaviors. Without a deep association with and understanding of the situational environment, the leader must focus instead on learning "on the job," and the time required for this learning is taken from other, perhaps more urgent tasks. Inextricably linked to the ability to "view the dance floor from the balcony," and to understand the intricacies of the dance and of the dancers below, are superior abilities in the realms of communications and listening and, more generally, in the area of interpersonal relations.[4] These are all pieces of the same puzzle: the ability to see the larger picture and to understand its organizational implications, as well as the skill to communicate effectively across a diverse range of publics, are main ingredients.

The second factor that appears related to global thinking is an exposure to the top of the organization early in one's career, a feature that five of the six individuals had in common. Such exposure to the overall structure of an enterprise contributes to a formative understanding of how all the pieces fit together within the organization and of how the organization relates to external entities. It allows a promising young person to develop a network of high-level support that enhances the ability to advance in the organization. More importantly, exposure to the top enables young people to witness and to absorb the broadest strategic thinking of the organization, seeing how the top managers decide on policy and how it is implemented and modified at various levels of the enterprise. It also gives the organization an opportunity to evaluate the young leader.

Self-awareness, an understanding of one's strengths and weaknesses and limitations, of how information is gathered and processed, of how one deals with ambiguity and stressful situations, and of how one is perceived by others, is an indispensable asset in leading complex organizations and in the interpretation of events as one sits in the "helicopter." In Shakespeare's *Hamlet*, Polonius' advice to his son Laertes includes this bit of advice about self-awareness:

> This above all—to thine own self be true,
> And it must follow as the night the day,
> Thou canst not then be false to any man.[5]

Mature leaders quickly point out and acknowledge, without much prodding, their limitations and they tend to discuss them rather openly. They are self-disclosers in the best sense of the term, opening up their behaviors and tendencies to outside scrutiny, which strengthens their interpersonal connections, making them seem more human to their associates. Knowledge of oneself—self-awareness, self-insight, self-understanding—is essential to one's productive personal and interpersonal functioning and understanding and empathizing with other people. It is a particularly useful trait that enables strong leaders to surround themselves with equally strong individuals who might not share their specific strengths and who in fact might be more proficient than they are at a variety of tasks and functions.

Biological imperatives—limited life and work spans—clearly indicate that leadership and followership activities are ultimately temporary. But the self-interest of followers also suggests that leadership does not last forever in any setting. Individual self-interest frequently trumps overall goals and interests of a group (or of a leader) as individuals eventually return to their personal concerns and put aside group priorities. And in some organizational settings, particularly in organizations like universities, where many organizational goals are vague (for example, "great teaching" or "the model land-grant university for the twenty-first century") or not widely held, the effects and consequences of leadership may be even shorter. Leaders of complex enterprises therefore understand the virtues of persistence and advantages of physical endurance and psychological stamina in achieving goals and objectives. And the pace and demands of leadership imply a need for renewal and preservation, a time and place for sanctuary where reflection about self and about the institutional sense of purpose can occur.

SPECIFIC PATTERNS

One sees in the case studies several specific patterns and issues worthy of recapitulation. They can be usefully divided into patterns and commonalities common during childhood and early lives and those during adulthood and their actual periods of leadership. From their early lives and backgrounds emerge the following patterns, characteristics, and behaviors:

1. **Importance of historical contexts and environmental influences.**
   Kerr, Friday, and Hesburgh witnessed problems attending the Depression—the unemployment, the labor tensions and its graphic violence,
   the human despair from a lack of opportunity, the desperate circum-
   stance of individuals fighting for a chance at a better life. These experiences affected materially how they viewed their world and colored
   many of the decisions they would make. In the case of Hanna Gray
   one finds the impact of immigration and the impact of "tradition and
   translation," of living two sets of lives, the one from the "old country" and the one from America. John Slaughter's childhood in Topeka,
   Kansas, the home of *Brown v. the [Topeka, Kansas] Board of Education*,
   was rich with stories about the historic plight of African Americans
   and the struggle for civil rights and social justice.

2. **Exceptional intelligences and gifts in the realm of communication
   and public speaking.** Hanna Gray was fifteen when she entered college; Friday, Kerr, and Bowen were class presidents; Hesburgh and
   Slaughter both distinguished themselves early on in various ways academically. Bowen was the youngest full professor in Princeton history. Three of them were chosen by their teachers and professors to
   speak at their commencements.

3. **Adversity or conflict as children and adolescents at home.** The six
   cases developed or exhibited the patterns of response and unusual perseverance that research on resiliency has uncovered. Many strengths
   and proclivities existed from early in their lives, from Kerr's unusual
   intellect and negotiating skills to Bill Friday's interpersonal impact on
   others around him to Bill Bowen's propensity for hard work and leadership skills from an early age. That kind of consistency and enduring
   persistence seems characteristic of some individuals who overcome the
   obstacles or challenges between them and extraordinary achievement.

4. **Extraordinary attention in the home to education and to reading.**
   This is true in virtually all cases, with the possible exception of Bowen,
   who notes that neither of his parents pushed him in any form to study,
   although several of his mentors in high school did so. It is more notable when compared to contemporary families in similar conditions
   and economic situations.

5. **Hard work at an early age.** Most of the leaders highlighted here had
   to work as youngsters and they worked hard. They had the physical
   capacity to do so and in the process learned about the value of time
   management. All of them have remained extraordinarily active long
   after normal retirement age.

6. **Travel and exposure to different cultures before adulthood.** Travel is
   an element in the ability to "translate" behaviors across diverse cultures

or in understanding and empathizing with people and events from other backgrounds. The act of reading enabled some to "lead other lives," but most, either because of the war, or Hitler, or their religion, or discrimination, traveled significantly outside their immediate geography and were exposed to different cultures at a relatively early age. Most of the individuals highlighted here were able to observe, and to compare and contrast, different "versions" of the world and to understand their distinctiveness through interactions with social or religious groups.

7. **Opportunities to develop the art and skill of communication.** Bill Friday still recalls some of the speeches his father Lath had him practice over and over. Kerr's conversion to Quakerism similarly put him in front of audiences in his youth. Hesburgh's grandfather instilled in him a curiosity for and later the love of foreign travel and languages; Hesburgh's rigorous preparation by the Jesuits reinforced these tendencies.

8. **Significant mentors.** Each leader can point quite specifically and without prodding to individuals at various stages of their careers who were special to their development—an elementary school teacher, an assistant dean, a professor. For some, this mirrors research findings indicating that resilient children have a radiance or an ensemble of traits that attracts adult mentors to them. A related theme is an ability to develop, maintain, and significantly expand connections or networks over their lives: each of the individuals studied have been excellent at networking from an early age, maintaining in contact with significant adults who kept them in mind as their careers progressed.

9. **Unusual achievements compared to their peers.** Most of the individuals studied here had achieved things that their peers had not at an early age. For example, several were chosen to speak at their commencements, were class presidents, or had reached educational or professional stages much faster than their peers.

10. **Early exposure to the top.** Five of the six individuals studied here had opportunities to observe at close hand the operation of their organizations from a high vantage point early in their careers. This enabled them to learn about the overall structure of the organization and exposed them to trustees and other senior officers, who in turn were able to evaluate their skills and promise. Through these exposures to the top of organizations, and also due to non-trivial elements of luck and chance, opportunities arose and these individuals were able to recognize these opportunities and to do something with them.

The more common elements from adulthood and from their leadership periods included the following:

1. **Connectedness to their organizations.** This is perhaps the most striking feature in the ability to achieve extraordinary results as illustrated
by the six cases studied here. All except Slaughter grew professionally
and managerially at the same institution and if they left, like Gray,
they returned relatively quickly. They were very familiar with the culture of their organizations and were well known to others in their
communities. They understood one of the paradoxes of leadership: the
leader is an indispensable part of an organization, but only a part, and
a small part at that. Much depends on them, but it is never about
them. At the same time, however, all were exposed in significant and
meaningful ways to other institutions and other ways of doing work
and things. For example, Hesburgh, though he began his career at
Notre Dame and remained there, traveled widely and served on several presidential commissions and national committees; Hanna Gray
was at Northwestern, Yale, and Harvard, and served as chair of the
prestigious Association of American Universities (AAU). Friday also
chaired the AAU and the American Council on Education and served
three very different institutions and later thirteen additional even
more diverse ones. Kerr went from Swarthmore to Berkeley, and from
one coast to the other, bringing with him strong traditions about liberal education on a more human scale, a background that helped him
shape several of the campuses of the University of California.

2. **Strong interpersonal relations.** The interpersonal skills of Bill Friday
and Father Ted are renowned, but all six cases, as might be expected
given their achievements in very public arenas, are gifted in the realm
of interpersonal relations. Several of them, including Gray and Kerr in
particular, have an excellent sense of humor, Kerr's often leaning more
toward commentary. Bowen is one of the most "connected" people in
the United States, with friends and contacts literally all over the world,
and Slaughter is disarmingly friendly and caring in his interactions.

3. **Ability to work long hours very effectively.** All had the physical
stamina to work fairly long hours and they were all excellent managers of their time.

4. **Optimism and perseverance.** Invariably, these six individuals tended
to focus on the positive aspects of an issue. For example, Slaughter, on
the attack on affirmative action programs, says: "The good thing is that
we're now talking about these issues." Hesburgh on the impact of technology: "Did you ever stop to think that when the Lord was talking in
the Sermon on the Mount, he could only talk to those people who
heard his voice? He may have rung in a little miracle or two, but today,
the Pope talks to a million people, no sweat." Bill Friday continues to
have an impact on the conduct of intercollegiate athletics through his
Knight Commission work two decades after retirement and Bill Bowen

continues to speak out for excellence in education and for social justice and opportunities for minorities nationally.

5. **An "aerial" or global understanding of the relationships among different parts of the enterprise and the larger environment.** They understood the "gestalt" was more than the sum of the parts and how the
   different pieces fit together internally and how the entire enterprise relates to external entities.

6. **Management styles suited to the needs and demands of their respective institutions and their organizational cultures.** There was no
   "right" management style: Hesburgh's charismatic, take-charge style
   worked well at Notre Dame but would not have functioned at the
   University of California. At the same time, however, they all exhibited certain leadership traits in common.

7. **Cadence of life and systematic renewal.** The ability to remain at the
   top of their games required the periodic physical and psychic renewal.
   Routine exercise, prayer, fishing, gardening, and reading all served the
   purpose for most of the leaders.

8. **Uselessness of the concept of the "ubermanager" or the "superleader."**
   When effective leaders accomplish extraordinary things, they do so
   with innate talents and basic skills often perfected from childhood;
   with a deep connection to, and considerable knowledge of, their organization and its culture; with superb associates; with outstanding communication skills; and with a great deal of hard work and perseverance.
   All of them sought consensus and agreement, excepting perhaps Hesburgh, who as a "founding" (or at least a "reinventing") president with
   a great deal of charisma and power, occasionally moved forward without much consultation, particularly during the early stages of his presidency while the Notre Dame faculty and the governing processes were
   being strengthened.

9. **Strong and trusted associates.** Most of the presidents attracted strong
   associates and worked with highly effective teams. Their working relations seemed to be characterized by a high degree of trust, cordial-
   ity, and mutual admiration. They were also not afraid to establish and
   empower faculty commissions to recommend courses of action to deal
   with important organizational challenges.

10. **Gender and race.** The obstacles that hurt and separate are still present
    at all levels of society. One gets the sense from a review Hanna Gray's
    successful career that women are evaluated more carefully than are men
    for leadership positions and that their behaviors and actions are ques-
    tioned more frequently. The case of John Slaughter painfully demon-
    strates the effects of racism on leadership success, but it also underscores
    the heavy demands (for public appearances, speeches, committee mem-
    berships, for example) on those few minorities who make it to positions

of power and influence. Gender and race issues are understudied topics in leadership and would benefit from further research attention.

11. **Absence of behaviors that often derail careers.** Just as important as the traits and patterns that the six case studies exhibit are those behaviors that are absent. In general, based on personal interviews as triangulated with written materials and interviews with associates, most of the individuals studied showed a high "emotional intelligence," to use the phrase popularized by Dan Goleman, referring to "people skills" and qualities like the ability to read social situations, understanding one's own experiences, empathy toward others, and regulation of emotions in effective and useful ways.[6] There was a general absence of certain behaviors commonly associated with executive derailment:[7]

   - Self-enriching behaviors such as extravagant spending on office décor, personal trips, or other personal remuneration or benefits
   - Arrogance
   - Mercurial personality and moodiness
   - Aloofness, insensitivity, or disengagement from others
   - Perfectionism
   - Eagerness to please or win "popularity contests"
   - Over-ambition
   - Passive aggressiveness
   - Distrust and focus on negative aspects of situations
   - Difficulty molding a staff

CHANGES AND TRENDS

The past, as Hanna Gray observes, is often more heroic than the present. Many people look back with nostalgia at some golden age of university "giants" who were great institutional leaders as well as great public figures.[8] A hundred years ago, Gray wryly observed, "presidents were normally expected to have three names. That stately catalog would include Charles William Eliot, Daniel Coit Gilman, William Rainey Harper, David Starr Jordan, Benjamin Ide Wheeler, and later, Nicholas Murray Butler, Arthur Twining Hadley, James Roland Angell, and Robert Maynard Hutchins."[9] With the recent corporate scandals at companies like Enron and Tyco, the yearning for these three-name university presidents probably has equivalents in business and in other institutions, such as Roberto Goizueta in private industry or Katharine Graham in the print media or Thomas Alva Edison in entrepreneurship and invention.

The presidency and the presidents have indeed changed. The president is no longer head and shoulders above other members of the university family: even as presidents' salaries have escalated tremendously in recent years relative to the pay for senior professors at their own universities, the dean of their medical schools and their football coaches typically make more money and are much more likely to be on television and in the newspapers. Outstanding university leaders might continue to exist today, but current pressures and trends such as the shortening of presidential tenures at the public universities or the increased prominence of external fund-raising functions make it more difficult for leaders to assume the multiple roles of institutional builders and public figures and spokespersons. And this is the dilemma, for while the presidency is not inherently more difficult today, it is different. And it still needs the "giants." Unlike the situation during the Great Depression or during the late 1950s, when major economic and demographic changes were recognized and anticipated and plans were developed to address them, it is not clear that the emerging trends affecting universities today have been fully identified or comprehended. Howard Gardner makes a related point:

> In the absence of institutional leaders who are willing to seize the bully pulpit, unhappy consequences are likely to ensue. Either their institutions go undefended and undescribed; or they are poorly described; or their public depiction is left to the media, which can hardly be expected to go beyond caricature. Stereotypical counterstories seize the day, whether they depict spoiled professors, overly rich museums, selfish corporations, or ivory-towered foundations.[10]

Thus, the need for more effective, if not "giant," university presidents who deeply comprehend the purposes of their institutions and who can communicate their value to society becomes essential as conflicting messages and the competing claimants on resources proliferate, particularly during times of rapid change. Universities continue to serve remarkably crucial public functions, just as they have always done, and their future depends on a public appreciation of these functions and on the importance attached to them. And because of the changes identified earlier, it seems these arguments apply with even greater force to the public, rather than to the private, universities.

FURTHER IMPLICATIONS

The six cases presented in this book admittedly represent extraordinary individuals at one extreme in a scale of achievement and accomplishment and it is reasonable to ask how their personal histories and voyages can suggest a path toward a better life for a more general audience or toward a better understanding of the forces of leadership and followership. A partiality toward successful leaders is evident among the presidents highlighted here and some of the findings flowing from their stories might not be representative. Contradictory examples probably exist and might undermine some generalizations. This is as it should be. This is the way disciplines advance and the edge of the knowledge envelope is pushed outward. But leadership is too often filled with false dichotomies, an "either/or" mindset that focuses thinking too narrowly. A compelling finding from the case studies is that the "made or born" schism is not particularly relevant. There is a universal advantage for everyone, leaders and followers, to learn more about the skills and behaviors and processes associated with this universal phenomenon.

In fact, several specific patterns from the six case studies are of guiding value in the development of talent and human potential, no matter what the starting point is: the importance of a strong emphasis on education, and reading in particular, at home; development of certain leadership skills during youth, such as debate and public speaking; the benefits of work while growing up; the usefulness of mentoring; and the broadening impacts of travel and of learning about foreign cultures while young. For leadership scholars, this study has revealed the usefulness of the case study approach as a valuable adjunct to more quantitative approaches and has identified several areas for further study, including the broad topics of resiliency and mentoring, topics about which comparatively little is still known. In addition, the relations between situation, power, and charismatic leadership, connectedness to one's organization and knowledge of organizational culture and processes, early exposure to the top of the managerial structure, and the impact of travel at an early age all would profit from further analysis to determine how they interact with leadership effectiveness.

The foregoing chapters additionally point to benefits in developing managerial talent internally and in providing mentoring opportunities for promising young colleagues that expose them to the highest levels of the organization. This presents learning opportunities for potential future leaders and chances for the institution to observe and evaluate individuals as they operate within the administration, looking for strengths in the areas of interpersonal relations, communications, physical and psychological stamina and for the absence of behaviors that tend to derail managerial careers. There is evidence, both from the case studies examined here and from other reports, about appreciable differences in the presidential transitions of public and private universities. The leadership transitions in the private universities appear in many cases to be much smoother, more like the handing off of a baton during a race than the stopping of one race and the starting of another. In spite of highly successful presidencies, the end of the Kerr and Slaughter presidencies were obviously traumatic spectacles, and even Friday's was not lacking in some controversy. On the other hand, the transitions of Bowen, Gray, and Hesburgh were relatively uneventful and allowed sufficient time for their respective universities to plan for an effective succession.[11] It may just be in the nature of public universities to be more politicized and for their succession events to be somewhat more complicated, with the involvement of many groups of interested stakeholders, but it would be useful for public trustees to study how to make their presidential transitions as smooth as possible.

NOTES

1. Ronald A. Heifetz, *Leadership Without Easy Answers* (Cambridge, MA: Harvard University Press, 1994), 251.

2. William J. Clinton, *My Life* (New York: Alfred A. Knopf, 2004).

3. Neil J. Smelser, foreword to Clark Kerr, *Academic Triumphs*, Vol. 1 of *The Gold and the Blue: A Personal Memoir of the University of California, 1949–1967* (Berkeley: University of California Press, 2001), xxvi.

4. Ronald Heifetz uses the dance floor and balcony metaphors in his *Leadership Without Easy Answers* (Cambridge, MA: Harvard University Press, 1994), 252–253.

5. While these words are often used to illustrate the value of self-awareness, the quote also comes from a play in which characters act with questionable morality and justify their deeds regardless of the ethics involved.

6. Daniel Goleman, *Emotional Intelligence* (New York: Bantam, 1995).

7. See, for example, Ellen Van Velsor and Jean B. Leslie, "Why Executives Derail: Perspectives Across Time and Cultures," *Academy of Management Executives* 9, no. 4 (1995); Barbara E. Kovach, "Successful Derailment: What Fast-Trackers Can Learn While They're Off the Track," *Organizational Dynamics* 18, no. 2 (Autumn 1989): 33–47.

8. Hanna Gray, "On the History of Giants," in *Universities and Their Leadership,* edited by William G. Bowen and Harold Shapiro (Princeton, NJ: Princeton University Press, 1998), 114.

9. Ibid., 101.

10. Howard Gardner, "The Vehicle and the Vehicles of Leadership," *American Behavioral Scientist* 42, no. 6 (March 1999): 1009–1023.

11. There are of course certain tensions and concerns in all transition events and in their timing, particularly if there are individuals who are especially interested in succeeding the departing presidents or if stresses have built up over the years between the departing president and some of the trustees. But these relatively minor transition issues do not have the same impact on the organization's continuity and morale as do sudden, unannounced departures or firings, for example.

REFERENCES

Abbott, Philip. *Strong Presidents: A Theory of Leadership*. Knoxville: University of Tennessee Press, 1996.

Albert, Robert S. "Family Positions and the Attainment of Eminence: A Study of Special Family Positions and Special Family Experiences." *Gifted Child Quarterly* 24 (1980): 87–95.

Anderson, B. Robert. "Bowen of Princeton." *College Management* 9, no. 2 (1974): 22–25.

Ashby, Warren. *Frank Porter Graham: A Southern Liberal*. Winston-Salem, NC: John F. Blair, 1980.

Barrier, Smith. *On Tobacco Road: Basketball in North Carolina*. New York: Leisure Press, 1983.

Bass, Bernard, and R. M. Stogdill. *Bass and Stogdill's Handbook of Leadership*. 3rd ed. New York: The Free Press, 1990.

Baumol, William J. "Jacob Viner at Princeton." *Journal of Political Economy* 80, no. 1 (1972): 12–15.

Ben-David, Joseph. *Centers of Learning: Britain, France, Germany, United States*. New York: McGraw-Hill, 1977.

Bennis, Warren. *On Becoming a Leader*. Reading, MA: Perseus Books, 1994.

Bennis, Warren, and Patricia Ward Biederman. *Organizing Genius: The Secrets of Creative Collaboration*. Reading, MA: Addison-Wesley, 1997.

Bennis, Warren, J. Parikh, and R. Lessem. *Beyond Leadership: Balancing Economics, Ethics, and Ecology*. Cambridge, MA: Blackwell Business, 1994.

Bergmann, Barbara R. "Do Sports Really Make Money for the University?" *Academe* 77, no. 1 (1991): 28–30.

Bérubé, Michael. "Why Inefficiency Is Good for Universities." *Chronicle of Higher Education*, May 27, 1998, B4–B5.

Blau, Peter M. *The Organization of Academic Work.* New York: Wiley, 1973.

Blumenstyk, Goldie. "Money-Making Champs." *Chronicle of Higher Education,* April 19, 1996, A49–A50.

Boulding, Kenneth E. *The Management of Decline.* Association of Governing Boards Reports 17, no. 5 (September–October 1975): 4–9.

Bowen, William G. "Economic Problems Confronting Higher Education: An Institutional Perspective." *American Economic Review* 67, no. 1 (1977): 96–100.

————. *Ever the Teacher: William G. Bowen's Writings as President of Princeton.* Princeton, NJ: Princeton University Press, 1987.

————. "When a Business Leader Joins a Nonprofit Board." *Harvard Business Review,* September 1994, 38–43.

Bowen, William G., and Derek Bok. *The Shape of the River: Long-Term Consequences of Considering Race in College and University Admissions.* Princeton, NJ: Princeton University Press, 1998.

Bowen, William G., and Harold T. Shapiro. *Universities and Their Leadership.* Princeton, NJ: Princeton University Press, 1998.

Bressler, Marvin. *The Report [to President William J. Bowen] of the Commission on the Future of the College.* Princeton, NJ: Princeton University, 1973.

Bromley, D. B. *The Case-Study Method in Psychology and Related Disciplines.* Chichester, UK: John Wiley and Sons, 1986.

Brown, Edmund G. *Reagan and Reality: The Two Californias.* New York: Praeger, 1970.

Burgen, Arnold, ed. *Goals and Purposes of Higher Education in the Twenty-First Century.* Bristol, PA: Jessica Kingsley, 1996.

Burns, James MacGregor. *Leadership.* New York: Harper and Row, 1978.

————. *Transforming Leadership.* New York: Atlantic Monthly Press, 2003.

Byers, Walter. *Unsportsmanlike Conduct: Exploiting College Athletes.* Ann Arbor: University of Michigan Press, 1995.

Campbell, Tracy. *Short of the Glory: The Fall and Redemption of Edward F. Prichard, Jr.* Lexington: University Press of Kentucky, 1998.

Carbone, Robert F. *Presidential Passages.* Washington, DC: American Council on Education, 1981.

Carson, Clayborne, et al., eds. *Eyes on the Prize: America's Civil Rights Years.* New York: Penguin Books, 1987.

"Chronology of Events: Three Months of Crisis." *California Monthly,* February 1965.

Clark, Kenneth. "Prejudice and Your Child." In *Eyes on the Prize: America's Civil Rights Years,* edited by Clayborne Carson et al. New York: Penguin Books, 1987.

Cohen, Michael D., and James G. March. *Leadership and Ambiguity: The American College President.* New York: McGraw-Hill, 1974.

Conant, James Bryant. *My Several Lives: Memoirs of a Social Inventor.* New York: Harper and Row, 1970.

Conger, Jay A. "Qualitative Research as the Cornerstone Methodology for Understanding Leadership." *Leadership Quarterly* 9, no. 1 (1998): 107–121.

————. "Charismatic and Transformational Leadership in Organizations: An Insider's Perspective on These Developing Streams of Research." *Leadership Quarterly* 10, no. 2 (1999): 145–169.

Csikszentmihalyi, Mihaly. *Creativity: Flow and the Psychology of Discovery and Invention.* New York: HarperCollins, 1996.

Csikszentmihalyi, Mihaly, Kevin Rathunde, Samuel Whalen, and Maria Wong. *Talented Teenagers: The Roots of Success and Failure.* Cambridge: Cambridge University Press, 1993.

Daft, Richard L. *Leadership: Theory and Practice.* Fort Worth: Dryden Press, 1999.

Davis, Ralph M. "Institutional Renewal: What the Corporate Model Can't Tell You." In *Applying Corporate Management Strategies,* edited by Roger J. Fecher, 5–12. San Francisco: Jossey-Bass, 1985.

Dawkins, R. *The Selfish Gene.* New York: Oxford University Press, 1976.

De Vries, Manfred. *Life and Death in the Executive Fast Lane.* San Francisco: Jossey-Bass, 1995.

Drucker, Peter F. "The Coming of the New Organization." *Harvard Business Review,* January–February 1988, 45–53.

Ehle, John. *Dr. Frank: Life with Frank Porter Graham.* Chapel Hill, NC: Franklin Street Books, 1993.

Eibl-Eibesfeld, I. *Human Ethnology.* Chicago: Aldine, 1989.

Ericson, John. "Real World; Pretend Universities." *Educational Record* 74, no. 1 (1993): 43–48.

Erikson, Erik H. *Identity: Youth and Crisis.* New York: W. W. Norton, 1968.

Farrell, Charles. "Colleges Eye Limit on Time Players Give to Sports, Tougher Tests for Drug Abuse." *Chronicle of Higher Education,* July 9, 1986, 23–24.

————. "A Long Summer for Maryland's Chancellor." *Chronicle of Higher Education,* September 10, 1986, 30–33.

Finkelstein, S., and D. C. Hambrick. *Strategic Leadership: Top Executives and Their Effects on Organizations.* Minneapolis: West Publishing, 1996.

Freeman, Joan, Pieter Span, and Harald Wagner, eds. *Actualizing Talent: A Lifelong Challenge.* London: Cassell, 1995.

Gardner, David. *The California Oath Controversy.* Berkeley: University of California Press, 1967.

Gardner, Howard. *Creating Minds: An Anatomy of Creativity.* New York: Basic Books, 1993.

————. *Extraordinary Minds: Portraits of Four Exceptional Individuals and an Examination of Our Own Extraordinariness.* New York: Basic Books, 1997.

————. "The Vehicle and the Vehicles of Leadership." *American Behavioral Scientist* 42, no. 6 (1999): 1009–1023.

Gardner, Howard, with Emma Laskin. *Leading Minds: An Anatomy of Leadership.* New York: Basic Books, 1995.

Gardner, John W. *On Leadership.* New York: The Free Press, 1990.

Garmezy, N., and A. Masten. "Chronic Adversities." In *Child and Adolescent Psychiatry,* 3rd ed., edited by M. Rutter, L. H. Taylor, and E. Taylor, 191–208. Oxford: Blackwell Scientific Publications, 1994.

Goffee, Robert, and Gareth Jones. "Why Should Anyone Be Led by You?" *Harvard Business Review* 78, no. 5 (September–October 2000): 62ff.

Goines, David L. *The Free Speech Movement: Coming of Age in the 1960s.* Berkeley, CA: Ten Speed Press, 1993.

Goldin, Claudia, and Lawrence F. Katz. "The Shaping of Higher Education: The Formative Years in the United States, 1890 to 1940." *Journal of Economic Perspectives* 13, no. 1 (1999): 37–62.

Goodall, Jane. *The Chimpanzees of Gombe: Patterns of Behavior.* Cambridge, MA: Belknap/Harvard University Press, 1986.

Goodman, Walter. "*Brown v. Board of Education:* Uneven Results Thirty Years Later." In *Eyes on the Prize: America's Civil Rights Years,* edited by Clayborne Carson et al. New York: Penguin Books, 1987.

Gragg, Charles I. "Because Wisdom Can't Be Told." In *Case Method at the Harvard Business School,* edited by M. P. McNair. New York: McGraw-Hill, 1954.

Graham, Hugh Davis, and Nancy Diamond. *The Rise of the American Research University.* Baltimore: Johns Hopkins University Press, 1997.

Gray, Hanna Holborn. Inaugural Address. University of Chicago, October 1978.

———. "The Leaning Tower of Academe." *Bulletin: The American Academy of Arts and Sciences* 49, no. 7 (1996): 34–54.

———. "On the History of Giants." In *Universities and Their Leadership,* edited by William G. Bowen and Robert Shapiro. Princeton, NJ: Princeton University Press, 1998.

Green, Madeleine F. *The American College President: A Contemporary Profile.* Washington, DC: American Council on Education, 1988.

Gruber, Howard E. *Darwin on Man: A Psychological Study of Scientific Creativity.* 2nd ed. Chicago: University of Chicago Press, 1981.

Haggerty, Robert J., L. Sherrod, N. Garmezy, and M. Rutter. *Stress, Risk, and Resilience in Children and Adolescents: Processes, Mechanisms, and Interventions.* New York: Cambridge University Press, 1994.

Harding, Vincent. "Introduction—We the People: The Long Journey Toward a More Perfect Union." In *Eyes on the Prize: America's Civil Rights Years,* edited by Clayborne Carson et al. New York: Penguin Books, 1987.

Haskins, Charles H. *The Rise of Universities.* New York: Peter Smith, 1923.

Heifetz, Ronald. *Leadership Without Easy Answers.* Cambridge, MA: Harvard University Press, 1994.

Heifetz, Ronald A., and Donald L. Laurie. "The Work of Leadership." In *Harvard Business Review on Leadership.* Cambridge, MA: Harvard Business School Press, 1998.

Hesburgh, Theodore M. *The Hesburgh Papers: Higher Values in Higher Education.* Kansas City: Andrews and McMeel, 1979.

Hesburgh, Theodore M., with J. Reedy. *God, Country, Notre Dame.* New York: Doubleday, 1990.

Hogan, Joyce. "Personological Dynamics of Leadership." *Journal of Research in Personality* 12 (1978): 390–395.

Hogan, Robert, G. Curphy, and J. Hogan. "What We Know About Leadership, Effectiveness, and Personality." *American Psychologist* 49, no. 6 (1994): 493–504.

Hogan, Robert, and Robert B. Kaiser. "What We Know About Leadership." *Review of General Psychology* (forthcoming).

James, Estelle. "Product Mix and Cost Disaggregation." *Journal of Human Resources* 13, no. 1 (1978): 157–186.

Joseph, Joanne. *The Resilient Child: Preparing Today's Youth for Tomorrow's World.* New York: Plenum Press, 1994.

Judge, T. A., J. E. Bono, R. Ilies, and M. Gerhardt, "Personality and Leadership: A Qualitative and Quantitative Review." *Journal of Applied Psychology* 87 (2002): 765–780.

Judge, T. A., R. Ilies, and A. E. Colbert. "Intelligence and Leadership: A Quantitative Review and Test of Theoretical Propositions." *Journal of Applied Psychology* 89 (2004): 542–552.

Kao, John. *Jamming: The Art and Discipline of Business Creativity.* New York: Harper Business, 1996.

Katz, Mark. *On Playing a Poor Hand Well: Insights from the Lives of Those Who Have Overcome Childhood Risks and Adversities.* New York: W. W. Norton, 1997.

Kernan, Alvin. *In Plato's Cave.* New Haven, CT: Yale University Press, 1999.

Kerr, Barbara A. *Smart Girls: A New Psychology of Girls, Women, and Giftedness.* 2nd ed. Scottsdale, AZ: Gifted Psychology Press, 1995.

Kerr, Clark. *Academic Triumphs.* Vol. 1 of *The Gold and the Blue: A Personal Memoir of the University of California, 1949–1967.* Berkeley: University of California Press, 2001.

———. *The Great Transformation in Higher Education, 1960–1980.* Albany: State University of New York Press, 1991.

Kerr, Clark, and Marian L. Gade. *The Many Lives of Academic Presidents: Time, Place and Character.* Washington, DC: Association of Governing Boards of Universities and Colleges, 1986.

Kerr, Clark, with Marian L. Gade and Maureen Kawaoka. *Higher Education Cannot Escape History: Issues for the Twenty-First Century.* Albany: State University of New York Press, 1994.

———. *Political Turmoil.* Vol. 2 of *The Gold and the Blue: A Personal Memoir of the University of California, 1949–1967.* Berkeley: University of California Press, 2003.

———. *Troubled Times for American Higher Education: The 1990s and Beyond.* Albany: State University of New York Press, 1994.

Kotter, John P. *A Force for Change: How Leadership Differs from Management.* New York: The Free Press, 1990.

———. "What Leaders Really Do." In *Harvard Business Review on Leadership,* 37–60. Cambridge, MA: Harvard Business School Press, 1998.

Ledeen, Michael A. *Machiavelli on Modern Leadership.* New York: St. Martin's Press, 1999.

Lederman, Douglas. "Many Faculty Members Seek Greater Role in Athletic Decision Making on Campuses." *Chronicle of Higher Education*, February 4, 1987, 29–30.

———. "Reform of Big-Time College Athletics a Subject of Growing Concern in Congress." *Chronicle of Higher Education*, May 31, 1989, A1+.

Link, William A. *William Friday: Power, Purpose, and American Higher Education*. Chapel Hill: University of North Carolina Press, 1995.

Lord, R. G., C. L. DeVader, and G. Alliger. "A Meta-analysis of the Relation Between Personality Traits and Leader Perceptions." *Journal of Applied Psychology* 71 (1986): 402–410.

Mann, R. D. "A Review of the Relationship Between Personality and Performance in Small Groups." *Psychological Bulletin* 66 (1959): 241–270.

March, James G., and Johan P. Olsen. *Ambiguity and Choice in Organizations*. Bergen: Universitetsforlaget, 1976.

Martin, James, and James E. Samels, eds. *Presidential Transition in Higher Education: Managing Leadership Change*. Baltimore: Johns Hopkins University Press, 2004.

McLaughlin, Judith Block, and David Riesman. *Choosing a College President: Opportunities and Constraints*. Princeton, NJ: Carnegie Foundation for the Advancement of Teaching, 1990.

Melcher, Arlun. "Leadership: A Functional Analysis." In *Leadership: The Cutting Edge*, edited by James Hunt and Lars L. Larson. Carbondale: Southern Illinois University Press, 1977.

Middleton-Moz, Jane. *Will to Survive: Affirming the Positive Power of the Human Spirit*. Deerfield Beach, FL: Health Communications, Inc., 1992.

Mintzberg, Henry. "Covert Leadership: Notes on Managing Professionals." *Harvard Business Review*, November–December 1998, 140–147.

Monaghan, Peter. "The Long Honeymoon of Occidental College's John Slaughter." *Chronicle of Higher Education*, October 3, 1990, A3.

Morgan, G., and L. Smircich. "The Case for Qualitative Research." *Academy of Management Review* 5, no. 4 (1980): 491–500.

Murphy, William Michael, and D.J.R. Bruckner, eds. *The Idea of the University of Chicago: Selections from the Papers of the First Eight Chief Executives of the University of Chicago from 1891 to 1975*. Chicago: University of Chicago Press, 1976.

Nason, John W. *The Nature of Trusteeship: The Role and Responsibilities of College and University Boards*. Washington, DC: Association of Governing Boards of Universities and Colleges, 1982.

O'Brien, Michael. *Hesburgh: A Biography*. Washington, DC: Catholic University of America Press, 1998.

Offerman, L. R., and M. K. Gowing. "Organizations of the Future." *American Psychologist* 45 (1990): 95–108.

Padilla, A. "Passing the Baton: Leadership Transitions and the Tenure of University Presidents." In *Presidential Transition in Higher Education: Manag-*

ing *Leadership Change*, edited by James Martin and James E. Samels. Baltimore: Johns Hopkins University Press, 2004.

Padilla, A., and D. Baumer. "Big-Time College Sports: Management and Economic Issues." *Journal of Sport and Social Issues* 18, no. 2 (1994): 123–143.

Padilla, A., and S. Ghosh. "Turnover at the Top: The Revolving Door of the Academic Presidency." *The Presidency*, Winter 2000, 30–37.

Paige, Glenn D. *The Scientific Study of Political Leadership.* New York: The Free Press, 1977.

Perkins, James A., ed. *The University as an Organization.* New York: McGraw-Hill, 1973.

Piaget, Jean. *The Origins of Intelligence in Children.* New York: International Universities Press, 1952.

Putnam, Robert D. "Bowling Alone: America's Declining Social Capital." *Journal of Democracy* 6, no. 1 (1995): 65–78.

Readings, Bill. *The University in Ruins.* Cambridge, MA: Harvard University Press, 1996.

Rosenzweig, Robert. *The Political University.* Baltimore: Johns Hopkins University Press, 1998.

Rutter, M., L. H. Taylor, and E. Taylor, eds. *Child and Adolescent Psychiatry.* 3rd ed. Oxford: Blackwell Scientific Publications, 1994.

Schaller, George B. *The Mountain Gorilla: Ecology and Behavior.* Chicago: University of Chicago Press, 1963.

Schlereth, Thomas. *The University of Notre Dame: A Portrait of Its History and Campus.* Notre Dame: University of Notre Dame Press, 1976.

Scott, W. Richard. *Organizations: Rational, Natural, and Open Systems.* 3rd ed. Englewood Cliffs, NJ: Prentice Hall, 1992.

Shapiro, Harold T. "University Presidents—Then and Now." Speech delivered at Princeton Conference on Higher Education, Princeton, New Jersey, March 1996. http://www.princeton.edu/pr/hts/9603-thennow.html.

Sinclair, Upton. "The Rah-Rah Boys." In *The Goose-Step: A Study of American Education* (1923). Reprinted in *Academe* 77, no. 1 (1991): 31.

Slaughter, John Brooks. "After a Steady Diet of the Big-Time, Small College Football Has Its Rewards." *Chronicle of Higher Education*, January 4, 1989, A52.

———. "A Call to Leadership." *Educational Record* 77, no. 2–3 (1994): 85–86.

———. "Science and Social Consciousness." *Journal of College Science Teaching* 22, no. 4 (1993): 204–205.

Smith, C. Fraser. *Lenny, Lefty, and the Chancellor: The Len Bias Tragedy and the Search for Reform in Big-Time College Basketball.* Baltimore: Bancroft Press, 1992.

Sorenson, Georgia. "An Intellectual History of Leadership Studies: The Role of James MacGregor Burns." Paper presented at the annual meeting of the American Political Science Association, Washington, DC, September 2000.

Sperber, Murray. "Why the NCAA Can't Reform College Athletics." *Academe* 77, no. 1 (1991): 13–21.

Stadtman, Verne A. *The University of California, 1868–1968*. New York: McGraw-Hill, 1970.

Sternberg, Robert J. *The Nature of Creativity: Contemporary Psychological Perspectives*. Cambridge: Cambridge University Press, 1988.

Stigler, George J. *The Intellectual and the Market Place and Other Essays*. London: The Free Press of Glencoe, 1963.

Stogdill, Ralph M. "Personal Factors Associated with Leadership: A Survey of the Literature." *Journal of Psychology* 25 (1948): 35–71.

Stoke, Harold W. *The American College President*. New York: Harper and Brothers, 1959.

Strong, Edward. "Student Demonstrations at Berkeley: A Report to the Regents," December 16, 1964. Reprinted in Verne A. Stadtman, *The University of California, 1868–1969*. New York: McGraw-Hill, 1970.

Stuart, Mary Clark. "Clark Kerr: Biography of an Action Intellectual." Ph.D. diss., University of Michigan at Ann Arbor, 1980.

Tannenbaum, Robert, and Warren H. Schmidt. "How to Choose a Leadership Pattern." *Harvard Business Review*, May–June 1973, 162–175.

Underwood, John. *Spoiled Sport: A Fan's Notes on the Troubles of Spectator Sports*. Boston: Little, Brown, 1984.

Van Maanen, J. "The Fact of Fiction in Organizational Ethnography." *Administrative Science Quarterly* 24, no. 4 (1979): 539–550.

Vest, Charles M. "Reflections on Institutional and Individual Leadership." Address to Alumni/ae Leadership Conference, Cambridge, Massachusetts, September 16, 1995. http://web.mit.edu/president/communications/ALC-9-95.html.

Weber, Max. *The Theory of Social and Economic Organizations*, trans. A. Henderson and T. Parsons. New York: The Free Press, 1947.

Wellman, Harry. "Teaching, Research, and Administration—1925–1968." Berkeley: University of California Oral History, Bancroft Library.

Wills, Garry. *Certain Trumpets: The Call of Leaders*. New York: Simon and Schuster, 1994.

Wilson, Edward O. *Sociobiology*. Cambridge, MA: Harvard University Press, 1980.

Young, Charles E. "Clark Kerr: A Quiet Force." *Chronicle of Higher Education*, December 19, 2003, B10–B11.

Yukl, Gary A. *Leadership in Organizations*. 2nd ed. Englewood Cliffs, NJ: Prentice Hall, 1989.

INDEX

dence, 158–59, 162–63; managerial style, 158–59, 161–62; mentors, 153; presidency, 154–64; student protests, 157–60; training for priesthood, 145–49; World War II, 149–50
Hesburgh, James, 144
Hesburgh Library, 141, 154–55
The Higher Learning in America, 219, 245 n.2
Hill, Watts, Jr., 131, 138 n.26
Hitler, Adolf, 223
Holborn, Hajo, 223–24
Holy Cross College, 149
Holy Cross Seminary, 145
Homer, 42
Humer, Franz, 34, 59
Hutchins, Robert Maynard, 219, 245 n.1, 256

The Iliad and *The Odyssey* (Homer), 42
Intercollegiate athletics. *See* Athletics, intercollegiate

Jenkins, Leo, 109
Johnson, Lyndon B., 59
Jones, Charlie, 162–63
Jordan, John, 120
Joyce, Father Ned, 156–57
Joyner, Felix, 130

Kansas, as a "free state," 168–69
Kelley, Stanley, Jr., 214
Kenefrick, John, 196, 197
Kennedy, John F., 1, 49; *Profiles in Courage*, 6
Kennedy, Ted, 176
Kernan, Alvin, 217 n.4; on the Princeton graduate school, 4
Kerr, Barbara, 54, 58
Kerr, Catherine (Kay) Spaulding, 87
Kerr, Clark, 7, 71–74, 252–54; chancellorship at UC-Berkeley,

89–91; childhood and family, 80–82; college education, 82–86; on communism, 86–87, 88–89; early career, 87–89; humor, 83–84, 106, 254; leadership challenges, 88–89, 90–96, 98–105; management style, 96–98, 105; mentors, 84, 85, 86; presidency, 91–106; Quakerism, 81, 82–84; on the university, 19; volunteerism, 83, 84–85; work ethic, 81, 97–98
Kerr, Samuel William, 80–82
King, Arnold, 134, 135
Kirk, Grayson, 157
Kirwin, Brit, 178, 179, 189–90
Knowledge workers, 28–30
Kuralt, Charles, 133

Labor struggles, 86, 114
Leader-member exchange theory of leadership, 43
Leadership: cadence of life, 60, 255; communication and interpersonal skills, 58–60, 250, 252, 253; education and mentors, 8, 56–58, 249, 253; evolutionary roots, 50–52, 248; family influences, 8, 52–56, 248; and followership, 40, 43, 49, 248; goals of, 49, 251; patterns identified, 249–56; as persuasion, 48, 248; promotion from within, 21–22, 250, 253, 254; temporary nature, 47, 49, 251; transactional and transformational, 44–45
Leadership theories, 41–43; qualitative and quantitative approaches, 41–44, 50, 68–71; as a topic of study, 39–46, 68–71
Leahy, Frank, 153
Lee, Eugene, 97